Brother and Sister Boer

Brother and Sister Boer
A Family's Struggle Against the British During the Boer War

The Petticoat Commando or Boer Women in Secret Service
Johanna Brandt

On Commando
Dietlof van Warmelo

Brother and Sister Boer
A Family's Struggle Against the British During the Boer War
The Petticoat Commando or Boer Women in Secret Service
by Johanna Brandt
and
On Commando
by Dietlof van Warmelo

First published under the titles
The Petticoat Commando or Boer Women in Secret Service
and
On Commando

FIRST EDITION

Leonaur is an imprint
of Oakpast Ltd

Copyright in this form © 2013 Oakpast Ltd

ISBN: 978-1-78282-182-3 (hardcover)
ISBN: 978-1-78282-183-0 (softcover)

http://www.leonaur.com

Publisher's Notes

The views expressed in this book are not necessarily those of the publisher.

Contents

The Petticoat Commando or Boer Women in
Secret Service   7

On Commando   287

The Petticoat Commando

or

Boer Women in Secret Service

THE WRITER

Contents

Foreword	13
Introduction	15
The Scene of Action	17
How the Mines Were Saved	27
The Surrender of the Golden City	33
Martial Law Under the Enemy	40
Only a Bit of Ribbon Gay!	47
Passes and Permits	50
Postage by Strategy	57
Outwitting the Censor	62
Jan Celliers, Poet and Patriot	69
A Little Adventure With the British Soldier	76
Prisoner of War	84
The Concentration Camps	93
A Consular Visit to Irene Camp	107
New Developments	114
The Formation of the National Scouts Corps	123
A Consignment of Explosives	128
The First Interview With Spies, Introducing Two Heroes	131

The Case of Spoelstra	138
Diamond Cut Diamond!	148
Thanksgiving and Humiliation	153
Flippie and Co.	158
The Secret Railway Timetable	165
System Employed by the Secret Committee	171
The Death of Adolph Krause	177
The Shoemaker at Work	183
Bitten by Our Own Dogs	187
The Betrayal of the Secret Committee	191
Hansie Earning the Vote	199
A War-Baby and a Curious Christening	206
Forming a New Committee	213
"Tea For Two"	218
Kidnapping Mauser the Kitten	221
The First Spies at Harmony	228
The Captain's Visit	235
Memories Bitter-Sweet	242
A Silent Departure. "Fare Thee Well"	245
Betrayed	250
The Raid on Harmony	256
The Watchword	263
Peace, Peace—and There is No Peace!	272
Conclusion	285

To
Hansie's Mother
As a Peace-Offering
For Having Brought Her Into Publicity
In Direct Opposition
To Her Wishes

Foreword

In introducing the English version of this book I venture to bespeak a welcome for it, not only for the light which it throws on some little-known incidents of the South African war, but also because of the keen personal interest of the events recorded. It is more than a history. It is a dramatic picture of the hopes and fears, the devotion and bitterness with which some patriotic women in Pretoria watched and, as far as they could, took part in the war which was slowly drawing to its conclusion on the *veld* outside.

I do not associate myself with the opinions expressed by the writer as to the causes of the war or the methods adopted to bring it to an end, or as to the policy which led to the concentration camps, and the causes of the terrible mortality which prevailed during the first months of their existence. On these matters many readers will hold different opinions from the writer, or will prefer to let judgment be in suspense and to look to the historian of the future for a final verdict. We are still too near the events to be impartial. But this book does not challenge or invite controversy. Fortunately for South Africa, most of us on both sides can now discuss the events of the war without bitterness and understand and respect the feelings of those who were most sharply divided by these events from ourselves.

The greater part of the narrative comes from a diary kept during the war with unusual fullness and vividness. The difficulty experienced by the writer of the diary in communicating to friends outside Pretoria information about what was passing inside, and in unburdening herself of the feelings roused in her by the events of the war, made the diary more than usually intimate. To understand fully many of the narratives which have been transferred from it to this book, it must be remembered that one is reading, not something written from memory years after the event, but rather the record of a conversation at the time, in which the diarist is describing the events as if to a friend who shares to the full all her own feelings and to whom she can speak without reserve.

Much has happened in the ten years, (as at time of first publication), which have passed since the end of the war. The country which was distracted by the conflicting ideals and interests of its different governments and peoples has become the Union of South Africa. It is now one State. It remains that it should call forth a spirit of patriotism and nationality which will unite and not divide its people.

Patrick Duncan.

Johannesburg, 1912.

Introduction

If, by inspiring feelings of patriotism in the hearts of some of my readers, especially those members of the rising generation to whom this story of adventure may appeal, I succeed in raising the standard of national life, this book will have achieved the purpose for which it was written, and I shall feel more than compensated for having set aside the reluctance with which I faced the thought of the publicity when first I began the work.

I have tried to give the public some idea of what was done by Boer women, during the great Anglo-Boer war, to keep their men in the field and to support them in what proved to be a hopeless struggle for independence and liberty.

As far as I was able I have also described the perils and hardships connected with the Secret Service of the Boers and the heroism and resource displayed by the men.

Although it is with the knowledge and consent of the Boer leaders that I give publicity to what is known to me of the methods employed in the Secret Service of the Boers, I do not wish to convey the impression that these events of the war at any time bore an official character.

It is a purely personal narrative and has only been written at the repeated request, during the last ten years, of the many friends associated with the experiences of the diarist and of the principal characters appearing in this book.

In order to preserve the historical value of the book no fictitious names have been employed.

There are, as far as we know, very few records of this nature in existence, owing to the dangers connected with keeping a diary under martial law, and it seemed a pity, therefore, to withhold from the public materials which may be of use to those who are interested in studying or writing the history of those critical years.

I cannot vouch for the truth of every war rumour related here, nor for the accuracy of the information which I have obtained from other people, but the experiences of the diarist, as they were recorded from day to day, are correct in every detail.

My Dutch edition of this book, *Die Kappie Kommando*, is now appearing in the Dutch South African bi-monthly journal, *Die Brandwag*, and will, when completed, be published in book form in Holland.

In conclusion, I should like to take this opportunity of expressing my thanks to the Honourable Sir Richard Solomon, G.C.M.G., etc., for the help and assistance which he has so kindly given me in connection with the publication of my book.

The Writer.

Johannesburg, 1912.

Chapter 1

The Scene of Action

When, on October 11th, 1899, shortly before 5 o'clock in the afternoon, martial law was proclaimed throughout the Transvaal and Orange Free State, South Africa, and after the great exodus of British subjects had taken place, there remained in Pretoria, where the principal events recorded here took place, a harmonious community of Boers and sympathisers, who for eight months enjoyed the novel advantage of Boer freedom under Boer martial law.

The remaining English residents were few in number, and kept, to all appearance, "strictly neutral," until the morning of June 5th, 1900, when the British troops poured into the capital.

The two people chiefly concerned in this story, mother and daughter, lived in Sunnyside, a south-eastern suburb of Pretoria, on a large and beautiful old property, appropriately called Harmony, one of the oldest estates in the capital.

This historical place consisted of a simple, comfortable farmhouse, with a rambling garden—a romantic spot, and an ideal setting for the adventures and enterprises here recorded.

At the time our story opens, the owner, Mrs. van Warmelo, was living alone on it with her daughter, Hansie, a girl of twenty-two, the diarist referred to in the introduction.

The other members of the family, though they took no part in those events of the war which took place within the capital, were so closely connected with the principal figures in this book that their introduction will be necessary here.

The family consisted of five, two daughters and three sons. The elder daughter was married and was living at Wynberg near Cape Town, the younger, as we have seen, was with her mother in Pretoria during the war, while of the sons, two, the eldest and the youngest,

Dietlof and Fritz, were on commando, having left the capital with the first contingent of volunteers on September 28th.

The third brother, Willem, who had been studying in Holland when the war broke out, had, with his mother's knowledge and permission, given up his nearly completed studies and had come to South Africa, to take part in the deadly struggle in which his fellow-countrymen were engaged.

In order to achieve his purpose, he had taken the only route open to him, the eastern route through Delagoa Bay, and had joined his brothers in the field, after a brief sojourn with his mother and sister at Harmony.

Considering the circumstances under which he had joined the Boer forces and the sacrifice he had made for love of fatherland, it was particularly sad that he should have been made a prisoner at the last great fight at the Tugela, the battle of Pieter's Height in Natal, on February 27th, after a very short experience of commando life.

He was lodged in the Maritzburg jail at this time, where things would have gone hard with him, but for the loving-kindness of his cousin, Miss Berning, now Lady Bale, who frequently visited him with her sister, and provided him with baskets of fruit and other delicacies, which helped greatly to brighten the long months of his imprisonment.

Later on, through the influence of his brother-in-law, Mr. Henry Cloete, of "Alphen," Wynberg, he was released on parole, and allowed to return to Holland to complete his studies. His name therefore will no more appear in these pages.

He was "out of action" once and for all, and could not be made use of, even when, later on, through the development of the events with which this book deals, his services were most required by his mother and sister.

The other two brothers, as we have said, had left Pretoria with the first volunteers.

It is strange that the first blood shed in that terrible war should have been that of a young Boer accidentally shot by a comrade.

As a train, laden with its burden of brave and hopeful *burghers*, steamed slowly through the cutting on the south-eastern side of Pretoria, volleys of farewell shots were fired.

It is customary to extract the bullets from the cartridges on such occasions, but one of the *burghers* must have omitted to do this, with the result that the bullet, rebounding from the rocks, penetrated a carriage window, and seriously wounded one of the occupants.

Was this event prophetic of a later development of the war, when, as we shall see, Boer shed the blood of brother Boer in the formation of the National Scouts Corps?

Mrs. van Warmelo was a "*voor-trekker*," a pioneer, in every sense of the word. As a girl of fourteen she had left Natal with her parents and had "trekked," with other families, through the wild waste of country, into the unknown and barbaric regions in which she was destined to spend her youth.

She had watched the growth of a new country, the building up of a new race. She had known all the hardships and dangers of life in an unsettled and uncivilised land, had been through a number of Kaffir wars and could speak, through personal experience, of many adventures with savage foes and wild beasts. Her children knew her stories by heart, and it is not to be wondered at that they grew up with the love of adventure strong in them. And above all things, they grew up with a strong love for the strange, rich, wild country for which their forefathers had fought and suffered.

Mrs. van Warmelo was the eldest daughter of a family of sixteen. Her father, Dietlof Siegfried Maré, for many years *Landdrost* of Zoutpansberg, that northern territory of the Transvaal, was a direct descendant of the Huguenot fugitives, and was a typical Frenchman, short of stature, dark, vivacious, and exceedingly humorous, a man remembered by all who knew him for his great hospitality and for the shrewd, quaint humour of his sayings.

Some years after their arrival in Zoutpansberg, Mrs. van Warmelo had married a Hollander, a young minister of the Dutch Reformed Church. Of him it is not necessary to speak in this book.

He had taken his part in the first Anglo-Boer war and had passed away in Heidelberg, Transvaal, leaving to the people of his adopted fatherland and to his children a rich inheritance in the memory of a life spent in doing noble deeds—a life of rare self-sacrifice.

His family had left Heidelberg a few years after his death, and had taken up their abode in the capital in order to be near Mrs. van Warmelo's married daughter, Mrs. Cloete, who then lived close to Harmony, in Sunnyside.

It was a wild, romantic suburb in those days, being still almost entirely in its natural state. Grass-covered hills, clumps of mimosa, and other wild trees, with here and there an old homestead picturesquely situated in isolated spots, were all there was to be seen.

Mrs. van Warmelo.

Of all the private properties in this suburb, Harmony was the most overgrown and neglected when Mrs. van Warmelo first took possession of it.

It was bounded at the lower, the western end, by the Aapies River, a harmless rivulet in its normal state—almost dry, in fact, during the winter season—but in flood a most dangerous and destructive element, overflowing its banks and sweeping away every obstruction in its wild course.

The property was overgrown with rank vegetation and reminded one of the impenetrable forest abode of the "*Sleeping Beauty*" of fairy-tale fame.

Friends wondered that Mrs. van Warmelo had the courage to live alone with her daughter Hansie in such a wild and desolate spot, and they wondered still more when they heard of the alarming experience the two ladies had the very first night they spent in their new home.

On their arrival, there were still workmen busy repairing the house, and Mrs. van Warmelo pointed out to one of them that the skylight above the bathroom door had not yet been put in. The man nailed a piece of canvas over it, with the remark that that would do for the night, and that he would put in the skylight on his return the next day. Mrs. van Warmelo was only half satisfied, but left the matter there.

During the night one of her own servants, a sullen, treacherous-looking native, recently in her employment, entered the bathroom by putting a ladder against the door and tearing away the canvas from the skylight.

He must then have unlocked the door on the inside, striking about a dozen matches while he was in the room, and carried various portmanteaux out into the garden, where he slashed them open at the sides and overhauled their contents for money and valuables.

Early the next morning Mrs. van Warmelo was roused by old Anne Merriman, the only woman servant on the place, who came in from the garden with articles of wearing apparel which she had picked up under the trees, and which she held up to astonished gaze of her mistress. On investigating further, they found the garden littered with articles of clothing, valuable documents, and title-deeds, which the thief had thrown aside as worthless, in his search for money.

The only things of value which he had taken with him were a set of pearl ear-rings and brooch, and a beautiful lined "*kaross*," or rug, made of the skins of wild South African animals. Nothing was seen of him again, but Mrs. van Warmelo immediately got a revolver and kept watch for him, hoping, yet fearing, that he would return for more plunder.

This was a sad beginning, and old Anne added to their fears by predicting every imaginable calamity to the inhabitants of Harmony. She was gifted with second-sight, so she said, and often saw a man in grey about the place; his presence "boded no good," and old Anne soon after left the place, with many warnings to her mistress to follow her example, before she could be overtaken by disaster.

All this had taken place long before the war broke out. Harmony had in the meantime been vastly improved, the dense undergrowth having been cut away, and the row of enormous willow trees, with which the house was overshadowed, having been removed, while large flower and vegetable gardens had been laid out, where once a jungle-like growth of shrubs and rank grass had abounded.

Much of the natural beauty still remained, however, and Harmony was a favourite resort for many people in Pretoria. Young and old visited the place, especially during the summer months when the garden was laden with its wealth of fruit and flowers; and of these friends of the family many figure in these pages, while some do not appear at all, having had no part in the stirring events with which this book deals.

Amongst the most frequent visitors at Harmony were the Consul-General for the Netherlands, Mr. Domela-Nieuwenhuis and his wife, and other members of the Diplomatic Corps with their families.

These friendships had been formed before the war, and it was only natural that they should have been strengthened and deepened by the trying circumstances of the years during which the country was convulsed by such unspeakable tragedies.

Although the position held by these men debarred them from taking any part whatsoever in the events of the war, their sympathies were undoubtedly with the people of South Africa. They suffered with and for their friends, and they must frequently have been weighed down by a sense of their powerlessness to alleviate the distress around them, which they were forced to witness; but they were, without exception, men of high integrity, and observed with strict honour the obligations laid upon them by their position of trust.

Needless to say, they were not aware of the conspiracies which were carried on at Harmony; to this day they are ignorant of the dangers to which the van Warmelos were exposed and the hazardous nature of many of the enterprises in which mother and daughter were engaged, and I look forward with delight to the privilege of presenting each of these gentlemen with a copy of this book, in which they will find so many revelations of an unexpected and startling nature.

It is not my intention to go into the details of the first encounters with the enemy, nor to describe the siege-comedy of Mafeking, where Baden-Powell, as principal actor, maintained a humorous correspondence with the Boers; nor of Kimberley, where Cecil Rhodes said he felt as safe as in Piccadilly; nor of Dundee, where the Boers were said to have found a large number of brand-new side-saddles, originally destined to be used by British officers on arrival at the capital, where they hoped to take the ladies of Pretoria riding, but ultimately consigned to the flames by the indignant brothers and lovers of those very ladies; nor of the fine linen, silver, cut-glass, and fingerbowls found and destroyed by the Boers in the luxurious British camp at Dundee. I shall not dwell upon the glorious victories of the first months, the capture of armoured trains, the blowing up of bridges, the besieging of towns, the arrival in Pretoria of the first British prisoners and the long sojourn of British officers in captivity in the Model School—from where, incidentally, Winston Churchill escaped in an ingenious way—and the crushing news of the first Boer reverses at Dundee and Elandslaagte.

Are these historical events not fully recorded in other books, by other writers more competent than myself?

A three-volume book would hardly contain the experiences Hansie had, first in the Volks Hospital in Pretoria and later in the State Girls' School, as volunteer nurse, but I shall pass over the events of the first eight months of war under Boer martial law and introduce my reader to that period in May 1900 shortly before the British took possession of the capital.

The two remaining brothers van Warmelo were at this time retreating with the now completely demoralised Boer forces, before the terrific onslaughts made upon them by the enemy.

Blow after blow was delivered by the English in quiet succession on their forced march from Bloemfontein to Pretoria, and it was on May 25th that the roar of Boer cannon reached the capital for the first time.

Looking south-east from Harmony, Mrs. and Miss van Warmelo were able to watch the Boer commandos pouring into the town—*straggling* would be a better word, for there was no one in command, and the weary men on their jaded horses passed in groups of twos and threes, and in small contingents of from fifty to a hundred.

Mrs. van Warmelo fully expected to see her sons among the number and made preparations to welcome them, for under the roar of cannon the fatted turkey had been killed and roasted and a large plum-pudding made.

Suddenly two men on horseback turned out of the wayside and rode straight up to the gate.

"Perhaps these men are bringing us news of our boys," Mrs. van Warmelo said to her daughter, who was watching them with anxiety at her heart.

The men dismounted at the gate and walked up to the two women, leading their horses slowly over the grass.

No one spoke until the men were a few yards off, when Hansie exclaimed, with unbounded joy and relief, "Why, they *are* our boys!"

With unkempt hair and long beards, covered with dust, tattered and weary, no wonder mother and sister failed to recognise them at first!

When the first greetings were over, the young men gave what news they could—stupefying news of the advance of the enemy in overwhelming numbers, and of the flight and confusion of what remained of the Boer forces.

"What are you going to do?" their mother asked.

"Rest and feed our horses first of all, mother," Dietlof, the elder, replied. "They are worn out and unfit for use. And when we have equipped ourselves for whatever may be in store for us, we must join some small commando and escape from the town. Little or no resistance is being offered by our men, and it is evident that Pretoria will not be defended. All we can do is to escape before the English take possession."

Mrs. van Warmelo then told her sons of the retreat of the President from the capital, with the entire Government, by the eastern railway route.

The greatest consternation had been caused by this flight at first, but subsequent events went to prove that this was the wisest course which could have been pursued.

In this decision the President had been urged by his wife, and Mrs. van Warmelo went on to tell how the brave old lady had said to her in an expressive way, on the occasion of her last visit at the President's house:

"My dear friend, do not fear. No Englishman will ever lay his hand on the coat-tails of the President."

It is quite impossible to describe the confusion that ensued during the next few days.

No one knew what to do; there were no organised Boer forces to join, there was no one in command, and, after long deliberation, the two young men, urged by mother and sister, came to the conclusion that, whatever other men might be doing, *their* duty was to get out of Pretoria and join whatever band of fighting burghers there might still be in the field.

The same spirit of determination not to fall into the hands of the enemy while the Boer Government was free, and could continue organising the war, prevailed amongst most of the men in Pretoria, and daily small parties could be seen leaving the town, in carts, on horseback, on bicycles, and even on foot. Where they were going and when they would return no one knew.

On the morning of June 4th, the necessary preparations for the departure of the young men having been made, as they were sitting at what proved to be their last meal together for such long and terrible years, they were suddenly startled by the sound of cannon-firing and the whistling of a shell through the air.

They listened, speechless, as the shell burst on Schanskop Fort, on the Sunnyside hill, just beyond Harmony, with an explosion that shook the house.

It was followed by another and yet another.

So little were the inhabitants of Pretoria prepared for this that everyone at first thought that the shells were being fired, for some unaccountable reason, by the Boers, from the Pretoria Forts, until a few of them burst so close to the houses that the fragments of rock and shell fell like hail on the iron roofs. The other members of the family followed Mrs. van Warmelo into the garden: and when it became evident that the enemy was bombarding the Pretoria Forts, the two young men immediately saddled their horses and rode out in the direction in which they thought it most likely that some resistance would be offered, after having advised their mother and sister to flee to some place of refuge in the centre of the town.

There was no doubt that Harmony was directly in the line of fire, and as the great shells went shrieking and hurtling through the air, the very earth seemed to shake with the force of each explosion.

Mrs. van Warmelo hastily packed a few valuables into a hand-bag, and fled into town with her daughter, leaving their dinner standing almost untouched on the table. On their way to town, they found many terrified women and children huddled under bridges for safety.

The bombardment continued all the afternoon, and ceased only when darkness fell.

That night, when the van Warmelos returned to their deserted home, they found the house still standing and no trace of the bombardment except pieces of shell lying in the garden.

They were much surprised a few hours later, by the return of their two warriors, weary and desperate after a hopeless attempt to keep back the English with a handful of *burghers*, and the news they brought was to the effect that Pretoria was to be surrendered to the enemy the next morning. Once more they expressed their determination to escape to the Boer lines, wherever they might be.

Only a few hours' rest for them that night and then they rode away at dawn, in the Middelburg direction, on that dark and dreadful June 5th.

It was Fritz's twenty-second birthday on that cruel mid-winter's morn, and when Hansie saw him again he was a man of twenty-six, with the experiences and suffering of a lifetime resting on his shoulders.

The fate of the two young men remained a mystery to their dear ones for many months of agonising suspense, and they pass out of these pages for a time while we turn our attention to the relation of events within the capital.

Chapter 2

How the Mines Were Saved

Before we begin relating the events with which this book is actually concerned, and which took place, as we have said in the previous chapter, exclusively in and around the capital, I must ask my reader to turn his attention for a few moments to that great mining centre, Johannesburg, "The Golden City" of South Africa.

If it was hated by the Boers before the war as the cause of all the unrest in their beloved country, the unwelcome revolution in the calm simplicity of their hitherto peaceful life, it is not to be wondered at that their hatred and resentment had been intensified by the way in which the war was brought about.

This feeling had risen to its height of concentrated fury when it became known to the *burghers* that the sweeping advance of the British forces in overwhelming numbers would soon make it possible for the English to take full possession of those coveted mines.

At the time of the Republican successes there had been no suggestion that it would be politic to destroy the mines, but as reverses became more frequent, and it became evident beyond a doubt that the British troops were about to cross the *Vaal*, strong section of the government, supported by popular feeling, openly advocated the destruction of the mines as well as the town of Johannesburg. The precedent quoted for such a course was the burning of Moscow by the Russians, in order to retard the victorious advance of Napoleon.

Very soon it became apparent that the members of the government who were advocating this policy were gaining the upper hand, as instructions were actually given to certain officials of the Mines Department to make the necessary arrangements for blowing up the mines. Another section of the government, among whom were General Louis Botha and Dr. F.E.T. Krause, strenuously opposed the carrying out of this policy.

This section eventually gained the upper hand at the time when Commandant Schutte was compelled to relinquish the position of Special Commandant for the Rand, and Dr. Krause was appointed in his stead, although the circumstances leading to this change had at first in some measure strengthened those who advocated destroying the mines. The change was brought about in consequence of the terrible explosion at Begbie's Engineering Works, which had been converted into a bomb factory by the government, and where several persons were killed and many injured.

The cause of this explosion after investigation was alleged to have been the work of British spies, and it was only natural that those persons advocating the destruction of the mines should avail themselves of this circumstance to further their scheme, but the bold and determined opposition of Dr. Krause, supported as he was by the mines police, a special body of men organised for the purpose of protecting the mines, had the effect of inducing the "Destroyers" to mature their scheme in secret.

The probable fate of the mines was openly and freely discussed in the capital, and I have a faint recollection of a debating society having taken for its subject, at this time, the question, "Would the result of blowing up the mines be beneficial or detrimental to the Boer cause?" Many were the pros and cons, and what conclusion was arrived at I do not know.

At Harmony, mother and daughter followed the subject with the keenest interest and anxiety, realising the important effect which the destruction of the mines would have on the later development of the war.

There were several weighty considerations which the "Destroyers," in their thirst for revenge, seemed to have overlooked entirely.

In the first place, the blowing up of the mines would have failed in its object of punishing the mining magnates against whom the resentment of the Republicans was specially directed, and the chief sufferers would be innocent shareholders in every part of the world, members of the middle-classes who had invested their little all in the fabulously rich gold mines of the Rand. Another very important consideration which was discussed by the more thoughtful section of the community was the probable destruction of the farms by the British forces by way of retaliation for the fate of the mines. Could the *burghers* have foreseen that the entire country would be laid waste in any case as the war proceeded, nothing could have saved the mines. But the devastation of Boer homesteads was not to begin until a much later period, and to this fact the "Destroyers" no doubt owed the frustration of their schemes.

I have to thank friends who were principally concerned in the matter for the following account of how the mines were saved and for the interesting description of the surrender of the Golden City, appearing in Chapter 3.

******

At this time the British troops were advancing rapidly. The Boers were panic-stricken, and had it not been for the determined efforts of the administration in Johannesburg, chaos would have resulted.

About ten days before the surrender of the town, the scheme of the "Destroyers" was unwittingly disclosed through the foolishness of the man who had been apparently chosen to carry it out. Judge Kock, who was a friend of Dr. Krause's, came over to Johannesburg for the purpose of making a last and determined effort to destroy the mines. Being a great friend of the Krauses, he was invited to stay at their house. In a burst of confidence he produced a letter signed by a very high-placed official of the Executive Council, whereby he was empowered, in indefinite terms, to call for the co-operation of any military official whom he pleased. He showed Dr. Krause this letter and requested him to instruct the mine police and certain other mine officials to assist him. He was met with a blank refusal, and a threat that if he persisted in this undertaking he would be arrested. Judge Kock, or, as he then styled himself, "General" Kock, had gathered together a cosmopolitan force of about 100 men.

About this time events were rapidly changing. The determined advance of the British forces and the panic-stricken retreat of the Boers had the effect of encouraging "General" Kock and his men. Dr. Krause's hands were full in attending to the military necessities of the situation. Urgent messages from Botha and the President were hourly passing over the wires. General French, who was advancing on Johannesburg from the east, had pressed forward to such an extent that the Boers retreating from Vereeniging were practically hemmed in by the British columns.

Commandant Krause on the Sunday afternoon hastily gathered as many fighting men as he could muster, and with them occupied the hills surrounding Van Wyk's Rust, in order to check the advance of French and give the Boers an opportunity of retreating safely. On the Monday, while fighting was going on, he was obliged to leave his men—who by that time had been reinforced by the retreating Boers—for Johannesburg, on receiving an urgent message that chaos was reigning in town, and that the goods sheds at the station, where Government provisions and food-stuffs were stored, were being looted. On his return order was speedily restored.

Tuesday, May 29th, was the eventful day in the history of the saving of the mines, as on this date Dr. Krause personally arrested "General" Kock and dispersed his band of followers. It happened in this way.

During the progress of the war the government had been working some of the mines, and, at the time of the rapid advance of the British from Bloemfontein, instructions were given that all the gold should be conveyed to Pretoria. The week before the surrender of Johannesburg, Dr. Krause had given the necessary instructions for doing this, and had received a report that all gold had been transported. Now, it appears that Kock had taken advantage of the commandant's absence from Johannesburg to further his scheme of destruction, and the first mine he went to with that purpose in view was the Robinson. On arriving there he accidentally discovered that about 120,000 ounces of gold, valued at about £400,000, were still stored on the mine. He was evidently so perturbed about this that he momentarily forgot his purpose, and galloped post-haste with the greater number of his men to the commandant's office. His men were drawn up outside; he dismounted and found Dr. Krause in consultation with Commandant L.E. van Diggelen, the energetic officer in command of the Mines Police. Kock adopted a threatening and bullying attitude, and demanded the reason why so much gold had been left on the mine, and where the treachery lay.

During the course of his angry outburst he disclosed the fact that he had proceeded to the mine for the purpose of destroying it, and had discovered the presence of the gold. It may be mentioned here that Dr. Krause, in the course of the morning, had been in telegraphic communication with General Botha, who was then in the vicinity of Eagles' Nest, and had informed him that it would probably be necessary to take violent measures against Kock, which might lead to bloodshed. General Botha's reply was: "I hold you responsible for the safety of the mines and the town of Johannesburg, and I leave everything in your hands."

When, therefore, "General" Kock disclosed his purpose, Dr. Krause jumped up, closed the door, confronted him, and, before he could realise his position, had him under arrest, calling upon van Diggelen to disarm him. Kock made an attempt to escape, but he was powerless in the hands of two determined men. Some time elapsed before he realised the hopelessness of the situation, as his last attempt to induce Commandant van Diggelen to deliver a note to his men outside was met with a blank refusal. The next thing to be done was to get rid of these men, who evidently had been instructed by their "General" not to leave without him, he probably fearing that something unforeseen might happen to him. How now to get rid of these men? The following ruse was adopted: Dr. Krause took up some telegrams, and, waving these in the air, rushed out to where they were stationed, demanding to know who the officer in charge was. He was met by a confusion of voices calling out, "Where is our general?"

"Oh!" was the reply, "your general is still in my office, consulting on military matters, and I have just received information that the British are advancing on the town from the direction of the Gueldenhuis. Your general commands you to proceed in that direction to reinforce the Boers, who are trying to stop the advance. We will follow immediately with the rest of the men. Now! who is in command?"

"I am, sir—Captain McCullum."

"Now, Captain," the doctor said, "ride for your life and do your duty."

The ruse was successful, and in a few minutes not a single man of the band was in sight. The next question was, what was to be done with Kock. The following plan was adopted: The arrest took place shortly before the luncheon hour, and as the offices were generally closed from one till two, Kock was detained in the *commandant's* office until one. All officials were then ordered to leave. Van Diggelen ordered his dog-cart to be brought round, Kock was told to step in, and was quietly driven to the fort, where he was detained by the officer in charge.

During the afternoon General Botha and his staff passed through Johannesburg, and came to see Dr. Krause, who reported what had happened. General Botha approved of and confirmed his action in every respect. The conference between the two officers did not last long, and resulted in Dr. Krause being definitely instructed to remain in Johannesburg in order to protect the town and its inhabitants, and to see that all fighting *burghers* immediately left for their respective commandos. The same evening Kock was sent to Pretoria, escorted by several police, and handed over to the authorities there.

The great danger which had threatened the safety of the mines was in this way averted.

Before closing this chapter, mention should be made of the excellent work done by the Mines Police in the protection of the mines, and in this connection especially to name Commandant L.E. van Diggelen and Lt. W. Vogts, the energetic Secretary of the Force.

The gold found on the Robinson Mine was on the same Tuesday sent by Dr. Krause to Pretoria in charge of Captain Arendt Burkhardt and several members of the Field Police, and was duly delivered by them to the authorities there.

> *Note.*—The subsequent career of Kock was an eventful one. He lost his father, J.H. Kock, at the Battle of Elandslaagte. This and other matters so preyed upon his mind that eventually he became subject to delusions, and is at present, (as at time of first publication), confined in the lunatic asylum at Pretoria.

Chapter 3

The Surrender of the Golden City

In attempting to chronicle the events which surround the surrender of Johannesburg, the mind involuntarily pauses, and a picture, which reminds one of the fairy-tales of one's childhood, is called up in imagination.

In 1886 Johannesburg could only boast of a few tin shanties—the beginnings of a mining camp; fourteen years later the British troops marched through the streets of a modern city. And what has been the history of these fourteen years?

In the history of the older European nations development and progress are slow, and social and economic cause and effect can be traced with almost scientific accuracy. In Johannesburg, however, ordinary human agencies do not seem to have been at work. The man who has the leisure at his disposal to ascertain the true facts of that period before the war, would present to the world a history so interesting and fascinating that he would be accused of having indulged in fiction in his narrative of events. It would be out of place in this book, however, to enter into these historical events, and we must confine ourselves to the details of the period with which this story deals.

Ever since the beginning of the war it was the intention of the Republican Government to defend both Pretoria and Johannesburg, and had the outbreak of the war not been precipitated, and the necessary cannon ordered from France arrived in time, this would have been done. Even after the fall of Bloemfontein the idea was not entirely abandoned, and Commandant Krause was instructed to provision the Johannesburg Fort and make other necessary preparations. A promise was made that several cannon would be left at Johannesburg by the Boers during their retreat. It was hoped that such defence would retard the British advance and enable the Boers to recover from the panic which had seized them ever since the surrender of Cronjé at Paardeberg.

When, however, General Botha on Tuesday, May 29th, 1900, passed through Johannesburg, Commandant Krause was ordered to abandon the defence of the town, to distribute all provisions collected amongst the families of the men on commando, and to get rid of all men capable of fighting. These orders were promptly carried out.

On the following day, Wednesday, May 30th, between ten and eleven in the morning, Major Francis Davis appeared with a flag of truce and requested to see Dr. Krause. At the time the commandant was at the fort attending to General Grobelaar and about 500 men who were retreating in the direction of Pretoria. During the day bodies of armed *burghers* were continually passing through the town.

On arrival at his office Dr. Krause found Major Davis in the company of two old Johannesburg residents. The latter were dressed in mufti. Both these men had taken an active part in the agitation which preceded the war.

Major Davis in soldierly manner addressed Dr. Krause by saying that he was commanded by Lord Roberts to demand the immediate and unconditional surrender of the town, in the name of Her Majesty Queen Victoria.

Dr. Krause's reply was very short: "No, sir, not immediately and not unconditionally."

Major Davis thereupon said that Lord Roberts had also expressed a desire that the *commandant* should grant him an interview, at which the matter could be discussed. Dr. Krause assented to this proposition.

What the Boers wanted was delay—and if Commandant Krause could delay the forward advance of the British troops a great advantage would be gained.

Lord Roberts was encamped just above the Victoria Lake, close to Germiston. On arrival at the camp Dr. Krause was met by Lord Roberts on the verandah of the house occupied by him and his staff.

A private interview then took place between the two officers, at which the terms of surrender of Johannesburg were agreed upon, and which will be found in the letter set out hereunder.

The chief reason for an armistice advanced by the Boer commandant was that if the British were at once to enter the town, street-fighting would undoubtedly take place, as the many armed *burghers* passing through the town would only obey the orders of their own respective *commandants* and field-cornets. Such street-fighting would be a serious menace to the women and children and to the other peaceful citizens of the town. Lord Roberts agreed to this, adding that he had once, in Afghanistan, experienced street-fighting and would not like to see it again.

Another incident of this interview is worth recording, *viz.* the protest made by Dr. Krause at the presence of the two civilians who accompanied Major Davis. Lord Roberts asked for the reason of this protest, and was informed that, according to the view of the people in Johannesburg, these men, through the part they played in the mendacious political agitation which was carried on prior to the war, were partly responsible for the war, and further that he (Dr. Krause) had in his possession a warrant for the arrest of one of these men for high treason, issued prior to the commencement of hostilities, and consequently their presence in the town was looked upon with a great deal of disfavour and resentment.

Lord Roberts expressed his regret, and said that these men had accompanied his officer only because he was told that they would be excellent guides, knowing the locality and the officials.

The terms of surrender were agreed to, including an armistice of twenty-four hours. This delay undoubtedly helped to save the Republican forces from utter destruction and certainly enabled General Botha and the other Boer officers to retreat with their men beyond Pretoria and to collect their scattered forces.

Dr. Krause returned to Johannesburg after this interview and immediately set about making the necessary arrangements to carry out his part of the bargain. A Proclamation was issued, calling upon all armed *burghers* and other capable men to leave the town; all officials were ordered to be in readiness the next day at the respective offices, for the purpose of handing over their administration to their successors.

Early the next morning Mr. William Shawe, the deputy sheriff, was dispatched to Lord Roberts, with a formal letter, confirming the terms of surrender agreed to at the above interview. This historical document is, I believe, here printed for the first time and reads as follows:

Johannesburg,
May 30th, 1900.

Lord Roberts,
Commander-in-Chief of Her Majesty's troops in South Africa.
Your Lordship,
Referring to the verbal interview I had with Your Lordship this morning, with reference to the surrender of the town, Johan-

nesburg, I now wish to confirm the following in writing:

(*a*) That all officials and other government employees will be treated with the necessary respect and consideration. On their behalf I can give Your Lordship the assurance, that until the surrender is complete, everything will be done by them to facilitate Your Lordship's work, in so far as their honour allows.

(*b*) With reference to the protection of women and children (including the women and children of *burghers* on commando),—that these persons will not be molested by the troops,—Your Lordship having already given the necessary instructions in this connection.

(*c*) That property will be protected, also forage, except in so far as military requirements necessitate it.

(*d*) That as regards the 13,000 *kaffirs* still on the mines, the necessary precautions will be taken by Your Lordship:—in this respect the Special Mine Police corps, till now under my command, will render Your Lordship all assistance.

(*e*) Enclosed I send Your Lordship a copy of a notice distributed by me, which speaks for itself, and from which Your Lordship will learn that all fighting and armed *burghers* have been ordered to leave the town at once.

(*f*) It grieves me to have to inform Your Lordship, that notwithstanding our arrangement, that no armed men would enter the town till tomorrow at 10 o'clock, several armed persons entered the town (evidently without Your Lordship's knowledge, and contrary to instructions), and several of whom are under arrest; one who attempted to disarm a *burgher* was wounded, and is at present in the hospital here.

Finally, I must request Your Lordship not to enter the town with too great a force (for reasons already communicated to Your Lordship). I shall send some one who will conduct Your Lordship personally (or the officer in command) to the government offices to there carry out and complete the necessary formalities of handing over the town. All chief and other officials have been notified by me of this arrangement, and they have been ordered to hold themselves in readiness to hand over their offices to the persons appointed thereto.

    I have the honour to be,
        Respectfully yours,
    (Signed)   F.E.T. Krause. Acting Special Commandant.

On the morning of May 31st, 1900, the sun rose in his bright winter splendour—the sky was blue, and not a cloud appeared upon the horizon. Mother Nature seemed to emphasise the darkness and bitterness in the hearts of the staunch and free Republicans by her dazzling brightness. The new era had dawned, heralding the victory of the invading forces and giving practical proof of the old adage, "*Might is right.*"

At about 10 o'clock Commandant Krause received a message from Lord Roberts announcing his presence on the outskirts of the town (at Denver) and expressing a desire that the *commandant* should personally come and meet and conduct him to the government offices, there to hand over the "keys" of the city. This request was complied with. The British were then seen entering the town, headed by Lord Roberts, Lord Kitchener, and Commandant Krause. On arrival at the government offices the different officials were presented to Lord Roberts, who requested them to remain in office until they were relieved of their duties by an English officer.

The surrender of the Golden City was an accomplished fact!

In conclusion, and as a contrast to this terrible period for the Republicans, I may here be permitted to publish a letter written by Lord Roberts to Dr. Krause, which will show in what manner the Golden City was previously administrated and afterwards handed over to the British troops on May 31st, 1900.

> Army Headquarters,
> Johannesburg,
> June 2nd, 1900.
>
> Dear Dr. Krause,
>
> I desire to express to you how fully I appreciate the valuable assistance you have afforded me in connection with the entry into this town of the force under my command.
>
> I recognise that you have had *difficulties of no ordinary nature to contend with of late,* and any weakness in the administration of the town and suburbs at such a juncture would doubtless have been taken full advantage of by the disorderly element which necessarily exists in an important mining community. Thanks to your energy and vigilance, order and tranquillity have been preserved, and I congratulate you heartily on the result of your labours.
>
> Permit me also to tender to you my personal thanks for the

The Surrender of the Golden City

great courtesy you have shown me since I first had the pleasure of meeting you.

Believe me to be,
    Yours truly,
        Roberts, F.M.

CHAPTER 4

Martial Law Under the Enemy

After her brothers' departure, described in Chapter 1, Hansie fastened her "*Vierkleur*," a broad band of the Transvaal colours, round her hat, and announced her intention of going into town to see the British troops come in.

Her mother thought it a most unseemly proceeding, and declined to accompany her wilful daughter, but the latter did not wish to miss what she knew would become an historical event of great importance, and rode away on her bicycle, accompanied by her faithful retriever, Carlo.

The thought of the conspicuous band of ribbon round her hat, in green, red, white, and blue, gave her a certain feeling of comfort and satisfaction.

At least none of the friends she might chance to meet that day could suspect her of being in town to *welcome* the enemy.

The air was charged with the electricity of an excitement so tense, so suppressed, that it struck her like some living force as she rode through the thronged, though silent streets.

In the heart of the town, as she neared Government Square, a change was noticeable—a change that she could not define until it was borne in upon her that it originated in the attitude of the black and coloured part of the community.

They had come out in their thousands—the streets literally seethed with them, the remarkable part of this being that they were all on the pavements, while their "white brothers" walked in the middle of the road.

For the sake of the uninitiated I must explain that under the Boer regime no black or coloured person was allowed on the pavements, nor to be out at night, nor to walk about without a registered pass.

There was no "black peril" then.

This noisy, unlawful demonstration was an expression of joy on their part at the prospect of that day being set free from Boer restrictions, a short-lived joy, however, for they became so lawless and overbearing that it was found necessary, within a very few days, to re-enforce the Boer laws and regulations.

★★★★★★

In perfect order, but weary unto death, the British troops marched in. Thousands and thousands of soldiers in khaki, travel-stained, foot-sore, and famished, sank to the ground, at a given command, in the open square facing Government Buildings.

Some of them tried to eat of the rations they had with them, others, too exhausted to eat, fell into a deep sleep almost at once, and one old warrior, looking up into the face of the girl standing above him, said, in a broken voice, "Thank God, the war is over."

Hansie bent towards him and answered, in a voice vibrating with passionate feeling, "Tommy Atkins, *the war has just begun.*"

He looked at her in puzzled surprise, and sighing heavily, closed his eyes.

Ah, unknown soldier, did you in after years, I wonder, remember the prophetic words spoken by the lips of a girl that day?

At three o'clock that afternoon the Union Jack was hoisted on Government Buildings!

Those of my readers whose love of home, kindred, traditions, ideals—patriotism—belong to other countries can draw a mental picture of what a similar experience would mean to them. One day to be full of hope that a beloved country and independence would be restored to its people, the next with those hopes laid low in the dust, shattered, destroyed for ever, by the sight of a small, unfamiliar flag standing out against the blue sky.

In time of great shock or crisis, merciful Providence numbs our keenest sensibilities and the brain acts and thinks mechanically. The inevitable comes, however, and we wonder at finding ourselves still breathing, after passing through that fire of mental agony.

Our young patriot's heart was torn and bleeding, but her sufferings then were as nothing compared to those she endured in later months and years, when the incidents of that winter's day would pass in review across her brain, haunting her sleeping and waking thoughts like some hideous nightmare.

It is not for me to describe the scene: the cheering of the multitude, the parade of haggard troops—the soul-sickening display of imperial patriotism.

As if ashamed of having witnessed it, the sun, suddenly grown old and grey, hid himself behind a passing cloud, and in the shadows which enveloped her the girl seemed to feel the hand of Nature, groping for hers, to convey its silent message of sympathy.

The crowds dispersed and the troops withdrew to the outskirts of the town to pitch their tents for the night.

When Hansie arrived at Harmony she found all the open space around it occupied by troops, and camps erected at the very gates, while, all along the roads and railway lines, fires were burning and soldiers were engaged in tending their horses and preparing their rations.

The air was so heavy with smoke and dust that it seemed as if a dense fog were resting on the town, but an order and discipline prevailed which could not be surpassed.

Mrs. van Warmelo was standing at the gate with a loaded revolver in her hands, keeping the entire British Army at bay with a pair of blazing eyes.

She had already spoken to the officer in command, who, on hearing that two unprotected ladies were living alone on the property, had immediately issued orders that no man was to enter Harmony on any pretext whatever. Somewhat reassured, mother and daughter retired into their stronghold, barricading doors and windows and ordering Carlo, the good watch-dog, to preserve an extra vigilance that night.

Brave old Carlo! from that moment he seemed to understand that his duty was to protect his beloved mistresses from their mortal foe, and nothing could equal his dislike and distrust of anything connected with the unwelcome visitors around his hitherto peaceful abode. For a long time, he valiantly withstood temptation in the form of titbits offered him by soldiers, not at any time responding to the many advances made by them, and my reader will agree with me, as this story unfolds itself, that no dog could have developed more useful qualities.

The first few weeks after the occupation of Pretoria were spent in settling down and finding accommodation for the thousands of British officers and men, and it soon became evident to the inhabitants of Harmony that Sunnyside had been chosen as a suitable suburb for the more important members of the military forces.

To give the reader some idea of how Harmony was hemmed in by troops on every side, I have drawn the annexed chart, and, though some alterations were made as the months went by, this was practically the position of our heroines during the greater part of the war.

On the eastern side were encamped the Military Mounted Police; on the west, on the banks of the Aapies River and adjoining the Berea Park, lay Kitchener's bodyguard; on the south were established the Montmorency Scouts; and on the north, commanding the principal entrance to Harmony, the Provost-Marshal, Major Poore, had taken up his abode in the comfortable residence of the ex-Mayor of Pretoria, Sir Johannes van Boeschoten, who was knighted on the occasion of the recent visit to South Africa of the Duke of Connaught.

Opposite the provost-marshal, in a house belonging to Mr. B.T. Bourke, the War Office, as we called it, was established; and still a little farther north, in the British Agency, vacated by Sir Conyngham and Lady Lily Greene when martial law was proclaimed, Lord Roberts and his staff were installed, until better quarters could be found for them. The Military Governor, General Sir John Maxwell, then took possession of the British Agency and remained there, as far as I know, until the end of the war.

During the first half-year after the British entry into Pretoria Harmony's front gate was blocked by the tent of the military post office, the ropes of which had been fastened to the posts of the gate. Although the inhabitants of Harmony found it inconvenient to squeeze through the small opening at the side of the gate, Mrs. van Warmelo made no objection to the arrangement, because it safeguarded the property to some extent from possible intruders.

Other houses in the immediate neighbourhood of Harmony were occupied at different times by Lord Kitchener of Khartoum, the Duke of Westminster, and many other distinguished personages, with their staffs. From this it will readily be understood that in the whole of Pretoria no spot could have been more completely hemmed in by the vigilant military than Harmony.

How this vigilance was evaded by two Boer women, and how Harmony became the centre of Boer espionage as time went on, will be the theme of this story; but I wish my reader clearly to understand that from beginning to end there was no treachery, no broken promises of peace and good behaviour.

It was simply taken for granted that the two women in question were hopelessly cut off from all communication with their friends in the field, and utterly helpless and incapable of assisting their fellow-countrymen.

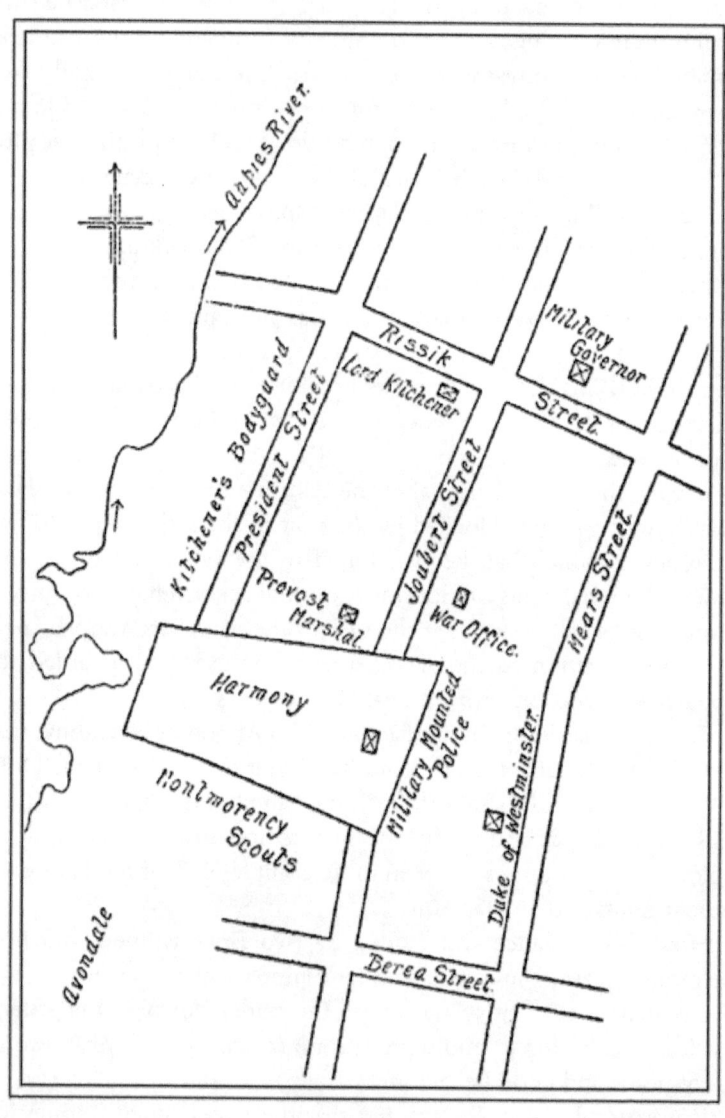

There were no conditions attached to the privilege of remaining undisturbed in their home, and, though it was well known that their menfolk were among the fighting burghers and that they themselves entertained the strongest feelings of antagonism towards the British, they were quietly left in peace.

Whether the fact that Mrs. van Warmelo's elder daughter was married to Mr. Henry Cloete, of Alphen, Wynberg, had anything to do with this unexpected and altogether undeserved leniency, I do not know. It certainly could not be put down to the credit of our heroines that Mr. Cloete had at one time been Acting British Agent at Pretoria, nor that he had shown the British Government such services as earned for him the distinction of having the Order of Companion of St. Michael and St. George conferred upon him.

All I can say is that if the van Warmelos owed their security to these facts, we can only look upon that as one of the fortunate circumstances of war over which we had no control. Other Boer residents in Pretoria fared less fortunately.

A great many "undesirable" families were put over the border at once; and of the remaining *burghers*, some took the oath of allegiance for purposes of their own, on which I am not in a position to pass judgment, others, the greater majority, took the oath of neutrality, and a few, in some mysterious way or other, avoided both these oaths, and remained in the capital, without pass, without permit, until time and occasion presented themselves for a sudden and unaccountable disappearance. In another chapter I shall endeavour to describe the dangers and difficulties which one of these men escaped from British martial law to the free life of the Boer commandos.

Although houses were "commandeered" right and left, and officers quartered on private families, as is the custom in every well-conducted war, Harmony was left in peace, only one mild attempt being made a few days after the occupation of Pretoria, by the officer in command of the Montmorency Scouts, to obtain entrance for himself and fellow officers at Harmony's inhospitable door.

"Only three officers," he said—"no men; and we shall give no trouble."

It was Hansie's duty to refuse, and refuse she did, firmly, patiently, without betraying her inmost fear that he could, and probably would—like the American darkie preacher, who announced to his flock that a certain meeting would take place "on Friday next, de Lord willin', an' if not, den on Sat'dy, whedder or no"—take possession of her home, "whedder or no" she gave her consent.

It is still a source of surprise that he did not, that, instead, he descended to argument, to beseechings.

"Our tents are bitterly cold at night," he said at last. "Let us at least sleep in the house."

"My brothers in the field have no tents," Hansie answered, "they sleep under the open sky. Do you think that we are going to allow British officers to sleep in their beds? Allow me to tell you that we are red-hot Republicans."

He departed, and, though Mrs. van Warmelo and Hansie lived in some trepidation for the next few days, no second attempt was made to commandeer Harmony.

The incident of the large number of side-saddles found in the British camp at Dundee had given Hansie food for much thought, and had caused her to plan her own future line of action long before the British officers entered Pretoria.

"They will want to enjoy themselves with our girls," she told her mother.

"They will be found at tennis-parties, at social evenings, and at concerts. They will want us to go out riding and driving with them, but, mother, I vow I shall never be seen with a khaki officer as long as our men are in the field." And, as far as she was able, she kept her word until the war was over.

This was not always easy, for many temptations were brought in her way, and she soon found it necessary to give up riding and tennis altogether in order to keep to her resolution.

CHAPTER 5

Only a Bit of Ribbon Gay!

The conspicuously bright hues of the "*Vierkleur*" round Hansie's hat attracted the attention of the new-comers in Pretoria, and she was often asked what they represented. In course of time other girls donned their colours, flaunting them in the face of the enemy on every possible occasion.

Now perhaps this was indiscreet, but, after all, what harm could it do?

It was a certain comfort to them, and there could be no objection to their taking a public stand for their own, under British martial law. At least, *we* thought so. Not so the enemy!

About three weeks after the British entry into the capital, the van Warmelos were told that orders had been issued that no Transvaal *burgher* in Pretoria would in future be permitted to wear the "*Vierkleur.*"

"Impossible! I do not believe it," Hansie exclaimed.

"What are you going to do?" her mother inquired.

"Go out as usual with my '*Vierkleur*' on, and see what happens," she said.

She went out and nothing happened, so she went out again next day, and the next.

In the meantime she heard that dozens of women and girls had been stopped in the streets and marched off to the various Charge Offices, where their colours were forcibly removed and detained as contraband articles of war.

Her mother warned her not to run the risk of losing her precious ribbon, and advised her to put it away, but Hansie was determined to wear it until *compelled* to submit. For a few days she rode about as usual, accompanied by Carlo, without being molested in any way, and she was just beginning to feel reassured, when, one day, a petty officer rode up to her in the street and ordered her to take off her Transvaal colours. She was on her way to Consul Cinatti's house, and was walking, for the Portuguese Consulate was quite close to Harmony.

With the horse prancing before her, she could not very well proceed on her way. She stopped and looked up at the soldier. She did not like his face at all, and changed her mind about what she meant to say to him.

"Why don't you do as I tell you? Take off that ribbon at once," he commanded.

"Why don't you go and conquer the Transvaal?" she asked.

"I have my orders," he said, with a black look, "and if you don't remove those colours from your hat immediately, I shall send some one to take them off by force."

"Take the Transvaal first," she said persuasively, "then you will be quite welcome to my bit of ribbon."

He wheeled round suddenly and tore off to the Sunnyside Charge Office, lashing his poor horse savagely and looking round at her with a watchful eye every few yards.

Hansie walked faster, and had nearly reached the side gate of the Consulate, when she saw him returning with two other mounted soldiers.

She dived through the gate, and running through the garden, unceremoniously entered the house at a side door.

"Oh, Celeste!" she said to the astonished Miss Cinatti, "there are three men after me!"

"Three men after you! What do you mean?"

"They want my precious '*Vierkleur.*' What shall I do?"

"Take it off!"

"Never!"

Here they were joined by Mr. Cinatti, who waved his arms and stamped his feet when he heard the story, and got so excited and indignant that he spluttered even more than usual in his broken English.

"What meant it all? What impudent impertinence was dis? It was nothing but one big mean trick, a prying trap," etc., etc.

When the storm was over (and his storms were usually of brief duration) he asked Hansie, with a gesture of comical despair:

"What are we going to do now?"

"I don't know."

"Will you take off dat ribbon?"

"I will not."

Hugely delighted, he clasped his hands in well-assumed agony of mind.

"Stay here and go home in de dark?"

"No," Hansie laughed.

"I'll tell you. Celeste will give you anudder ribbon to put over dat one."

"Thank you very much," Hansie said. "Yes, that is a good idea."

Miss Cinatti fastened a broad white ribbon over the "*Vierkleur*," and Hansie bade her an affectionate farewell. The Consul escorted her to the gate, where they found one of the mounted soldiers guarding the entrance, while the second had been stationed at the side gate into which Hansie had been seen to disappear. The man who had addressed her first was nowhere to be seen. Mr. Cinatti glared at the soldier, who backed away from the entrance, and allowed the girl to pass. He did not look triumphant—on the contrary he saluted respectfully; but the other Tommy at the side gate laughed when he saw the white ribbon on her hat, and I am afraid that Hansie felt very much inclined to say, "I've got my '*Vierkleur*' on still!" But she wisely refrained, walking on stiffly without so much as a glance at the man. That night she slowly and sadly took off her 'bit of ribbon gay,' replacing it by a black band in token of mourning and bereavement.

There was too much at stake, and she felt it would be better to keep the ribbon in safety at home than to run the risk of being deprived of it by force.

A sympathetic friend afterwards painted two crossed flags, the flags of the Transvaal and the Free State, on her band of black, and this she wore unmolested until the end of the war.

CHAPTER 6

Passes and Permits

At this time the procuring of passes and permits became the order of the day, and it is inconceivable the amount of red-tape that had to be gone through in the process.

For women living alone and having no menfolk to send to the offices, this was especially annoying.

Hours were spent in waiting, and applicants were frequently sent from one official to another, and from one department to another, on unimportant matters.

This brought Hansie into touch with the very men whose society she had resolved to avoid.

It took her three or four hours to get a permit for her bicycle and as many days to get permission to retain her Colt's pocket-pistol, for the officers in charge of the rifle department refused to let her keep it and she eventually decided to go straight to headquarters, *viz.* the Military Governor, General Maxwell.

Orders had very rightly been issued that all firearms should be delivered to the military authorities, but in this case Mrs. van Warmelo thought an exception should be made, because two unprotected women, living in an isolated homestead, could hardly be considered safe in times of such great danger unless sufficiently armed and able to defend themselves.

Other matters, of minor importance, could be overlooked, but it was to this question of retaining weapons that she and her daughter owed their acquaintance with the charming and affable Military Governor.

The two women were received with great courtesy, and when they had explained that they had a Mauser rifle in their possession, a revolver, and a pistol, begging to be allowed to keep them for self-defence,

General Maxwell instantly granted them permits for the revolver and pistol, but asked them to give up their rifle. He gave them a written promise, signed by himself, that the rifle would be returned to them after the war—which promise, I may add, was faithfully kept. General Maxwell asked many questions about their fighting relatives, and, when they were departing, said he hoped they would come straight to him if at any time they got into trouble.

This kindness opened the way to many subsequent visits, and brought about a friendly understanding between the officials in the Governor's Department and Mrs. and Miss van Warmelo.

The latter, upon whom naturally devolved the task of procuring the necessary passes and permits, was always well received, and never kept waiting, although she made no secret of her feelings towards the British, and frankly gave vent to her opinions on every subject connected with the war. This state of affairs was brought about all the more easily by the fact that General Maxwell and his A.D.C., Major Hoskins, invited her opinions on every possible occasion.

Mutual respect, and a sincere desire to alleviate the suffering caused by the war, formed the basis of the somewhat incongruous friendship between the high British official and the Republican girl, especially as time went on and the appalling problem of the concentration camps presented itself. Then it was that General Maxwell, pacing up and down in his office, his brow drawn with care, and every movement betraying his distress, frankly discussed the situation with Hansie and invited her confidence. As she had no secrets of importance at this time, these interviews were marked by a spirit of mutual understanding, and she learnt more and more to admire and respect the governor for his humanity and nobility of character; but the time was soon to come when the demands of her land and people called her to more dangerous fields of labour, and then it became difficult, well-nigh impossible, to meet the searching eye of the military governor.

Her visits became less frequent, of her own free will, and in time ceased altogether.

Soon after the rifle incident Hansie had to call on General Maxwell, as Secretary of the Pretoria Ladies' Vocal Society, for a permit to hold rehearsals. She found him alone and disengaged, for a wonder, and so evidently pleased to see her again that she entered into conversation with him unhesitatingly.

After she had explained the object of her visit and apologised for troubling him about such a trifle, she told him that she had been informed in other departments that as there was no institution for granting permits to hold rehearsals, she would have to get a special permit from the Military Governor.

"Why," he exclaimed in surprise, "can you not rehearse without a permit?"

"No," Hansie answered laughingly. "Do you not know that two or three may not gather together except in the name of the governor under the new regulations and since the execution of Cordua? Why, we may be conspiring against your life instead of rehearsing our songs, and at the present moment we can hardly put our noses out-of-doors without being asked whether we have permits for them."

"You are right," he answered; "I did not think of this. Well, you may have your permit on condition that you promise to talk no politics and to be in your own homes before 7 p.m."

Hansie gave the promise on behalf of the vocal society, and yet another war-permit was added to her curious collection! With all the friendliness existing between the governor and herself, I do not for a moment think that they ever trusted one another completely. Were they not both good patriots? Hansie knew by the questions he asked her that he was trying to extract information from her, and the governor only told her as much as he thought she could use to his own advantage.

On this particular occasion, when he parted from her, he asked in a fatherly, I-take-such-an-interest-in-you way whether she ever heard from her brothers.

"No," she exclaimed in innocent surprise. "How can I?" (and at the time she spoke truth). Whereupon he sympathetically murmured something about "a very trying time for you."

Permits everywhere and for everything!

Men were stopped in the streets to show their residential passes, private carriages were held up and the occupants requested to produce their permits for vehicle and horses, and cyclists had to dismount a dozen times a day at the sign of some khaki-clothed figure patrolling the streets.

The first British officers to cross Harmony's threshold as visitors and equals were a colonel and a young captain, who both came from Wynberg with letters of introduction from Mrs. van Warmelo's daughter, Mrs. Henry Cloete.

After the long months of irregular correspondence, always severely censored, it was such a relief to get news direct that the bearers were welcomed gratefully.

They called again, and the dignified presence of the colonel soon became a familiar sight at Harmony. With him it was quite possible to converse, for he avoided every painful topic with the utmost tact and good-breeding, but the captain was a veritable firebrand, and many were the heated arguments carried on during his visits.

As the weary, weary months dragged on, and the most sanguine could not see the end of the terrible war, it seemed as if feeling grew stronger and the power of endurance lessened.

Even the occasional visits of the British officers became trying to the van Warmelos, and one day her mother asked Hansie to request the captain not to come again, valiantly retreating to the garden when next he called, and leaving her daughter to fight it out with him alone.

"I am very sorry," he said, "but what have *I* done?"

"Nothing," Hansie answered, "but you see it is against our principles, and we would like you to wait until the war is over——" The hateful task was over, and the captain took his departure, not to return again.

Hansie refused obstinately to go over the same ground with the colonel. He came so seldom, and he was such a kind and courteous old gentleman, that it seemed unnecessary to put an end to his visits, and in time his own good feeling told him to discontinue them.

It was in the summer of 1901, when the days at Harmony were spent in the fruit-laden garden and great jars of apples, pears, peaches, and figs were being canned and preserved for winter use, that thoughts strayed most lovingly and persistently to the two hungry brothers in the field.

"Where are they, I wonder?" was a frequent exclamation. "Did they ever reach the Boer commandos, and oh, when shall we hear from them?"

Great were the rejoicings when Dr. Mulder, who was on his way to Holland, and had got permission from the British to pass through Pretoria from the Boer lines, arrived at Harmony with the news that he had seen the two van Warmelos in the English camp at Nooitgedacht, after its capture by the Boers under General Beyers. They were well and in good spirits then, and the delight their mother and sister experienced at seeing some one direct from the Boer lines can only be appreciated by those who know what it means to a Boer to be a captive under British martial law.

At this time Pretoria was almost completely surrounded by the Boers, and every precaution was being taken against a possible attack. Deep trenches were dug all round the town, electric wires put up, while the hills bristled with cannon and searchlights played from the forts incessantly at night.

The realities of war were forced upon one by the increased activity on the Eastern Railway line to Delagoa Bay, plainly visible from the side verandah at Harmony, and, daily, train loads passed of armed soldiers, or Boer women and children being brought in from the devastated farms.

Armoured trains and Red Cross carriages steamed in and out, horses, cattle, provision loads—everything that could remind one of the fierce strife raging throughout the land.

At this time it became evident that a thief or thieves were helping themselves at night to thoroughbred fowls and fruit at Harmony, and Mrs. van Warmelo asked the sergeant-major of the Military Mounted Police to consult with her about catching the miscreants.

She suspected *kaffirs*—certainly not the troops encamped about the place, for a more orderly set of soldiers it would have been hard to find. Their behaviour was always so exemplary that they were now and then rewarded with baskets of fruit and vegetables from Harmony's overflowing abundance.

It was therefore perfectly natural that the sergeant-major should hurry over to the house, indignant and sympathetic, to listen to Mrs. van Warmelo's grievances and to lay plans for the capture of the cunning thief.

That he came at dawn seemed evident, for though the police watched every night, they never caught sight of him, and yet there were fowls missing every morning. Things were beginning to look rather suspicious when, in spite of the vigilant watch kept by the police, there were only nineteen fowls left of the sixty. Mrs. van Warmelo made up her mind to watch for herself.

Early next morning, when a fine white cock had disappeared, she set out with one of the native servants, and, following the track made by the white feathers the bird had lost in its struggles, she came upon the thieves' den. An ideal spot in a little hollow by the riverside, surrounded by trees and shrubs! A small fireplace, a few old sacks and tins and a mass of feathers and bones told their own tale, and Mrs. van Warmelo went home well satisfied.

The sergeant-major, when he heard her story, said he thought it would be better to catch the thief red-handed in the fowl-run than to surprise him in his den, and the police were set to watch again that night.

In the morning two fine hens were missing! The remarks then made at Harmony on the vigilance of British soldiers in general and Military Mounted Police in particular were complimentary in the extreme.

Then Mrs. van Warmelo sent the boy to reconnoitre, and he soon came running back in great excitement, with the news that the thief, a young *kaffir*, was sitting beside a fire, eating fowls.

Armed to the teeth, the police set forth to capture him, and soon returned with the miscreant. Such a sight he was! Glistening with fat and covered with feathers, and, as one of the soldiers remarked, "with a corporation like the Lord Mayor." He was handcuffed and taken to the police camp, while the men had their breakfast before escorting him to the Charge Office.

Suddenly there was a fearful commotion.

The culprit had slipped off one of his handcuffs, crept through the wire fence unobserved, and was flying like the wind through the garden towards the river.

After him, in wild confusion, jumping over shrubs and furrows, followed half a dozen soldiers, a couple of natives, Carlo, and I don't know how many other dogs.

He was captured by the brave corporal as he was dashing up the bank on the other side of the river, and brought back to the camp, with his hands tied securely behind.

One month's imprisonment only and a change of diet were prescribed for him at the Charge Office that day.

This incident, though exciting at the time, would not have been worth recording here were it not for its connection with what happened afterwards.

Whatever suspicions the military may have had of intrigues at Harmony, these must have been removed by the fact of their having been requested by the inmates themselves to keep a watch over the property.

So the way was being unconsciously prepared for subsequent events.

As fruit was also being stolen from time to time, the soldiers maintained their watch over the garden, well knowing that their vigilance would be rewarded by a full share of the good things, while they would be the losers if the pilfering were allowed to continue.

When it became evident, a few months later, that another thief was helping himself to her fowls, Mrs. van Warmelo made up her mind to catch him red-handed, without the assistance of the Military Police.

She decided that he would not come back at once, and gave him two days to digest his spoil, and on the third day she got up very early in the hopes of being on the scenes before him, ready to receive him when he came.

She had only been in the garden a few moments when she saw some one, in a stooping posture, running swiftly towards the fowl-run. A moment later and he had seen her. He turned and ran in the opposite direction, Mrs. van Warmelo following closely on his heels, loading her revolver as she ran and calling out, "Stand, or I fire." On being warned a second time he stopped and turned round. Mrs. van Warmelo demanded what he was doing on her property, and he answered in good English that he had lost his way, upon which Mrs. van Warmelo offered to show him the way, and ordered him to march on ahead. With the loaded revolver between his shoulders, the culprit was forced to obey, and Mrs. van Warmelo had the satisfaction of handing him over to the sergeant-major "all by herself."

To save himself, the wily thief turned Queen's evidence and offered to conduct the police to a place where drink for natives was brewed and sold, but the soldiers, not relishing the idea of his escaping scot-free, first gave him a good thrashing before handing him over to be further dealt with by the provost-marshal.

CHAPTER 7

Postage by Strategy

Life at Pretoria was at this time far from pleasant for the Boers who remained loyal to their cause.

Most people who had the means, or were not bound to the country by the closest ties, let their houses and went to Europe until the war was over. Many of those who did not leave of their own free will were sent away to the coast, where they were considered safe from plotting against the British, and the few remaining Boer families were apparently on their best behaviour, above all dreading the fate of their fellow-countrymen.

The inmates of Harmony, perhaps more than any other Boers, feared being sent away, because they knew that watching events from afar would be a thousand times worse than enduring the restrictions of English martial law, and that banishment would make it impossible for them to render their fighting men any services. But they found the time of inactivity terribly trying, so much so that they began to cast about in their minds for work, for mischief—for anything, in fact, to relieve the daily, deadening suspense and the dread, of what they knew not, with which they were consumed.

Very galling was the severe censorship of their letters. Mrs. van Warmelo's high spirit rebelled against the continued surveillance of her correspondence and she determined to outwit the censor.

Then began an exciting period of smuggling and contriving, which led to the most complete independence on their part of the services of Mr. Censor, and ended in a well-organised and exceedingly clever system of communication with friends in every part of the world.

On one occasion a sympathiser, leaving the country for good, offered to smuggle through to Mrs. Cloete any document Mrs. van Warmelo might wish to send.

There was nothing ready at the time, but Mrs. van Warmelo decided to make use of this opportunity for some future occasion, and wrote to her daughter on a tiny piece of tissue-paper, "Whatever you may receive in future, marked with a small blue cross, examine closely."

This was smuggled through in some way unknown to the sender and safely delivered to Mrs. Cloete, for people were leaving Pretoria daily, and it was not difficult to find suitable envoys.

Hansie had—and has to this day in her possession as a priceless memento of the war—a small morocco case with a maroon velvet lining, which travelled backwards and forwards between Harmony and Alphen until some better way of communication was contrived. With a sharp instrument Mrs. van Warmelo had removed the entire tray-like bottom of the case, packed two or three closely-written sheets of tissue paper in the opening, and pressed the little tray firmly down in its place again. A tiny blue cross carelessly pasted on the bottom of the case carried its own message to the conspirator at Alphen.

A few weeks later the case came back to Harmony with an antique gold bracelet for Hansie and a long uncensored letter, in the snug hiding-place, for Mrs. van Warmelo.

The next adventure was with a charming lady, whom we shall call "the English lady," she was so *very* English. (If the truth were known, she was not really English, but Cape Colonial, and, as is often the case, more English than the English themselves, and more loyal than the queen.)

She unwisely said to a friend of Hansie's, who naturally repeated her words to Hansie, that she would take good care not to convey letters or parcels for the van Warmelos when she left for England, as she shortly intended doing, because she was quite sure they "smuggled," or, if she did consent to take anything, she would examine it thoroughly and destroy whatever it contained of a doubtful character.

When this reached Hansie's ears she made up her mind that "the English lady," and no other, would be her next messenger to Alphen. She dismissed the morocco case from her mind as unsuitable for the occasion, and deliberated long with her mother. At last she was sent to town to buy three medium-sized dolls.

It did not matter much what kind of dolls they were, but they had to have hollow porcelain heads, and they were to be bought from one man only, an indispensable fellow-conspirator in one of the principal stores in Church Street.

When she came home with the dolls her mother seemed pretty well satisfied with the heads; they looked fairly roomy from the outside, and so they were found to be when one of them had been carefully steamed until the glue melted and the head dropped off.

Hansie had been writing, without lifting her head, while her mother prepared the doll. The sheets of paper, rolled up into pellets, were then forced through the slender neck, and the dolls weighed to see if the difference in weight were noticeable. It was not. The head was glued on again, a blue cross was marked on the body, and the dolls were neatly wrapped in a brown-paper parcel.

"The English lady" soon after came to pay her farewell call. After the usual formalities had been exchanged she remarked that she hoped to visit Alphen soon after her arrival in Cape Town.

Mrs. van Warmelo was charmed and delighted, and asked whether she would be good enough to take a parcel of three dolls for Mrs. Cloete's little daughters.

There was just one moment's hesitation, then "the English lady rapidly made up her mind." "Yes, with pleasure, but I must have the parcel to-morrow, because my trunks have to be closed and sent on ahead."

Mrs. van Warmelo turned to her daughter in grave consultation. "Let me see, it is too late now, the shops will be closed, but you can perhaps go to town on your bicycle early to-morrow morning to buy the dolls and have them sent straight to Mrs. ———'s house."

"Yes, mother, I'll do that with pleasure, but I won't have them sent. I'll take them to her myself to be quite sure that she will have them before twelve o'clock."

The next morning Hansie took the dolls to her fellow-conspirator behind the counter and had them made up into an unmistakably *professional*-looking parcel, tied and sealed with the label of the shop.

Thus were the suspicions of "the English lady" lulled to rest. For her comfort, should this ever reach her eye, I may say that there were no dangerous communications in the doll's head, and should she feel resentful at having been outwitted, she should have known better than to *dare* one of her country-women under martial law.

On other occasions sympathetic friends were willingly made use of, and the methods of smuggling were so carefully planned in every case that none of the bearers ever got into trouble, with one exception.

A foreign gentleman of high position, through his own carelessness, found himself in a difficult and unpleasant situation. He was leaving for Europe and expressed his willingness to take letters or documents, provided they were packed so carefully that there would be no danger of their being discovered.

Mrs. van Warmelo asked him if he could let her have any little article in daily use and which he was in the habit of carrying about in his pockets. He said that he would think about it, and sent her, next day, a silver cigarette-case with a watered-silk lining. It did not take long to remove the lining and to pack the letters under it. When the lining was replaced and the cigarettes lay in neat rows against it, the most careful observer could not detect anything unusual. These letters were destined for Mr. W.T. Stead and contained a full account of the condition of the Irene Concentration Camp.

In addition to this, Hansie gave her friend a photo of herself in a sturdy frame, containing a hidden letter for Mrs. Cloete, whilst instructing him to destroy the epistle if he could not hand it over to Mrs. Cloete personally, moreover, not to remove the letter from the cigarette-case until he arrived in London.

At Cape Town he met at the hotel a man who professed to be a great pro-Boer and with whom he soon became so friendly that he, finding it impossible to go out to Alphen himself, indiscreetly entrusted Mrs. Cloete's letter into the hands of this stranger, with the result that it was taken direct to the military authorities.

Our friend was arrested the next day as he was boarding the ocean liner, and was kept under strict surveillance while his luggage was being overhauled.

We were told afterwards by friends who witnessed the scene that, during the process, he sat on deck with the utmost unconcern, smoking cigarettes and toying with a silver case! No further evidence having been found against him, he was allowed to sail away in peace, and Mrs. Cloete too escaped without so much as a warning, perhaps because the contents of the letter were not considered sufficiently incriminating.

Mr. Stead received the documents hidden in the cigarette-case in due time and made full use of their contents in his monthly magazine, *The Review of Reviews*.

Although, surprising to relate, no steps were taken against the conspirators at Harmony, they soon noticed an extraordinary increase in the vigilance of the censor, so much so, that the most harmless communications failed to reach their destination, and when by chance anything was allowed to pass through it was mutilated beyond recognition, whole sentences being smirched with printer's ink or pages cut away by the ruthless hand of the censor.

It may seem a small thing now, but this state of affairs, when letters and papers were the only consolation one had, became a source of such keen annoyance and distress that Hansie decided to approach the censor and ask him the reason for such petty persecutions.

The head censor being away at the time, she was shown into the presence of a man whose very appearance excited her strongest antipathy. In the first place he had a purely Dutch name, and she knew that he could not occupy a position of so much trust under the British without being a traitor to his own countrymen.

Secondly, he seemed to derive much pleasure from her visit and, when she told him who she was, had the audacity to say:

"I always enjoy your letters very much, Miss van Warmelo; they quite repay me for my trouble!"

When taxed with confiscating and mutilating them, he was all concern and innocence personified.

No, indeed, he could never be guilty of such a breach of gallantry and etiquette, the fault must lie elsewhere; he was her friend, and if she would promise to bring all her letters to him personally, he would see that they were passed.

"Miserable Renegade!" she thought, with boiling blood.

Instantly it flashed through her mind that it would be foolish indeed to make an enemy of this man. Her whole manner changed.

"How *very* kind of you!" she said. "Yes, I shall come myself if you are sure I shall not be giving you too much trouble."

"A pleasure, I assure you," bowing with great gallantry, and Hansie went home to tell her mother what had happened.

After this interview with the censor, he allowed their letters to pass with unfailing regularity.

True to her promise, Hansie took her European mail to him herself every week, and this brought her into contact with him frequently. He was always affable (hatefully affable) and obliging, and the thought of this man made it more and more difficult for her to write, especially those letters destined for the north of Holland.

One day she asked her mother to think of some plan by which she could use the censor for her own purposes, without his knowledge, and this set Mrs. van Warmelo's active mind and resourceful brain working, with what result we shall see in our next chapter.

CHAPTER 8

Outwitting the Censor

If the method of writing between the lines in chemicals presented itself to Mrs. van Warmelo's mind for a moment, it was dismissed as too crude and well-known, and, in consequence, too dangerous.

And yet she found her thoughts reverting persistently to chemicals as the only solution to the problem before her. One day she took the strained juice of a lemon and wrote a few words with it on a sheet of white paper. When dry, there was no trace of the written words to be seen until she had passed a hot iron over them. Imagine her joy and satisfaction when they showed up clear and distinct, in a colour of yellowish brown. Well satisfied with her experiment, she sought and found a square white envelope of thick paper and good quality, which she carefully opened out, by inserting and rolling the thin end of a penholder along the part that was glued. Spreading the envelope before her on the table, she wrote some sentences in lemon juice on the *inside*, folding it into shape again and pasting it down with great care and neatness. This envelope she placed in Hansie's hands, with an expectant look, when the latter came home that afternoon.

Hansie turned it over, examined it on all sides and shook her head, puzzled.

"Open it," her mother suggested, "and look inside."

Hansie opened it and, peering into it, shook her head again, more mystified than ever.

"I give it up, mother," she said. "Come, don't be so mysterious—tell me what it all means."

Mrs. van Warmelo then took the envelope, opened it with the penholder again, and, producing the hot iron which she had been keeping in readiness for the psychological moment, she ironed out the flattened sheet and revealed to the astonished gaze of her daughter the written words within.

At first Hansie was speechless with admiration; then she threw her arms round her mother and hugged her vigorously.

"Really, mother," she exclaimed, "I am proud of you. How we shall be able to dupe 'Miserable Renegade' now!"

The full importance of this discovery was not realised at the time, for all their smuggling had hitherto been carried on merely for pleasure and they had had no information of any importance to communicate to their friends across the seas; but, in the light of after-events, they realised that they had been led to make their preparations and to have their methods in full working order before the time came to use them in conveying dispatches from the Boer Secret Service to President Kruger in Holland.

They were now in the possession of a scheme which defied detection, and the next thing to be done was to inform some distant conspirator of this valuable discovery and instruct him in the use of it.

That this could not be done through the post, my reader will understand, and as reliable opportunities were becoming more rare, Hansie had to wait some months and to possess her soul in patience until at last some trusted friend, leaving the country, could be persuaded to convey the important instructions.

When and how they were eventually sent I cannot tell with positive certainty. There is a difference of opinion on this point between Mrs. van Warmelo and her daughter, and there is no way of settling the dispute, because Hansie's diary contains no word about the White Envelope, for reasons which it will hardly be necessary to explain.

Mrs. van Warmelo says the instructions were dispatched in a false double-bottom of an ordinary safety match-box. Hansie thinks they were either hidden behind a photo-frame or in a tin of insect-powder, both these methods having been employed on various occasions, but at present we are only concerned with the fact that the instructions reached their destination safely, and from that day until the end of the war a gloriously free and uninterrupted communication was kept up between Harmony and Alphen and one spot in the north of Holland, of which we shall hear more as our story unfolds itself.

Further experimenting showed that the lemon-juice became visible after a few days when written on certain papers, while on others there was nothing to be seen after many weeks, and this danger was immediately communicated to Holland as a very serious one, for it stands to reason that the danger connected with the sending of the

White Envelope *from* South Africa was nothing compared to the danger of receiving one and having it censored three weeks after it had been written.

One had to keep in mind that letters leaving the country would be censored immediately and would not be subjected to further scrutiny in Europe, whereas letters for South Africa ran every risk of being betrayed on examination, after a three-weeks' journey by land and sea.

When the smuggled instructions were well on their way, the first White Envelope was written to Holland, and carelessly thrust amongst a pile of other letters by the quaking Hansie when next she handed her mail to "Miserable Renegade."

He glanced through them all without examining them, merely putting the mark of the censor on them and assuring Hansie that they would be forwarded that very day.

No seven weeks could have been longer or more full of suspense than those which followed, and the excitement at Harmony when in due time a square White Envelope in the well-known hand arrived from Holland can better be imagined than described.

With what anxiety it was opened and how eagerly examined before the hot iron was applied! how keen the delight when nothing legible was found, even on the closest inspection! What relief, at last, when the written messages became not only legible, but clear and distinct!

So this method was going to answer beyond their wildest expectations!

To make assurance doubly sure, and because Hansie did not trust "Miserable Renegade" one jot, she sometimes made use of friends, going to Johannesburg, to post her White Envelope there, giving as her reason for doing so the difficulties she had had with the Pretoria censor.

Of course the secret of the White Envelope was not confided even to her most intimate friends.

This correspondence having been fairly established, there was nothing to prevent Hansie from using the European mail every week; but to avoid needless risks and the possible exposure of the valuable secret, it was agreed to use it only in cases of extreme necessity.

The sign of the White Envelope became an understood thing between the conspirators, and for all other correspondence grey and coloured envelopes were used.

The correspondent in the north of Holland was a young minister of the Gospel who had taken for years an unusual interest in Hansie's career.

At this point of our story the two young people, after some years of estrangement, brought about by an unfortunate misunderstanding on his part, pride and self-will on hers, had reached the delightfully unsettling stage of exchanging photographs, the sequel of which took place under the most romantic circumstances, not to be related in this volume.

"It is an ill wind that blows nobody any good," the young man must often have thought, as he faithfully carried out every instruction from the scene of action.

All communications for the President and Dr. Leyds were sent to him (through the White Envelope), because it was not considered safe to correspond with them direct, even through the medium of the lemon-juice discovery.

As time went on, this method of communication was used for many purposes and always with success, but some time after the war, when it was Hansie's right and privilege to go through the war correspondence of the young minister of religion, she came upon a letter from Dr. Leyds to him, in which she read, with growing interest, the following information:

"I cannot conceal from you that I was startled when I opened the last white envelope, for I was able to read the whole report, though the writing was faint, without applying the heating process to it. Perhaps this letter lay in a warm place near the engine-rooms on the voyage. Will you not send a timely warning? You could, for instance, say that the measles have come out and are plainly visible, even without the application of hot compresses. Those people are quite clever enough to understand what you wish to convey to them."

This warning did not reach Harmony at the time. Perhaps the censor, trained as he must have been in the art of reading dangerous meanings into seemingly harmless sentences, decided in his own mind that it would be advisable to keep the information about the measles to himself, and consigned the letter to the waste-paper basket.

In time experience taught the conspirators at Harmony that the greatest care would be necessary in the use of the White Envelope, and to this they probably owe the fact that it was never found out by the enemy.

The reproductions given here of specimens of the White Envelope, showing the address on one side and the written messages on the oth-

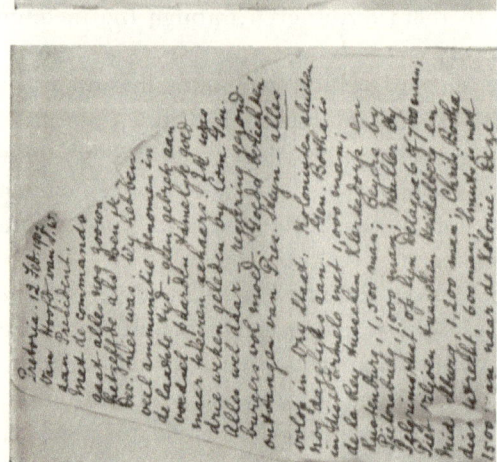

(1) Letter From Head of Secret Service to President.

(2) Letter From Head of Secret Service to President.

(3) Letter From Head of Secret Service to President.

er, will give the reader an idea of how this correspondence was carried on. We do not vouch for the accuracy of the information conveyed in the following translation of the contents of this envelope. The figures were quoted from memory, but the general impression conveyed in this report, of the condition of the commandos at the time, is reliable and correct. On the side flaps of the envelope certain love messages were written. These have been covered over with blank paper and are not for publication.

(TRANSLATION)
Contents of White Envelope
From Head of Secret Service to President

Pretoria, February 12th, 1902.

With Commandos all is still about the same as when I was here in December. Much ammunition has been taken from the enemy recently.

No want of food, horses fairly good, but clothing very scarce.

Three weeks ago I was with the Commandant-General. All well with him. Government in good health, *burghers* full of courage. Good tidings received from President Steyn.

Everything plentiful in Free State.

General Botha is now in Ermelo district with 1,000 men; de la Rey between Klerksdorp and Rustenburg, 1,500 men; Beyers near Pietersberg, 1,000 men; Muller near Pilgrim's Rest, on Delagoa line, with 600 or 700 men; Piet Viljoen between Heidelberg and Middelburg, 1,200; Christian Botha, district Utrecht, 600; Smuts has gone to the Colony with 1,500. These are the big Commandos only. There are many small forces of 100 or a few hundred men under petty officers. Engagements: January 15th General Botha defeated enemy. Three wounded on our side. Enemy's loss, 46 killed, 92 wounded, 150 prisoners. 200 horses taken, 15,000 rounds of ammunition. Great victory by Commandant-General on the 3rd inst. No full report received yet.

Everywhere small engagements.

Many prisoners taken from our ranks lately, through the poor condition of our horses. Things better now. De la Rey has had a few small victories. On December 25th engagement under de Wet near Frankfort. Our side victorious. A camp of 500 men taken, 150 killed and wounded, 200 captures, 2 Armstrongs taken with 400 shells; 1 Nordenbeldt with 2,500 maxim pom-poms; rifle ammunition 150,000; all the horses and cattle. The enemy is plundered daily. Health of *burghers* excellent. Plenty of fruit. Our losses, as usual, miraculously small.

Through perseverance and faith we hope to gain a certain victory.

Chapter 9
Jan Celliers, Poet and Patriot

That there is more than one man of the name of Jan Celliers in South Africa I know, but there is only one Jan Celliers who can be honoured by the title "Poet and Patriot," and that is the remarkable personality of our friend in Pretoria, J.F.E. Celliers.

I have chosen him as the subject of this chapter, not so much because of the important, I may almost say revolutionary part he has played in the building up of South African literature since the war, as on account of the unique patriotism displayed by him throughout the war under circumstances of the severest test and trial.

How he, after active service in the field since the beginning of the war, came to be locked up in Pretoria as an unseen prisoner of war, an unwilling captive between the green walls of his suburban garden, when the British took possession of the capital on that stupefying June 5th, 1900, we shall briefly relate in this chapter.

Mr. Celliers' experience was that of many good and faithful *burghers*.

The news of heavy Boer losses, the desperately forced march of the British troops from Bloemfontein to Pretoria, the crushing blows in quick succession, the departure of the Boer Administration from the seat of government, the demoralisation of the scattered forces, and the painful uncertainty of what the next step was to be—these things, combined with the fact, in Mr. Celliers' case, of having no riding-horse or bicycle on which to escape from the town, caused him to be surprised by the wholly unexpected entry of the British forces into the capital. Just a brief period of dazed inaction, a few hours of stupefied uncertainty, and he found himself hopelessly cut off from every chance of escape.

He planned escape from the beginning, for conscientious scruples forbade his taking the oath of neutrality. Of the oath of allegiance there was no question whatever.

There was nothing for it but to keep himself hidden until an opportunity for escaping to his fellow-countrymen in the field presented itself.

The first three weeks were spent in the garden, but it soon became evident that listening ears and prying eyes were being paid to discover his whereabouts, and closer confinement was found necessary. Thereafter he sat between four walls, reading and writing during the greater part of the day, keeping a watchful eye on the little front gate through a narrow opening in the window-blind and disappearing, through a trap-door, under the floor as soon as a soldier or official entered the gate.

When darkness fell he left his cramped hiding-place, and gliding unseen through the house and yard, this weary prisoner occupied himself with exercises for the preservation of his health, running, jumping, standing on his head, and plying the skipping-rope vigorously, under the protecting shadows of the dark cypress trees.

The weeks went by, broken once by the intense excitement of a visit of one of the *burghers* from the field.

Mrs. Celliers' brother, M. Dürr, had crept into town at dead of night between the British sentinels on a dangerous mission for the Boers. A short week he spent with his brother-in-law, sharing his confinement and making plans for his escape. Then he was gone, and the old deadly monotony settled over the house once more.

July went by, and August was nearly spent when at last an opportunity presented itself, and Mr. Celliers, in woman's garb, bade wife and children a passionate farewell, not to see them again for nearly two years.

With a cloak over his shoulders and a high collar concealing his closely cropped hair, his wife's skirt on, and a heavy veil covering a straw hat, he stepped boldly into a small vehicle standing waiting before his gate and drove through the streets of Pretoria. For the time at least he too belonged to the "Petticoat Commando." Mrs. Malan was in the cart, and had been sent by Mrs. Joubert to escort him through the town.

The disguise was taken before a thought could be given to the possible consequences of such a step. Spurred by the heroic attitude and fine courage displayed by his wife, Mr. Celliers lost not a moment in availing himself of the long-looked-for opportunity.

The thrilling adventures and hairbreadth escapes he went through in that memorable flight for duty and freedom will no doubt be found accurately recorded in his book on the war, which I know to be "in the making" at the present moment. Suffice it to say that he reached the farm of a friend near Silkatsnek in safety, where, he had been informed, he would find Boer commandos in the neighbourhood.

Disappointment awaited him, however. The commando had withdrawn to the north, followed closely by thousands of British troops whose proximity to the farm made it dangerous, not only for him, but for the people who harboured him, to remain there longer than one night. A farm-hand, a trusted native servant, was asked to undertake the task of escorting Mr. Celliers to the Boer lines. After some hesitation he consented. The risk was great, but the promise of £20 reward when the war was over acted like a charm, and the two set forth before break of day on their perilous adventure.

Here and there the tiny light of an outpost on the open field warned them to make a wide *détour*. The crackling of the short burnt stubbles of grass under their feet caused them to hold their breath and listen with loudly beating hearts for the dreaded "Halt! Who goes there?"

When the light of day began to break over earth and sky, the *kaffir*, in evident anxiety, warned the *Baas* to hide in a large dense tree while he, the *kaffir*, went on ahead to reconnoitre. He departed—not to return again, base coward that he was, and the unfortunate man in the tree waited for hours until it dawned on him that he had been deserted at the most critical moment. He stepped from his hiding-place, quickly deciding to walk nonchalantly forward, the open *veld* leaving no possible means of pursuing his way under cover.

He passes many isolated homesteads, some ruined and deserted, others inhabited by aged people, delicate women, and little children only. One and all they shrink from him when he relates his story. They do not trust him—he may be in the employment of the British, a trap set for the unwary; their homes are closed to him. He pursues his way wearily. What is that approaching him in the distance? With straining eyes he is able to distinguish a group of horsemen coming towards him, and with lightning-like rapidity he turns from his course and jumps into the washed-out bed of a small rivulet flowing by. A group of startled Kaffir children gaze at him in astonishment. The riders come in clear view—not horsemen, but a number of *kaffir* women with earthenware pots on their heads. These they fill with water, and mounting their horses depart the way they came.

With renewed hope and thankfulness at his heart our traveller resumes his course in the lengthening shadows of the short winter afternoon. At last he reaches a German mission station.

No refuge for him here! For the inhabitants are "neutral," but he is informed that a few days before 20,000 British troops had passed that way in a northward direction, in hot pursuit of the Boer commandos fleeing to the Waterberg district. The benevolent old missionary directs him to a small farm in the neighbourhood where a Boer woman lives alone with her little children. Perhaps she can give him some idea of the safest route for him to take. But no, the woman turns from him in extreme agitation, refuses to answer his questions, and is so evidently distressed at his appearance that he turns away and withdraws to the *veld* to think. What now? What now?

He is sitting on the outskirts of the great bush-*veld*, that endless stretch of forest-growth, dense and dark as far as the eye can reach. Shall he enter that, unarmed, without provisions or water and totally ignorant of the direction to take? He shudders. The blackness of the night is creeping over the scene, and over his soul desolation and despair.

"I must return to the mission station," he decides at last. "Surely they will give me refuge for the night!"

Slowly he drags his weary limbs across the *veld*, hesitatingly he presents himself, falteringly he proffers his request. A moment's hesitation and the family circle opens to receive him, its members crowd round him with words of comfort and small deeds of love. They are not doing *right*, but they will do *well*. Nothing is left undone to restore and refresh the exhausted fugitive, who soon finds himself in a perfect haven of domestic happiness and luxury.

As the evening wears on, the small harmonium is opened, and while the younger members of the family are singing sweet part-songs together, our hero turns over the leaves of a small book he has found lying on the table, a book of German quotations. His eyes are attracted by the following lines by Dessler:

Lenkst du durch Wusten meine Reise,
Ich folg, und lehne mich auf Dich
Du gibst mir aus der Wolken Speise
Und Tränkest aus dem Felsen mich,
Ich traue Deinen Wunderwegen,

Sie enden sich in Lieb und Segen,
Genug, wenn ich Dich bei mir hab.

They are like balm to his troubled soul, and he commits them to memory for future use. God knows the future looks desperate enough to him, for he feels that he cannot remain in this haven of rest. Consideration for the safety of his kind friends forbids this. He soon departs, having heard that, for the present at least, the western direction is open to him, and, in taking this, his tribulations begin afresh.

Unused to exercise as he has been during the long months of his confinement, this traveller, in pursuing his course with so much patience and steadfast determination, now finds himself hardly able to walk. The tender feet are swollen and bleeding to such an extent that he finds it impossible to remove his heavy boots. Halting, stumbling, he continues on his way.

By good fortune he meets with another *kaffir* guide, who leads him to a small *kaffir* hut and revives him with a draught of *kaffir* beer. A few moments' rest, and they are on the way again.

The day was far spent when they reached a *kaffir kraal*, and here Mr. Celliers sank down in agony of mind and body, too great for words. More *kaffir* beer was respectfully tendered to him and he drank it gratefully, meanwhile watching with dull interest the *kaffir* babies, jet black and stark naked, except for a small fringe of blue beads about the loins, as they crept around him, like so many playful kittens.

He was not long allowed to rest, the good guide urging him to make a final effort, and encouraging him with the assurance that he would find a farm not far distant, the home of Mr. Piet Roos, of Krokodil Poort.

This goal was reached that night, and a cordial welcome given to the poor exhausted traveller, although he was warned that he could by no means consider himself safe on the farm, as the British passed it nearly every day. Nigh three weeks he spent there, taking refuge under the trees of an adjacent hill by day and sleeping under the hospitable roof by night. As time went on and the visits of the Khakis became rarer, he became more at ease, and often worked with the farmer and the women in the fields, helping them to dig sweet-potatoes, and assisting his host in the work of sorting, drying, and rolling up the leaves of the tobacco-plant. He also became an expert in the art of making candles, and took active part in the other small industries carried on in that frugal and industrious household, and the evenings were spent in poring over maps, geographical and astronomical, which his host happened to possess. Many were the questions put to him, and long the discussions about worlds and suns and planets, while the busy fingers plied and rolled tobacco leaves, but these discussions generally ended in a sigh, a shake of the head, and an unbelieving, "there *must* be something solid *under* this earth," from the sceptical host.

The time was now approaching for the fulfilment of his heart's ambition, but there is still one small incident to relate before we leave our hero. One day, while he was still on the farm, he was passed by a *kaffir*, whom he questioned as to his destination. The native replied that he was on his way to Pretoria, and the happy thought occurred to Mr. Celliers to ask this native to let his wife know that her husband was in perfect safety.

Now the remarkable part of this incident was, that that unknown native took the trouble to deliver his message faithfully and conscientiously, and it was only after the war that Mr. Celliers heard from his wife that she had received news of his successful escape from a strange *kaffir*, who said he had been sent by her husband. This is a striking instance, well worth recording here, of the sagacity and fidelity of some members of the heathen tribes.

It was on September 13th that unexpected deliverance came in the shape of a Boer waggon in search of green forage for the horses on commando. Mr. Celliers instantly decided to accompany the waggon back to the *laager*, and prepared himself for departure that very day. Tender, grateful leave was taken of the good friends who had harboured him so long, and he drove away, seated, with his few worldly possessions beside him, on the top of a load of green forage.

The next day he arrived at the *laager* of Commandant Badenhorst's commando on the farm Waterval near the "*Sein koppies*," and now we close the chapter with the following words, which I have translated from his diary:

"The crown has been set on my undertaking God be thanked, I find myself again amongst free men, with weapon in hand. For the first time in the past four months I feel myself secure. There is no one, on my arrival, who gives one sign of interest or appreciation; one *burgher* even asks me why I had not rather remained in Pretoria.

"This stolid and philosophic view of life is characteristic of the Boer and certainly does not discourage me.

"Excitement and enthusiasm do not appear to be the children of the great solitudes, the slumbering sunlit vastnesses; nay, rather do they spring from the unbroken friction of many spirits, sparks bursting from the anvil of the great, restlessly driven activity of the world."

Mr. Celliers remained in the field until the war was over.

CHAPTER 10

A Little Adventure With the British Soldier

The exquisite summer of 1901 was drawing to a close.

January and February had been months of unsurpassed splendour and riotous luxury in fruit and flowers, each day being more gorgeous than the last. The glorious sunsets, the mysterious and exquisitely peaceful moonlight nights were a never-ending source of joy to our young writer, thrilling her being with emotions not to be described.

Each morning at 5 o'clock, while the rest of the idiotic world lay asleep within its cramped boundary of brick and stone, Hansie revelled in the beauties of Nature, abandoning herself to at least one hour of perfect bliss before the toil and trouble of another day could occupy her mind.

The garden being so situated that its most secluded spots were far removed from any sights and sounds which could remind one of the war, Hansie had no difficulty in turning her thoughts into more uplifting channels during the peaceful morning hour, spent, when the weather permitted, in her favourite corner under the six gigantic willows below the orange avenue.

And the weather in those days nearly always permitted!

Most of the entries in her diary she made in this fair spot, alone, but for the sympathetic presence of her big black dog. The morning solitude was amply atoned for by the dozens of young friends who joined the "fruit parties" every afternoon, filling the air with their gay voices and wholesome, happy laughter.

Four or five young men and a bevy of beautiful young girls were amongst the most constant visitors at Harmony. The girls, often referred to in Hansie's diary as the "Four Graces," were certainly the

THE SIX WILLOWS, HARMONY.

most exquisite specimens of budding womanhood in Pretoria.

There was Consuélo, tall and slender, our languid "Spanish beauty," with her rich brown hair and slumbrous dark-brown eyes; there was our little Marguerite, fresh and fair as the flower after which she was named, an opening marguerite in the dewy daintiness of life's first summer morning; there was Annie, spoilt and wilful but undoubtedly the fairest of them all; and then there was her sister Sara, Hansie's favourite, with a girlish charm impossible to describe. Her creamy white complexion, her lovely soft brown eyes, her winning smile and tender voice—what could be more delightful than to sit and watch her as she moved and spoke with rare, unconscious grace, clad in a snowy dress of fine white muslin!

One sweet summer morn, a Sabbath, if I remember correctly, when the air was filled with the fragrance of innumerable buds and blossoms, Hansie sat in the accustomed spot, with her diary on her lap. She was not writing then, but, with a slip of paper in her hands and a gleam of mischief in her eyes, she was repeating with evident enjoyment a few catching lines.

"Oh, Carlo, this is lovely! I must learn these verses and recite them to the girls when they come this afternoon! Listen, Carlo."

From Kitchener to Secretary of State For War

Sunday
I am taking measures once for all to clear my reputation;
I swear to give de Wet a fall that means annihilation.

Monday
A brilliant action by Brabant, the enemy has fled,
Their loss was something dreadful; ours—one single kaffir dead.

Tuesday
De Wet is short of food-stuffs, his ammunition's done,
His horses are all dying, and he's only got one gun.

Wednesday
The cordon draws in round de Wet; he now has little room,
He only can escape one way—by road to Potchefstroom.

Thursday
De Wet is now caged like a rat, he's fairly in a box,
Around him grouped are Clements, Cléry, Methuen, French, and Knox.

Friday
An unfortunate event occurred—I report it with regret,

> *A convoy with five hundred men was captured by de Wet.*
>
> *Saturday*
>
> *A kaffir runner says he saw de Wet's men trekking west,*
> *With ammunition for two years, and food supply the best.*
>
> *Saturday (later)*
>
> *A loyal farmer told our Scouts de Wet was riding east,*
> *Each man, beside the horse he rode, was leading a spare beast.*

Carlo wagged his tail sympathetically.

✶✶✶✶✶✶

Overhead the sky was of the deepest, richest sapphire blue, paling away to the horizon to the most delicate tints, against which the distant hills showed up in bold relief.

"Gentleman Jim," one of the native servants, was evidently enjoying his Sunday too, for he loitered in the garden, plucking up a weed here and there and watching the bees at work, the busy bees who know of no day of rest.

"Bring me some grapes, please, Jim," Hansie called out to him.

"Yes, little missie," with alacrity. "What you like? Them black ones or them white ones?"

"Some of both."

He walked briskly to the house to fetch a basket and disappeared into the vineyard, returning shortly with a plentiful supply of luscious grapes.

"Thank you, Jim. Enough for a week!" Hansie laughed, and he looked pleased as he went off in the direction of the river.

A few moments later, half concealed by the shrubs and rank grass with which the lower part of Harmony was overrun, Hansie noticed two stooping figures in khaki, moving forward cautiously and then making sudden dashes at some object, invisible to the girl. She watched them intently, wondering who the intruders were and what their game could be, until they came so near that she was able to distinguish what it was they nourished in their hands. Butterfly nets!

A pair of harmless Tommies, spending their Sunday morning in catching butterflies and the other insects of which there abounded so large a variety at that time of the year.

They did not catch sight of the girl until Carlo sprang up barking furiously, and then they started back in consternation and surprise.

"Lie down, Carlo," Hansie commanded sharply. "Good morning," to the men.

"Good morning, miss," respectfully; "I hope we are not intrudin'."

"Certainly not. Are you catching butterflies? Show me what you have got."

The men produced their spoil with pride.

"Will you have some grapes?" Hansie asked, handing the basket to one of them, who helped himself gratefully and then passed it on to his comrade. The latter, evidently not of a very sociable disposition, took a bunch and walked off in pursuit of more butterflies.

The first soldier, however, squatted down on the ground at some little distance from the girl and began to talk, as he ate the grapes with great relish. At this point Carlo raised himself with the utmost deliberation, yawned, stretched himself, and sauntering (I cannot call it anything except *sauntering*) slowly towards his mistress, laid his full length on the ground between her and the Tommy. Then he went sound asleep to all appearances, but his mistress observed that when the soldier made the slightest movement, the dog's ears twitched or an eyelid quivered.

Slowly eating his grapes, the man glanced curiously at the book on Hansie's lap.

"Are you sketchin', miss?" he asked.

"No; writing."

"Poetry?"

There was no answer.

"I am one of Lord Kitchener's body-guard," he went on presently. "We are encamped near Berea Park on the other side of your fence. We were in Middelburg last week and I saw one of the Boer Generals, General Botha."

Hansie's heart bounded. She looked at the man incredulously.

"Indeed! How was that possible?"

"Quite simple, miss. Lord Kitchener invited the general into town to have an interview with him. His brother—I think his name is Christian—came with him. I acted as their orderly."

"Tell me more, tell me everything," the girl's voice shook with ill-controlled emotion.

"There were five or six other men with them. They arrived at about nine in the morning and stayed until half-past four that afternoon. They had lunch with Lord Kitchener. A fine man the General is, well set up, big and broad-shouldered."

"Yes, I know." Hansie *could not* withhold those words.

"You know!" he exclaimed in great surprise. "Do *you* know General Botha?"

"Yes, indeed. And what is more, he is *my* general."

The soldier looked at her in ludicrous amazement.

"Are you a Boer? You don't look like one, and I never heard any one speak better English."

"I don't know whether what you are saying is meant as a compliment to me, but I don't like being told that I don't look like a Boer, and I certainly would not be pleased if you took me for an Englishwoman."

The poor Tommy looked troubled and muttered something about "no offence meant, I am sure."

"Now please go on and tell me more about the general. Did you hear anything of what he said to Lord Kitchener?"

"Nothing, miss, except when he went away. They shook hands very hearty-like and the general said, 'Goodbye; I hope you will have good luck.' That was all."

"Good luck! What do you think he could have meant?"

"We don't know, miss, but we think he meant good luck in Natal, for Lord Kitchener went yesterday and I hear there is some talk of peace."

Hansie sat silent for a long time, turning these things over in her mind.

"But what is all this accursed war about, miss? We soldiers know nothing except that we have to fight when we are ordered to do so."

"Of course you know nothing. An English soldier is nothing but a fighting machine, not allowed to think or act for himself. Discipline is a grand thing, but Heaven protect a man from the discipline of the British army. The war? I will tell you if you want to know. The war is a cruel and unjust attempt to rob us of our rich and independent land, and England is the tool in base and unscrupulous hands. You suffer too, I know, and all my heart goes out in sympathy to the bereaved and broken-hearted Englishwomen across the seas. Their only comfort is their firm belief that their heroes died a noble death for freedom and justice. Did they but know the truth! They died to satisfy the lust for gain and greed of gold of mining magnates on the Rand."

"Suffer, miss! As long as I live I will not forget that march from the colony, through Bloemfontein to Pretoria. Fighting nearly every day and marching at least thirty miles a day, on *one biscuit*. There was no water to be had! Will you believe that for three days not a drop of water passed my lips? And I heard the other fellows say, not once, but a thousand times, 'Would to God that a bullet find me before night!' Our tongues were hanging from our mouths and our lips were cracked———"

"Stop!" Hansie cried, putting her hands to her ears. "I do not want to hear another word. These things cannot be helped, and your officers suffered too!"

"The officers! When at last the water-carts came, we had to stand aside and watch while bucketsful were being carried into the tents for their *baths*!"

There was silence again.

"If I were an English soldier, I would run away," Hansie said.

"I've had enough, God knows, and when I get home I mean to leave the army and take up my old work—carpentering. The war can't last very long. England is mighty—but I wish the bloomin' capitalists would come and do the fighting, if they want this country and its gold-mines."

"There are only a 'few marauding bands' left, so the English say," Hansie answered bitterly. "But remember what I tell you now. South Africa will be soaked in blood and tears, and a hundred thousand hearts will be broken here and in your country, before the mighty British Army has subdued those 'few marauding bands.'"

The soldier's face grew troubled once again.

It was a good, strong face—a patient face—and it bore the marks of much suffering, endured in silence and alone.

He rose and took off his cap.

"You've been very good to me, miss. I wish I could be of some use to you."

"Run away from Lord Kitchener!" she said, laughing. "I would be very sorry indeed if you fell by the hand of one of my brothers."

He looked at her sympathetically.

"How many brothers have you in the field?"

"God only knows," she answered sadly. "There were two left when last we heard of them. The third has been made a prisoner."

The soldier took his leave and Hansie lost herself in reverie.

And when at last she roused herself, she wrote with rapid pen:

"Two Tommies have been in our garden, catching butterflies———"
We know the rest.

******

That afternoon about ten or twelve young people assembled in the garden and were later joined by several members of the Diplomatic

Corps—Consul Cinatti, Consul Aubert, and Consul Nieuwenhuis, the most frequent visitors at Harmony.

The topic of conversation was connected with General Botha's visit to Lord Kitchener in Middelburg, and when Hansie told her friends what she had heard from the soldier that morning, they expressed their conviction that every word he said must have been true.

And the latest *official* war news, in rhyme, the dispatch from Kitchener to the Secretary of State for War, came in for its share of attention, occasioning no small amount of merriment.

Oh, happy afternoon! Oh, memories sweet! Oh, long departed days of good fellowship and mutual understanding! Bright spots of gold and crimson in our sky of lead!

******

Mrs. van Warmelo never at any time encouraged evening visitors. They were all early risers at Harmony and their life could not be adapted to the artificial, the unnatural strain of modern civilisation.

So the quiet evenings were spent by the mother in reading and writing, while the daughter gave herself up to the indulgence of her one great passion, music. Scales and exercises, Schubert and Chopin, and invariably at the end—before retiring for the night—Beethoven, the Master, the King of Music.

Chapter 11

Prisoner of War

How the routine of life at Harmony was broken in upon by news "from the front" that April month in 1901, I shall endeavour to relate.

Hansie coming home one morning from a shopping expedition, found her mother in a state of suppressed excitement.

Everything was as much as possible "suppressed" in those days—goodness only knows why, for surely it would have been better for the nervous and highly strung mind if an occasional outburst could have been permitted. Hansie suffered from the same complaint, and had to pay most dearly in after years for the suppression of her deepest feelings.

There is a Dutch saying which forcibly expresses that condition of tense self-control under circumstances of a particularly trying nature. We say we are "living on our nerves," and that describes the case better than anything I have ever heard.

Our heroines, like so many other sorely tried women in South Africa, were "living on their nerves," those wise, understanding nerves, so knowing and so delicate, which form the stronghold of the human frame.

The external symptoms of this state were only known by those who lived in close and constant intercourse with one another. Hansie therefore knew, by an inflection in her mother's voice, that something out of the way had happened when she said:

"I have had a note from General Maxwell."

"Indeed! What does he say?"

"He writes that Dietlof has been made a prisoner, and he encloses a telegram from the Assistant Provost-Marshal at Ventersdorp, in the name of General Babington, to say that Dietlof is well, as was Fritz when last seen. See for yourself."

Hansie grabbed—yes, grabbed—the papers from her mother's outstretched hand.

"'When last seen?' Mother, what can that mean? Why have the boys been separated?"

"That is what I should like to know," her mother answered. "I wonder how we can find out. We must ask to see General Maxwell at once."

That afternoon the two women called at the Government Buildings and were shown into the governor's office.

He seemed to be expecting a visit from them, and Mrs. van Warmelo apologised for troubling him, reminding him of the promise he had made on the occasion of their very first visit to him, that he would help them if they came to him in any trouble.

This he remembered perfectly.

"What is it you want me to do?" he asked.

"If you will be so good, we want a permit to visit our prisoner in the Johannesburg Fort, where he will probably be kept until he is sent to Ceylon or where-ever he may have to go."

"Certainly; I will do this with the greatest pleasure. But first we must wire and find out his whereabouts. I'll see about the matter and let you know at once."

Thanking him gratefully, mother and daughter took their leave.

"We should have asked permission to take a box of clothes and other little necessaries for our boy," the mother said.

"Yes, what a pity we did not think of it! But surely there could be no objection to that! Let us get everything ready at least, and ask permission when we hear from General Maxwell again."

The largest portmanteau in the house was overhauled and carefully and thoughtfully packed by the mother's yearning hands.

No article of comfort was overlooked, no detail of the wardrobe considered too small for her closest attention and care.

Presently Hansie came with *her* contribution, a thick exercise-book and a couple of pencils.

"Put these in, mother, if you still have room. I am going to ask Dietlof to write down all his adventures in this book for us to read afterwards. It will help him to get through his time of imprisonment."

(This small act, I may add here, led to the publication of her brother's book, *Mijn Kommando en Guerilla-Kommando leven—On Commando*, in the English edition—which was begun in Ladysmith and written in the Indian Fort at Ahmednagar and smuggled out to Holland under conditions of such romantic interest: the first book on the war, written *during* the war and devoured by the public in Holland long before it was allowed to reach South African shores—a book famed for its moderation and its truth, direct, sincere throughout.)

✶✶✶✶✶✶

That Saturday night poor Mrs. van Warmelo never closed her eyes. She feared, and she had good reason to fear, that her son would pass through Johannesburg, and be transported to some foreign isle, before a word of greeting and farewell could be made by her. The thought of the morrow's Sabbath rest and inactivity intensified her fears.

The first thing she said to Hansie next morning was:

"You must go to General Maxwell and ask whether there is no news for us."

"But, mother, this is Sunday!"

"I know that. You will have to go to his house."

"Oh, I could not possibly do that. What does he care about our anxieties? Besides, I think it would be most indiscreet."

"I don't care," shortly.

In the end Hansie had to go, and when once she had made up her mind she looked forward with some pleasure to her little adventure, for there was no one of the officials known to her for whom she had a more sincere regard than General Maxwell. His house was but a few minutes' walk from Harmony, and Hansie, looking up at the gathering clouds, hoped that she could be home again before the approaching storm broke loose.

Our "brave" heroine *trembled* when she rang the bell, for all her distaste of the task had returned with redoubled force, but her self-confidence was soon restored under the genial warmth of the General's greetings.

He did not seem to be the least annoyed or displeased at this intrusion on his Sabbath privacy. And he was quite alone—not, as Hansie had feared to find him, surrounded by a crowd of officers.

He told her that though he had not been able to get news of her brother direct, he knew that a large number of prisoners had arrived at the Johannesburg Fort from Ventersdorp. He thought her brother would probably be amongst them, and gave her special permits to Johannesburg and back, and also a letter of introduction to the Military Governor in Johannesburg, asking him as a personal favour to assist the ladies in their quest.

"If I were you, I would not wait for definite news, but go tomorrow on the chance of finding him. Delay might bring you great disappointment. But, tell me, Miss van Warmelo, are you not glad that your brother has been captured and is out of danger now?"

"Glad? No, how can I be glad? It means a man less on our side—and *he is a man*, I can assure you. If all the Boers were as brave and true—and such unerring marksmen—the war would soon be over."

The governor looked disturbed.

"It seems to me a strange thing for a girl like you to feel so strongly. Are all your women such staunch patriots?"

"Not all, perhaps, but there are many who feel even more strongly than I do."

The general kept her there and talked of many things, asked her innumerable questions on the country and its people, and drew her out upon the subject of the war.

Outside, the elements were raging, for the storm had broken loose, and the rain came down in torrents, while the crashing thunder pealed overhead.

Hansie looked anxious, and the governor said:

"It will soon be over. Are you afraid?"

"Oh no, I love our storms; but my mother is alone at home, and she does *not*."

She told him, toying with her permits, of her curious collection of passes and other war-curios, and he left the room with a friendly—

"Perhaps I can find something for you too," returning with a button from his coat and a colonel's crown.

"The storm is over; let us see what damage has been done," and he led the way into the garden, showed her the flowers, asked the names of shrubs unknown to him.

✶✶✶✶✶✶

"Oh, mother, the English must not be so good to us! It is not right to accept favours at their hands, for it places us in a false position. Don't ever ask me to go to General Maxwell again."

"Of course not. I quite agree with you, but I am very glad to have those permits. Did you ask about the portmanteau and box?"

"Yes. He said it was all right, and promised to give permits, so that they need not be examined."

They did not leave for Johannesburg, after all, on Monday, for a full list of the names of prisoners from Ventersdorp arrived, but there was no van Warmelo among them.

Telegrams were sent right and left, but there was something strange about the whole affair, and no satisfactory answers could be got until five days after the first tidings had reached Harmony. The prisoner was at Potchefstroom.

Two more days of suspense and a note from Major Hoskins came, enclosing a telegram—"Van Warmelo leaving tomorrow for Fort Johannesburg."

Great rejoicings! The women had begun to fear that their hero had been whisked away to some remote portion of the globe, without one word from them.

General Maxwell's letters of introduction acted like a charm when presented at the various military departments in the Golden City.

Colonel Mackenzie, the military governor, gave the women a letter of introduction to the O.C. troops, who directed them to the provost-marshal, Captain Short, informing them that they would find him at his office in the Fort.

The provost-marshal did not know that more prisoners from Ventersdorp were expected that day. He thought there must be some mistake—unless—yes, there would be another train at 5 o'clock that afternoon.

The ladies were advised to call again on Sunday morning and drove to Heath's Hotel, where they had taken up their quarters. How quiet and deserted the Golden City looked! How bleak and desolate, with the first breath of winter upon it!

Poor Hansie had a shocking cold, and as she drove through the silent streets with her mother all the miseries of the past eighteen months came crowding into her aching heart and throbbing brain.

What would the meeting be like tomorrow? Would he be changed? And what would he have to tell? The question still remained whether he would be allowed to tell them anything about the war at all——

Suddenly a brilliant thought flashed into Hansie's mind.

"Oh, mother, let us go to the Braamfontein Station and see the train arrive. I know we won't be allowed to speak to him, but we may at least wave our hands and *look* at him."

Her mother was delighted with the thought, and at 4 o'clock that afternoon they took a cab to Braamfontein Station.

The train had been delayed, and would be in at 6 instead of 5 o'clock, so they were told, but, for fear of having been misinformed, they decided to wait at the station.

Cold, dusty, pitiless, the keen wind blew on that unfriendly platform. There was no ladies' waiting room—in fact, it seemed as if the rooms had all been utilised for other, perhaps military, purposes.

It is incredible the amount of suffering that can be crowded into one hour of waiting!

Thank God, at last the train steamed in.

Armed troops and an unusually large number of passengers alighted on the platform, but there was not a prisoner to be seen. The desperate women walked up and down, keenly scrutinising every face they passed, until they heard a well-known, highly excited voice calling out "Mother! Mother!" to them from behind. They turned and saw their hero tumbling from the train, an armed Tommy at his heels.

There are no memories of the moments such as those which followed.

Things must have been rather bad, for when Hansie looked round again the armed soldier had turned away and was slowly walking in another direction. Blessed, thrice-blessed Tommy!

To this day when Hansie thinks of him she remembers with a pang that she did not shake hands with him.

"May we walk with the prisoner as far as the Johannesburg Fort?" Hansie asked.

"Certainly, miss."

How the people stared and turned round in the street to stare again!

And now that I come to think of it, it must have looked remarkable—a ruffianly-looking man, carrying a disreputable bundle of blankets, a tin cup and water-bottle slung across his shoulders all clanking together, and a small *Bible* in his hands, with a well-dressed lady on each arm and an armed soldier behind, guarding the whole!

The prisoner was a sight! The old felt hat was full of holes, through which the unkempt hair was sticking, and the dirty black suit was torn and greasy-looking—but the face, except for the moustache and unfamiliar beard, was the same, the look of love in the blue eyes unchanged.

It seemed like a dream, incredibly sweet and strange, to be walking through the streets of Johannesburg in uninterrupted conversation, carried on *in Dutch,* with him, and to be able to ask the burning questions with which their hearts had been filled all day—why he was alone, where he had left Fritz, how and where he had been captured.

Everything was explained on that memorable walk, simply and briefly explained, for the time was short, and under the circumstances

Dietlof would not give any details of information concerning the war, considering himself bound to silence by the guard's trust in him.

He had been promoted to the position of commandeering officer by General Kemp and had been in the habit, for some time past, of leaving his commando for days at a stretch on commandeering expeditions.

About four days before his capture he had left his people again for the same purpose, and on this occasion he had fled before the enemy for three days, falling into their hands through the death of his good horse through horse-sickness.

His brother Fritz was under General Kemp with Jan and Izak Celliers (this was the first news Mrs. van Warmelo heard of Mr. Celliers' safe arrival on commando, after the adventures undergone by him and described in Chapter 9), and a few others of his most trusted friends, but what they must have thought of his inexplicable non-appearance Dietlof did not know, but he feared they would be undergoing much anxiety on his account.

Near the entrance of the Fort mother and daughter took their leave, thanking the soldier warmly for his kindness to his charge, whom they hoped to see again the following morning.

Very different was the meeting then!

The prisoner, a forlorn object, stood between two guards, before the provost-marshal's office, when the cab containing the two women drove up.

Hansie jumped out and was going up to her brother, when one of the soldiers said to her:

"You may not speak to the prisoner."

"But I may kiss him!" Hansie retorted, throwing her arms round his neck and giving him a kiss which could be heard all over the Fort.

There was a general laugh, and Mrs. van Warmelo promptly followed suit.

Dietlof was called into the provost-marshal's office and cross-questioned, while his mother and sister waited outside impatiently. What a lengthy examination! Quarter of an hour, half an hour passed, then he appeared with a soldier, who said curtly:

"You may talk to the prisoner for half an hour *in English*!"

I forget how many minutes of the precious thirty were lost in groping desperately for some topic of conversation suitable to the occasion, and safe! but when at last they found their tongues, they talked so fast that it is doubtful whether the Tommies understood anything.

Hansie longed to ask her brother whether the provost-marshal knew anything of their escapade the night before, but dared not, hoping that the men concerned were under the impression that this was their first interview with the prisoner.

He told them some of his war experiences and the fights he had been in, for the provost-marshal had given him permission to speak of his personal experiences of the war.

One incident Hansie remembered particularly, because of a curious coincidence connected with it.

In describing the Battle of Moselikatsnek, under General de la Rey, in which he and Fritz had taken an active part, he told his mother and sister of a young English officer, Lieutenant Pilkington, whom he had found lying alone in a pool of blood among the rocks and shrubs. Dietlof tended him, giving him brandy from a flask which he always carried with him for such purposes, and laying grass under him on the hard rocks. The poor man was shockingly wounded, and it was evident that his case was hopeless. He held Dietlof's hand, imploring him not to leave him, but Dietlof was the forerunner of the seven *burghers* who were forcing their way wedgelike through the English ranks in order to compel the enemy to surrender by attacking them from behind. He considered it his duty to go forward, but assured the dying man that the comrades who were following in his wake could speak English and would care for him. The donga was strewn with dead and dying English.

In the meantime the younger brother Fritz was tending a soldier with a terrible wound in the head. The seven men were now advancing steadily from one ridge to the other, but Dietlof had reached a point on which the *burghers* from behind were bombarding with their cannon, and as the rocks flew into the air he found it impossible to proceed.

He therefore returned, and the captain sent a dispatch-bearer down with orders that the cannon-firing should cease.

For a moment Dietlof went back to the wounded lieutenant, where he found some of his comrades assembled, and while they stood there the unfortunate man, exhausted by loss of blood, drew his last breath.

Through incredible dangers the seven *burghers* forced their way through the *donga* until they reached the point from where they could attack the enemy from behind. It was a most critical moment, for they were exposed to the constant fire of their own *burghers*, under Commandant Coetzee, as well as that of the enemy, but soon they were relieved to see the white flag hoisted, and were then joined by the rest of the commando.

The English could not believe that the party which had attacked them from behind had consisted of only seven men.

Colonel Roberts, Lieutenant Lyall, and Lieutenant Davis were taken with 210 men of the Lincolnshire Regiment. One officer escaped while the *burghers* were disarming their prisoners and yielding themselves to the spirit of plunder with which every man is possessed after a severe struggle for victory.

Of dead and wounded the *burghers* had lost thirteen or fourteen men, but the seven forerunners, who had been exposed to the greatest dangers, escaped without a scratch, while the enemy, in spite of the fact that they had been under cover throughout, lay dead and dying in large numbers.

Strange to relate, a letter from an English officer fell into Dietlof's hands some weeks later, and in glancing over it his eye fell on the words, "Lieutenant Pilkington is also dead—you know that famous cricketer."

And still later Hansie heard from her brother that one of the seven men, Field-cornet von Zulch, who afterwards joined him as prisoner of war in the Ahmednagar Fort, told him that he had received a letter from Lieutenant Pilkington's mother, begging for more particulars of her son's last moments.

Many wonderful experiences were related, many glimpses given into the conditions of commando life. The young man dwelt lightly for a moment on his hardships and privations, saying, "Mother, do you know those woollen *kaffir* blankets with yellow stars and leopards, and red and green half-crescents?"

"Yes," his mother answered expectantly.

"Well, I once had a pair of trousers made of that material."

Everyone laughed.

"But there are worse things than *that*," he continued; "unmentionable horrors—things you pick up in the English camps and can't get rid of again——"

Hansie understood.

"You will find a tin of insect-powder in that wonderful Indian juggler of a portmanteau," she said, "and don't forget to use the blank exercise-book."

The thirty minutes were over, and they were considerately left alone for a few moments——

CHAPTER 12

The Concentration Camps

For a small moment have I forsaken thee; but with great mercies will I gather thee. In a little wrath I hid My face from thee for a moment; but with everlasting kindness will I have mercy on thee, saith the Lord thy Redeemer.—Isa. *liv.* 7 and 8.

The hand which holds my pen today trembles.

From the beginning it was not my intention to touch upon the concentration camps, but this story of the war would be incomplete without at least a brief outline of that which played so important a part during the war.

After the occupation of Pretoria, and when it was found that hostilities, instead of coming to an end, were continued under what the English called a system of "guerilla" warfare, and that the Boer forces, instead of being compelled to surrender through starvation or exhaustion, continued to thrive and increase in numbers, the military authorities found it necessary to adopt entirely new tactics. But subsequent events showed that no greater strategical error was ever committed.

Let me explain briefly for the benefit of those of my readers who have forgotten the details of the great South African war.

The Boer Republics had no organised force. In the event of war against natives or against some foreign power, the *burghers* were called up from their farms, the husbands, fathers, sons of the nation, to fight for home and fatherland. This left the women and children unprotected on the farms, but not unprovided for, for it is an historical fact that the Boer women in time of war carried on their farming operations with greater vigour than during times of peace. Fruit trees were tended, fields were ploughed, and harvests brought in with redoubled energy, with the result that crops increased and live-stock multiplied.

From the natives they had nothing to fear—in fact, their work was carried on with the help of native servants only. It soon became evident to the British military authorities that the Boer forces were being supplied with necessaries in the way of food and clothing by the women on the farms.

From the Boer point of view this was right and good, but it was perfectly natural that the English should resent it, and, in isolated cases, where it was known beyond doubt to have taken place, the houses were destroyed, and the women and children removed to the towns as prisoners of war.

As time went on and the women continued to provide their men with the necessaries of life, the British authorities decided to lay the entire country waste, with the intention of depriving the Boer commandos of all means of subsistence and forcing them, through starvation, into a speedy surrender.

A systematic devastation of the two Boer Republics then took place. Only the towns were spared; for the rest, the farms and homesteads and even small villages, throughout the length and breadth of the country, were laid waste. Trees were cut down, crops destroyed, homes, pillaged of valuables, burnt with everything they contained, and the women and children removed to camps in the districts to which they belonged.

Now, we are well aware that a savage foe would have left these helpless victims of the unavoidable circumstances of war on the veld to die, but the English are not only not savages and heathens, but they are one of the most civilised and humane Christian nations.

Concentration camps were formed in every part of the country, and the women and children placed in tents on the open *veld*, near the railway lines where possible, or in close proximity to the towns.

The work of devastation, carried out by some British officers with loathing and distaste, and by others with fiendish exultation, was not completed in a few weeks or months. It was carried on right through from the time when the policy was decided on until peace was declared, and in the end nothing was left but the blackened ruins of once prosperous homes.

******

If ever there was a war of surprises, it was the Anglo-Boer war.
******

Instead of hostilities being brought to a speedy termination by the demolition of the farms, the Boer forces gathered and increased in strength and numbers by the addition to their ranks of men who had left the commandos and were again living on their farms.

Wives and children gone, homes devastated, there was nothing left for the men to live for.

Instead of being brought to submission by the drastic measures taken to compel them to surrender, they were transformed into raging lions, with but one object in view, the expulsion of their enemy from the land of their birth.

Not alone in the towns did the secret service do its work. As the camps grew in size and close supervision became more difficult, the spies crept in and out, bearing with them the information wanted by the Boer leaders, concerning the condition of the inmates.

In nine cases out of ten the earnest request of the women to their men was to fight to the bitter end—not to surrender on their account, but to let them die in captivity sooner than yield for the sake of them and their children.

Perhaps I may be allowed to say here that when Hansie was in the Irene Camp as volunteer nurse she knew nothing of the work of the spies.

Love and pity drew her to the scene of suffering.

******

The British did not count the cost when they began the system of gathering in the Boer families, any more than they did when they began their "walk over" to Pretoria.

Not only had they to support women and children for an indefinite period after the devastation of the farms, but the entire maintenance of the scattered Boer forces fell to their lot. During nearly two years the Boers lived on the enemy, took their convoys, wrecked their trains, helped themselves to horses, clothing, ammunition, provisions—everything, in fact, that they required for the continuation of the war. To tell the truth, there was hardly a Mauser rifle to be found in the possession of the Boers at the end of the war, they having destroyed the rifles with which they began the war, for want of Mauser ammunition, and using only the Lee Metfords of the enemy.

Sickness broke out in the camps—scarlet fever, measles, whooping-cough, enteric, pneumonia, and a thousand ills brought by exposure, overcrowding, underfeeding, and untold hardships.

Expectant mothers, tender babes, the aged and infirm, torn from their homes and herded together under conditions impossible to describe, exposed to the bitter inclemency of the South African winters and the scorching, germ-breeding heat of the summer, succumbed in their thousands, while daily, fresh people, ruddy, healthy, straight from their wholesome life on the farms, were brought into the infected camps and left to face sickness and the imminent risk of death.

Over twenty thousand dead women and children stand recorded in the books of the Burgher Camps Department today, as the victims of this policy of concentration.

Over twenty thousand women and children within two years! While the total number of fighting men lost on the Boer side, in battle and in captivity, amounts to four thousand throughout the entire war.

That this appalling result was wholly unlooked for, we do not doubt, but nothing could be done to prevent the high mortality until many months after the worst period was over and only the strongest remained in the camps. It was indeed a case of the survival of the fittest.

Let me briefly relate a tragic event of the war to show what the people of the camps went through and what little cause for surprise there is in the unprecedented death-rate.

During the winter of 1901 a blizzard passed over the High Veld, the site of so many Concentration Camps, in the Balmoral district, and overtook a young lieutenant, W. St. Clare McLaren, of the First Argyll and Sutherland Highlanders (the friend and playmate of Hansie's childhood's years at Heidelberg) with his men.

They were without shelter, their commissariat waggons being some way ahead, and crept under a tarpaulin for protection from the fierce and bitterly cold blast.

During that awful night Mr. McLaren took off his overcoat to cover up the perishing body of his major, and when morning came he was found dead with five of his men, while around them, stiffly frozen, lay the bodies of six hundred mules.

The brave and heroic heart was stilled for ever, a young and noble life was lost in performing an act of rare self-sacrifice; but far away in "bonnie Scotland" a widowed mother, smiling bravely through her tears, thanked God for the privilege of cherishing *such* a memory.

Small wonder to us then, when tragedies such as this were brought home to us, that in the camps the thin tents, torn to ribbons by the storm, afforded no protection to the scantily-clothed, half-famished inmates!

That the death-rate was not higher during the winter months we owe entirely to the overcrowding of the tents, there being in Hansie's ward at Irene many bell-tents, destined to accommodate six, holding from sixteen to twenty-three persons for many months. But what was an advantage during the winter months became a source of great danger when the heat of summer came.

To return to our story.

It was Hansie's privilege—yes, privilege—to act as one of the volunteer nurses from Pretoria during that very winter of 1901, and though it is not my intention to record in this book the experience connected with that period, I do not think it will be out of place here to mention an important result of that sojourn at Irene.

Mrs. van Warmelo visited her daughter in the camp for the first time on May 21st, and she was so much impressed by the misery she had witnessed that, on her return to Pretoria that night, she could not sleep, but tossed from side to side, thinking of some way to save her country-women from suffering and death.

Suddenly she was inspired by the thought, "Write a petition to the Consuls!"

It was 3 a.m. when she got out of bed to fetch her writing-materials from the dining-room, and she then and there wrote a passionate appeal for help to the Diplomatic Corps in Pretoria.

The Consul-General for the Netherlands, Mr. Domela Nieuwenhuis, to whom she took the petition the following morning, advised her to lay it before the Portuguese Consul, Mr. Cinatti, who, as the doyen of the Diplomatic Corps, would bring the matter before the other Consuls, if he thought it advisable.

Mr. Cinatti, after reading the petition, said the matter could certainly be taken up if Mrs. van Warmelo would get a few leading women in Pretoria to sign the petition.

This was done within a few days.

Under injunctions to observe the strictest secrecy, nine prominent Boer women signed the document, and it was once more laid before the senior member of the Diplomatic Corps, who immediately called a meeting of the consuls, the result of which was that a copy of the petition, translated into French, was sent by the first mail to each of the ten different Powers they represented and also to Lord Kitchener.

General Maxwell, soon after these were dispatched, asked Mr. Cinatti to see him at once in his office at Government Buildings, where, in a long interview with him, he demanded from Mr. Cinatti the names of the nine signatories.

Mr. Cinatti said he was not at liberty to disclose them—that, in fact, they were not known (with the exception of the writer of the petition) to the other consuls. General Maxwell then pressed him to give him that name only, as he particularly wished to know who had drawn up the petition.

This was refused, fortunately for Mrs. van Warmelo, for the penalty would have been great.

The military authorities left no stone unturned afterwards to find out who the women petitioners were, but without success, thanks to the great precautions taken by the Portuguese Consul.

A full month passed and no reply came from Lord Kitchener.

A second petition, more strongly worded than the first, was then drawn up, imploring the Consuls to intercede on behalf of the victims of the concentration camps and to inform the Powers represented by them, of the death-rate which threatened the Boer nation with extinction.

Again a meeting of the consuls was called, at which three of them were appointed to form a committee of investigation:

Consul Cinatti, Consul-General for Portugal.

Baron Pitner, Consul-General for Austria.

Baron Ostmann, Consul-General for Germany.

Some of the other members at the meeting were:

M. Domela Nieuwenhuis, Consul-General for the Netherlands.

M. Aubert, Consul-General for France.

Mr. Gordon, Consul-General for United States.

The latter lived in Johannesburg, but attended all the meetings held in Pretoria in connection with the Concentration Camps.

From General Maxwell the committee of investigation got permission to inspect the camp at Irene, called the "Model Camp," and with the statistics obtained there, as well as the official statistics of all the camps in the Transvaal, the Diplomatic Corps drew up a report, which went to prove that unless immediate steps were taken to arrest the appalling death-rate, the Boer population in the camps would be extinct within a period of three years.

Copies of this report were sent to the military governor and Lord Kitchener, and to ten foreign Powers, with copies of the second petition.

What diplomatic correspondence then passed between England and the foreign Powers we shall never know, for the utmost secrecy was observed throughout; but what we do know is, that the famous commission of inquiry, the "Whitewash Committee," so-called by the Pro-Boers in England, was very soon afterwards sent out. It consisted of six English ladies, and as a result of their investigations some of the inland camps were removed to the coast, the rations increased, additional medical and other comforts provided, and the general condition of the camps improved to such an extent that after some months the death-rate decreased considerably, continuing to do so until it became nearly normal.

But, as I have said before, not until over 20,000 women and children had been sacrificed as a direct result of being torn from their homes, exposed to the elements, and herded together under conditions which only the strongest could survive. It would take too much space to insert copies of the petitions here, but they are to be found in Hansie's Dutch book on the Irene Concentration Camp, published in Holland from her diary a year after the war.

The following statistics of what is known as "Black October 1901" are taken from the Blue Books of England and will give the reader an idea of the number of camps in the Transvaal alone, the number of their inhabitants, and the full death-rate within the period of thirty-one days:—

Total Census of Deaths, etc. etc., occurring in the Concentration Camps, Transvaal only, during the Month Of October 1901.

	Camps.	Census.	Deaths
1.	Barberton	1,907	12
2.	Balmoral	2,580	70
3.	Belfast	1,397	33
4.	Heidelberg	2,173	41
5.	Irene	3,972	101
6.	Johannesburg	2,937	29
7.	Klerksdorp	3,822	176
8.	Krugersdorp	5,500	90
9.	Middelburg	5,602	127
10.	Mafeking	4,783	410
11.	Nylstroom	1,819	52
12.	Pietersburg	3,598	41
13.	Potchefstroom	7,467	90
14.	Standerton	3,005	215
15.	Vereeniging	920	9

16. Volksrust	5,280	47
17. Vryburg	1,256	53
	58,018	1,596

During this terrible month there was a population of 112,619 in all the Concentration Camps in South Africa. There were 3,156 deaths, *i.e.* a death-rate of 28 per 1,000 per month. After "Black October" the mortality decreased steadily, as will be seen from the following figures:

	Population.	Deaths.
November 1901	117,974	2,807
December 1901	117,017	2,380
January 1902	114,376	1,805
February 1902	113,905	638
March 1902	111,508	402
April 1902	112,783	298
May 1902	116,572	196

Consular Report on the Concentration Camps

The following is the report on the concentration camps by the committee appointed by the Consular Corps of the Transvaal in response to a renewed appeal addressed to them by the Committee of Boer Women of Pretoria. The appeal was supported by three of the consuls.

The committee, which you have appointed to examine the situation in the prisoners' camps, where Boer women are concentrated, though they could not always obtain the required accurate information, have gained sufficient results to arrive at the conclusions as laid down in short in the following report:—

1.—In order to formulate a clear idea of the situation the committee has laid down the following tables:

(*a*) Showing the population and deaths in the camps during April 1901, compiled from the official reports of the inspector-general of the camps.

(*b*) The death-rate in the camps of the Transvaal calculated from Table A, as well as from reports published in the Official Gazette, and according to other trustworthy information.

(*c*) The death-rate in the camps at Bloemfontein and Kroonstad, compiled from the notices in the Official Gazette of the Orange Free State.

(*d*) Diseases and deaths according to Official Gazette.

2.—Although the returns are not complete through absence of returns for whole weeks in the official publications, we may arrive at the following conclusions:

1. That the death-percentage in the camps surpasses all hitherto-known proportions.
2. That the death-rate amounts to 14 times that of Pretoria, which has, according to Dr. Stroud, an average of 25 per thousand per year.
3. That the death-rate among the children confined to the camps has increased to an alarming extent.

The committee, basing their verdict partly on the repeated assertions of public opinion, on the communications of eye-witnesses, on the evidence given by certain witnesses in a case before the Military Court at Pretoria, and finally on the personal observations of four members of the Consular Corps, to whom permission was granted to visit the camp at Irene, feel compelled to believe the principal causes of diseases, carrying in their train such an abnormal death-rate, to be:

1. The difficulties and misery and privations to which the Boer families are subject after having been driven from their farms (their journeys often lasting about 20 days).
2. The insufficient quantity and frequently even bad quality of articles of food distributed among them. Often the food given to the children is in every respect inadequate to their wants.
3. The great fall in temperature during the night.
4. The insufficient protection against cold experienced in the tents by the healthy population, and all the more by the invalids.
5. The absence of clothing and blankets.
6. The insufficient providing for invalids and the inadequate state of medical stores.
7. The want of employees for the sanitary service in the camps.

In view of the importance of the problem put before the committee, they have drawn up the above report and have sent copies of same to all the members of the Consular Corps.

    (Signed)   S.S. Pitner.
                                              P. Cinatti.
                                              Bn. Ostmann.

Table A

Direct Causes of the Deaths in the Camps of the Imprisoned Boers, composed according to the Official Newspaper Articles till July 10th, 1901.

Diseases	Number of Deaths.
Measles	123
Inflammation of the lungs	60
Dysentery	45
Inflammation of the bowels	36
Consumption	33
Diarrhoea	29
Bronchitis	27
Old age	21
Inflammation of the stomach	16
Malaria	18
Cramps	15
Measles and bronchitis	14
Typhoid fever	14
Weakness (Debility)	13

Direct Causes of the Deaths in the Camps of the Imprisoned Boers, composed according to the Official Newspaper Articles till July 10th, 1901.

Disease	Number of Deaths
Heart disease	12
Croup	11
Old age	11
Cramps and inflammation of the stomach	10
Measles and weakness	11
Lying-in fever and child-birth illness	5
Measles and inflammation of the lungs	4
Inflammation of the brain	4
Diphtheria	4
Consumption and measles	4
Disease of the kidneys	6
Measles and diarrhoea	3
Measles and dysentery	3
Exhaustion	3
Inflammation of the bowels	3
Debility	2

Heart disease 4
Inflammation of the kidneys and debility, diseases
through teething, asthma, influenza 6
Various 26
Not classified 57

641

SUMMARY AND PERCENTAGE

	Cases	Percentage
Simple and complicated measles	149	23
Diseases of the respiratory organs	106	17
Diseases of the bowels	105	17
Fever	67	10
Debility, old age, consumption	75	12
Convulsions	15	2
Debility through old age	13	2
Heart disease	12	2
Not classified	57	9
Various	42	6

641 cases.

TABLE B
Death-rate of the Imprisoned Boers in the Camps of the Transvaal according to Official Reports and Trustworthy Information.

Camps and Months.		No. of Prisoners under 8 years.			Death-rate for the Period Indicated.						
					Under 8 years.			Per 1,000 per ann. Under 8 years.			
		Male.	Female.	Total.	Male.	Female.	Total.	Male.	Female.	pr. 1,000.
Middelburg	April	666	626	1,292	5	4	9	86	77	83
Potchefstroom	April	1,577	4,147	5,724	7*	17*	24	53	39	54
,,	May 1–17th	1,605†	4,207‡	5,812‡	8	17	25	106	86	94
Standerton	April	584	553	1,137	5‖	20‖	25	104	372	255
Volksrust	April	1,911	1,667	3,578	5	21	26	32	153	87
Irene	April	2,134	1,569	3,703	14*	35*	49	79	270	161
,,	May	2,364†	1,738†	4,102‡	19	49	68	58	331	200
,,	June	2,593†	2,007†	4,600‡	38*	97‡	135§	177	588	366
Johannesburg	April	1,705	1,465	3,170	9	82	91	62	681	349
,,	May 1–27th	1,770†	1,515†	3,285‡	12	67	79	94	598	325
All Camps in Transvaal	April	11,098	12,714	23,612	69	171	240	75	161	122

Without further comment the figures are borrowed from the official reports of the month of April or published in the *Official Gazette*.

* According to the proportion for the month of May.
† According to the proportion for the month of April
‡ Average number from April till July 9th.
‖ According to the proportion for Volksrust.
§ Statement by a nurse in service at Irene.

TABLE C

RETURN OF DEATHS OF THE IMPRISONED BOERS IN THE CAMPS OF BLOEMFONTEIN AND KROONSTAD (ORANGE FREE STATE) ACCORDING TO THE "OFFICIAL GAZETTE."

Camps.	Number of Deaths.				Causes of Death.				per 1,000.
	Men.	Women.	Children under 8 years.	Total.	Infectious Disease.	Lung and Heart Disease.	Typhoid, Dysentery, Diarrhœa.	Debility, Old Age.	
Bloemfontein from April 2nd till July 2nd, 1901	33	80	198	311	101	99	107	4	309
Kroonstad from April 1st till May 16th, 1901	8	8	41	57	15	16	24	2	195
Kroonstad from May 26th till June 23rd, 1901	9	12	26	47	18	14	15	6	213

Number of prisoners till June 1st: Bloemfontein, 4,339; Kroonstad, 2,638.

TABLE D

Returns of Deaths and Disease of the Imprisoned Boers in the English Camps of the Transvaal during April 1901.

Camps.	Number of Prisoners.				Number of Cases during April 1901.				Deaths during the Month.
	Men.	Women.	Children.	Total.	Men.	Women.	Children.	Total.	
Barberton	38	151	236	425	6	26	27	59	4
Middelburg	191	475	626	1,292	29	46	55	130	9
Irene	892	1,242	1,569	3,703	51	85	181	317	49
Johannesburg	505	1,200	1,465	3,170	3	26	110	139	90
Potchefstroom	322	1,255	4,147	5,724	3	30	29	62	24
Klerksdorp	120	350	521	991	—	7	12	19	2
Krugersdorp	234	381	473	1,088	—	—	2	2	—
Vereeniging	175	312	346	833	5	8	11	24	5
Heidelberg	377	327	432	1,136	13	21	32	66	2
Standerton	271	313	653	1,237	10	17	20	47	35
Volksrust	452	1,459	1,667	3,578	14	19	33	66	26
Mafeking	96	140	529	765	12	96	44	152	4
Total	3,673	7,605	12,664	23,942	146	381	556	1,083	250

This table is compiled from an official report by an attendant of the Prisoner-Camps.

Chapter 13

A Consular Visit to Irene Camp

The story of the petitions, related in the previous chapter, had, as I have said before, taken place during the time of Hansie's sojourn at Irene. She knew nothing about it at the time because, naturally, her mother's letters contained no hint of the agitation with the consuls at Pretoria, and she was absorbed in her own "agitations" in the camp, her stormy interviews with the commandant, her hopeless struggles against disease and death.

If ever a concentration camp was mismanaged, Irene was, and the six volunteer nurses, not being paid servants, but having taken up their work for love and at no small sacrifice to themselves, left no stone unturned to bring about the necessary improvements.

How futile their poor little efforts were! How powerless they found themselves against the tide of wilful misunderstanding, deliberate neglect, unpardonable mismanagement!

The number of deaths in the camps increased every day, and Hansie, wiping the hoar-frost from her hair when she woke, half-frozen, in her tent, wondered how many of her little patients had been mercifully released by death that night.

For always, when she resumed her work, there were *childish* forms stretched out in their last sleep.

One morning, when she found that there had been five deaths during the night, in her ward alone, she took the train to Pretoria, straight to General Maxwell's office.

"Come and see for yourself, General. The people are starving, and they lie on the cold ground with little or no covering. Fuel they have nothing to speak of, medical comforts are always out of stock———"

With a heavy frown he asked:

"Why are these things not reported to me?"

"I don't know," she answered miserably. "We thought you knew. We can do nothing with the *commandant*——"

A great deal more was said on both sides, revelations, not to be repeated here, made by the unhappy girl, and the governor's sympathetic face grew stern with righteous indignation as she proceeded.

"I will investigate the matter for myself," he said. "But you look ill—why don't you come home and take a good rest?"

"I am only sick with misery, General; but if you will speak to the commandant and insist on better management in the camp, we may still be able to save a great many lives. There is no time to lose. If the people are not provided with better food and warmer covering during this intensely cold weather, the mortality will be something appalling next month."

A few days later, one beautifully crisp and clear Sunday morning, General Maxwell and his A.D.C., Major Hoskins, rode over to Irene to pay the camp a surprise visit—and a "surprise" it must have been indeed, of no pleasant nature, to the *commandant*, judging by his black looks afterwards.

The general asked to see Miss van Warmelo and demanded to be shown through her ward, inspected her worst cases, visited the overcrowded tents. He seemed much impressed by the scenes he witnessed that day, and issued orders to the effect that all complaints from her ward were to be attended to promptly, and that a distribution of blankets and warm clothing should be made immediately.

There were no blankets "in stock" the day before, but they were produced on this occasion with remarkable alacrity.

The governor inspected the foodstuffs and the small supply of medical comforts (which was *always*, I may say here, kept in stock for inspection, and was not touched for the use of the inmates of the camp, when the stores ran out).

On leaving, the governor said to Hansie with marked emphasis:

"I shall be obliged if you will make your complaints *to me* in future."

Her ward was now in a somewhat better condition, and she was preparing to leave for home for a month's rest and recreation.

Although there were never more than six volunteer nurses in the Camp at a time, there were quite as many again in Pretoria, waiting to take the place of those obliged to go home on sick leave, and one of them was immediately sent to take charge of Hansie's ward.

Tragic were the parting scenes witnessed in that ward next day, and, as Hansie laughingly extricated herself from the crowd, she promised to come back "very soon," little thinking that she would be in their midst again on the morrow.

The new nurse, an inexperienced girl, after having gone through the ward once with Hansie, quietly fainted away.

"Shall I stay?" Hansie asked her, when she had recovered.

"Oh no; I must get used to it. But what must I do when the babies are dying like that?"

"You must pray to God to take them quickly. Very little can be done to save them. Report your worst cases to the doctor regularly every day; then, at least, the responsibility does not rest on your shoulders."

It was terrible, leaving them all in such a state.

Arrived at Harmony, Hansie found a note from Mr. Cinatti asking her to come over to the Consulate immediately, because Dr. Kendal Franks, who was visiting Irene next day, wished to see her before he left.

She went at once, and found a dinner-party in progress at the Consulate, the German Consul, Baron Ostmann, the Austrian Consul, Baron Pitner and his wife, one of the directors of the Dynamite Company, and Dr. Kendal Franks. She was shown into a private study, where Mr. Cinatti joined her, in great excitement.

"Come in to dinner," he urged, but Hansie wished to see only Dr. Franks and said she would wait.

"Tell me," she said before Mr. Cinatti left her. "Is there any danger for my mother in connection with those petitions?"

"Oh no, my dear, I think not. I hope not. The penalty" (he said "penality") "would be very great. You won't mention it to Dr. Franks, will you?"

"Of course not," Hansie laughed, and when he flew in a few moments later, with a silver dish containing *bonbons*, he whispered excitedly: "He's coming now. Be on your guard! Take some of these, they contain *rum*." Dear Mr. Cinatti, how he enjoyed an atmosphere of danger! How he revelled in secret adventures, and how he would have appreciated the conspiracies at Harmony, at a later date, if it had been possible for the van Warmelos to take him into their confidence!

✶✶✶✶✶✶

There was an atmosphere of serenity in the courtly, kindly presence of the great doctor.

"Have you any objection to being cross-questioned?" he asked, producing a notebook and pencil.

"Not at all," she said.

"General Maxwell told me to make a point of visiting your ward. I am sorry you will not be there. Would it not be possible for you to go over to Irene with me tomorrow? I am leaving by the early train."

Hansie hesitated.

"I have no permit, and it is too late now."

"Oh, that is easily remedied."

A messenger was at once dispatched to General Maxwell's house, almost next door, and he soon returned with the necessary permits and a cordial note from the governor, wishing them "good luck."

That was an eventful day at Irene!

The anxious face of the "new nurse" broke into a beaming smile when she saw Hansie on the scenes once more, the people crowding round her with their questions. Why did she come back? Was she going to stay? Didn't she go to Pretoria yesterday? Who was that with her? etc. Mothers pulled her aside and pointed in wordless grief to their tents, to what lay there in still repose since last night. Children clung to her skirts—"We thought you had gone for good."

"The people love you," the great doctor said.

"But not as much as I love them," the answer quickly came.

It was arranged that Dr. Franks should go through the hospital, the dispensary, and the store-rooms in the morning, with the matron and the doctors of the camp, and that after lunch he should inspect some of the tents in Hansie's ward.

This arrangement suited her to perfection, for she wished, after she had greeted her people in the camp, to write an important letter, destined for the north of Holland, for which she had had neither time nor opportunity for many weeks.

The doctor's "hour or two in the camp" lengthened to three, very nearly four, and during the greater part of this time Hansie, sitting in the tent which had been hers, wrote, without lifting her head.

"How shall I get this away? The censor must not set eyes on *this*," she mused as she folded the closely written sheets.

She put the envelope into her handbag, and just then "the girls" trooped in from the camp. Surprised greetings were exchanged and explanations made as they all went into the big marquee where the midday meal was being served.

The doctor was very hot and tired after his long visit of inspection, but highly satisfied with the number of notes he had made, and the meal passed off in animated conversation. When it was over, Dr. Franks and Hansie went through the long rows of tents in her ward—her "prize" tents she called them—and the doctor seemed much struck by the extreme poverty and misery of the inmates. In one tent two little boys were dying, and the distracted mother, when she heard the magic word "doctor," implored him to save them. She was a widow and these children were all she had. He knelt beside them and examined them with his strong and gentle hands, shaking his head. There was no hope.

"Your ward is in a shocking state. But things were not as bad in the dispensary and store-rooms as you made out last night," he said to her on their way to the station.

There was a touch of reproof in the kind voice.

"You saw the small supply which is always kept for inspection, doctor," she answered. "It is always there and is not touched when the stores run out."

His face wore a troubled look, but he said no more.

When they parted at the station he said he would report on his visit, to the governor, and Hansie laughingly replied that she would report too.

"For you are a Briton and I am a Boer. General Maxwell must have *two* reports."

She found the governor next day in the friendliest of moods and evidently satisfied when she thanked him for the improvements in her ward.

He told her that the *commandant*, who had been at Irene when first she came there, was going round the country to inspect all the camps and to write reports for him. Seeing the look of intense dissatisfaction on her face, he asked whether she did not think that Commandant —— would do it well.

"No, indeed," she replied. "I think I would do it a great deal better. Will you let *me* go round to all the camps also, to write reports for you?"

She spoke in jest, but to her surprise the governor immediately entered into the idea, saying that it would be a great help to him to know that he could rely on getting truthful reports.

"You must come and see me later," he continued. "I advise you to take a few weeks' rest before you begin this tour. Is there anything else I can do for you now, or, I should say, for your people, for I have done nothing for you."

"Not just now, thank you, General; but I will let you know when

I am able to go round to the camps, and when I take up my work again at Irene."

Suddenly she remembered the unposted letter in her handbag.

"But there *is* something else———" She hesitated.

"I have a private letter for Holland here. It contains no word about the war, but I cannot let it pass through the hands of the censor. May I ask you to send it for me? I can assure you———"

"With pleasure," he broke in. "I will see that it is dispatched safely."

"Thank you very much. Shall I tell you what it is about?"

"Oh no; I trust you."

He handed a piece of sealing-wax to her.

"What is this for?" she asked.

"To seal the letter," he replied; but she quickly answered, with a smile:

"Oh no; *I trust you*."

He gave her a long official-looking envelope, into which she placed her letter, and, when she had readdressed it, he closed it with the stamp of the military governor's office.

Now, this little scene could not have taken place a few months, or even a few weeks, later, but at the time Hansie had no secrets to conceal from the governor, and she had no reason to feel the slightest qualm in asking him to do her this personal favour.

But the time was soon to come, however, when she remembered the incident of the uncensored letter with no small degree of discomfort—when she found herself in the midst of conspiracies against the enemy, conspiracies of a far more serious nature than the harmless "smuggling" hitherto carried on by her and her mother.

"He would never believe that that letter contained no war news, if he were to find out what we are doing now," she thought then. "This kind of thing must cease—no more favours from the enemy, and, if I can help it, no more interviews with the governor. But there is this tour of inspection—no getting out of that, and I shall have to see a great deal of him. Well, as far as the camps are concerned, I can always 'play the game' to him. That is a thing apart."

A few days after this interview with the governor, Mr. Cinatti called at Harmony with the interesting news that General Maxwell had invited the entire Diplomatic Corps to spend a day with him at Irene.

"We are going tomorrow (July 13th)," he said. "Now, why are you not there?" looking dolefully at Hansie.

"Oh, why did I leave my little round tent at Irene Camp?" she wailed. "But I will give you a letter for Miss Findlay, Mr. Cinatti. She knows all my worst cases and she has many quite as bad in her ward. Ask to see her, and whatever you do, don't forget to ask for Dr. Neethling."

Dr. Neethling was the only Dutch doctor in the camp, and he was seldom in evidence when there was any question of inspection. That Consular visit to Irene must have been quite an event. General Maxwell, Major Hoskins, and all the Consuls in a body went through the camp and hospital, and made the usual inspection of foodstuffs and "medical comforts."

They were satisfied that great improvements had been made, but they did not see the volunteer nurses or Dr. Neethling, although Mr. Cinatti asked three or four times for Miss Findlay and all the consuls asked to see Dr. Neethling. These good people were not forthcoming, and there was so very much to see that it was time for the sumptuous lunch, with which General Maxwell treated the consuls at the railway station, before further questions could be asked.

On the return journey General Maxwell inquired of Mr. Cinatti what he thought of the camps, to which Mr. Cinatti replied, with that quaint mixture of pathos and humour which characterised him:

"General, your *tiffin* was a beauty, but your camp—was very sad!"

Mrs. van Warmelo laughed when Hansie repeated these words to her and said:

"Oh, you have no idea how funny he is," and then she related the following incident to her daughter with great relish:

After she had drawn up the first petition, she was out driving one afternoon with Mrs. General Joubert in the latter's carriage, going from house to house to get the signatures to the petition, and on the Sunnyside bridge they found the three inseparable consuls, Aubert, Cinatti, and Nieuwenhuis, out for their daily constitutional, leaning over the railings and looking down into the stream below. Approaching the bridge from the opposite direction were Lord Kitchener and his A.D.C. on horseback, and the three parties met, as luck would have it, in the centre of the bridge.

"The consuls took off their hats in greeting to the ladies in the carriage, and then turned in salutation to Lord Kitchener, but I wish you could have seen the look Mr. Cinatti gave me, Hansie, as he glanced from the document in my hands to Lord Kitchener's retreating form. It spoke volumes, and I had the greatest difficulty in preserving my gravity."

Chapter 14

New Developments

It was in the winter of 1901, while Hansie was at the Irene Concentration Camp, as one of six volunteer nurses from Pretoria, that Mrs. van Warmelo began her first adventures with the spies, and it has always been a source of keen regret to Hansie that she was not in Pretoria at the time. But one cannot have everything, and the knowledge she gained in the camp was more valuable to her than any other experience she went through during the war.

I have merely touched on the concentration camps in the previous chapter, for obvious reasons, and propose to entirely omit the events of the two months Hansie spent in the Irene Camp.

As the six volunteer nurses were soon after expelled from the camp by the military authorities, there was, fortunately for her, no opportunity of returning to her labour of love. Other duties awaited her at home, however, and by degrees she came into full possession of the facts connected with her mother's experiences during those months.

Amongst the men caught in Pretoria on June 5th, 1900, when the British first entered the capital, were two heroes of this book, Mr. J. Naudé and W.J. Botha.

These men were destined, through their indecision in allowing themselves to be caught like rats in a trap, to fulfil with honour a *rôle* of great importance in the history of the war—a *rôle* unknown to the world, and without which this book would probably not have been written. Mr. Naudé—who, by the way, was well known in town as beadle of the Dutch Reformed Church on Church Square immediately opposite the Government Buildings—had, after the first few days of uncertainty and remorse, no intention whatever of remaining long in durance vile.

With a few comrades in the same predicament as himself, amongst whom were Willem Botha and G. Els, he laid his plans for a speedy escape, and for the purpose of spying more effectually he used the tower of the sacred edifice for which he was responsible, as a point of vantage not only suitable but safe. With a strong telescope he took his observations, unobserved himself, from the highest point of the tower, with the result that a certain route was chosen as offering the best facilities for a safe exit from the town.

Mr. Botha should have accompanied him on this, his first enterprise; but because of Mr. Botha's physical weakness, he having been struck by lightning at Pieter's Heights while on commando, and being subject to severe headaches and unable to walk far at times, it was decided that he should wait in town until Mr. Naudé could come back from commando, bringing with him a horse for the use of his friend. It was as well that Mr. Botha did not expose himself to the hardships and perils of that first flight from the capital, for though Mr. Naudé, wearing an English officer's uniform and carrying his private clothes in a knapsack, escaped with the greatest ease and safety, he and his companion roamed about the *veld* for three days and nights without finding a trace of the Boer commandos which they were so eager to join.

They therefore ventured a return to their homes in Pretoria and accomplished this successfully at dead of night, except for a small adventure through having been delayed too long on their homeward journey, on account of which they reached the first outpost just as day was breaking.

Naudé's companion, in great anxiety, suggested making a *détour*, but Mr. Naudé, with the presence of mind which characterised his every action, answered firmly:

"No; we must go straight ahead. Perhaps the watch has already caught a glimpse of us, and any indecision on our part would be fatal."

Seeing some clothing hanging on a line to dry near a *kaffir* or *coolie* hut, Mr. Naudé annexed one or two garments, and, quickly changing his uniform for the civilian clothes he had with him, he made a bundle of his knapsack, uniform, and helmet, tying them up in the stolen articles. With this bundle under his arm and a handkerchief tied over his head, he and his companion lurched uncertainly over the *veld* towards the watch, after first having taken a draught from their spirit-flask.

"Halt! who goes there?"

Captain Naudé.

They halted, smiling at him in an imbecile manner.

"Show me your residential passes."

His comrade fumbled in his pockets and produced his, but Mr. Naudé fumbled in vain. He had no pass.

He shook his head. His smile became more inane. He muttered hoarsely:

"Can't find it. Must have lost it last night. We have been on the booze, old man."

"I can see *that*," the watch replied and signed to them to pass on.

That their reappearance caused a stir amongst their relatives and friends can easily be understood, and it was found necessary to keep them in hiding. The beadle had been missed from his post, and it was an open secret among his friends and certainly not unknown to the enemy, that he had made a dash for liberty. Under the circumstances he could not remain in Pretoria long, and after a few days of more spying from the church tower he made a second attempt in a different direction, with a comrade of the name of Coetzee, the first man having had enough of the dangerous game. This time their enterprise was crowned with success, and they were able to join a Boer commando under General Louis Botha, but not before they had gone through an adventure which might have cost them their lives.

They were captured by the Boers under Acting Commandant Badenhorst and detained as British spies, all protestations of their innocence proving futile, until Mr. Naudé informed the *commandant* that he had with him dispatches for General Botha.

Commandant Badenhorst demanded to see them.

He refused, saying that they were private documents for the commandant-general, and that he was not at liberty to deliver them to any one else.

His word was accepted, and he was sent to the High Veld with a guard of men on foot to escort him to the general.

The want of horses proved to be a serious drawback and hardship to these men, so they determined to provide themselves with horses, of the very best, and appointed Mr. Naudé as their leader.

Instead of proceeding straight to the High Veld, these enterprising and resourceful young fellows retraced their steps to the vicinity of the Pretoria West Station, where Mr. Naudé knew that the enemy kept a number of magnificent horses for the use of officers only.

With infinite caution they approached the spot, keeping under cover until they were well within rifle-range of the men on guard.

The movements of the latter were stealthily watched, and it was observed that the guard, consisting of two men, well armed, walked up and down before the stables in which the horses were kept. Meeting at a certain point, they turned abruptly and retraced their steps in the opposite direction, until they reached the limit of their beat and turned again.

Mr. Naudé's plans were quickly made, and his commands given below his breath.

There was to be no bloodshed, he said. The thing could easily be done without, if his instructions were well carried out.

Two of the men were ordered to level their guns at one of the guard when he had nearly reached the point farthest from his comrade, while the others stormed the stables.

It was the work of a few moments.

The first thing the unfortunate guard knew was that he was looking straight into the barrels of two guns.

Not a word was said on either side.

Those glittering rifles, held by unseen, steady hands, flashed the unspoken challenge, "Give the alarm, and you are a dead man."

The guard stood still as if rooted to the spot.

Swiftly and silently Mr. Naudé, with his few men, approached and entered the stables, cut loose the halters of the animals, and stampeded from the place.

And yet the guard stood still, transfixed by the unerring aim of those two deadly implements.

A moment more and every man was provided with a steed, another moment and they tore across the *veld* in mad, exultant flight, while behind them the shots rang out and the bullets fell beside them in the grass.

Eleven horses in all! Noble thoroughbreds, well trained and sensitive to voice and touch.

No fear of cruel treatment from your captors, beautiful steeds! The life you are entering upon may be full of hardship for you, but it will be free and wild, and you will be tended with all care and gentleness. These men are brave and strong, and it is only the cowardly and weak who would inflict on you one single unnecessary pain.

Serve your new masters well.

Be swift and sure when Death is on their track.

God only knows what the future holds for them of suffering and woe.

✶✶✶✶✶✶

Not on foot, but riding like lords, these men reached General Botha's force, and the two men Naudé and Coetzee, being among the only *burghers* on commando familiar with the route through the British lines, were thereafter employed by minor officers to travel backwards and forwards to the capital. At first their work consisted only of helping other *burghers* to escape, but as time went on their duties became more complicated and hazardous. There were countless commissions to fulfil and information to be obtained on every imaginable question.

The need of a body of organised men in town began to be felt more strongly in the field, and it was Captain Naudé who introduced the system of employing a set of reliable *burghers* as spies in the heart of the enemy.

For this purpose he once again went to Pretoria with the list of names of the men he wished to interview.

Mr. Botha was the first he approached, and the former was only half pleased when he heard that, instead of the escape from British martial law, for which he had been keeping himself in readiness so long, he was commanded to remain in Pretoria as the head of a body of Secret Service men.

He protested vehemently, but his objections were overruled by the argument brought forward by Naudé, a consideration for the state of his health. This was certainly a point which carried weight. He consented, and the names of the other men to be appointed as his co-operators were submitted to him for approval:

C.P. Hattingh, G. Els, W. Bosch, and J. Gillyland, a body of five men, which we shall know in future by the name of "the Secret Committee."

The Secret Service of the Boers was now well established, and could not have been entrusted into hands more capable, more undaunted, or more faithful.

Captain Naudé had in the meantime earned distinction for himself as the bravest and most enterprising emissary employed in the field. He was placed by General Botha at the head of a corps of scouts, including the men who had captured the British remounts, and it is on the foundation of his adventures as captain of this body of men that this story is built.

✶✶✶✶✶✶

We now turn to Mr. Botha and his first visit to Harmony.

It seems that Mrs. van Warmelo was one morning, during her daughter's absence at Irene, surprised by the appearance of a stranger at her house.

He introduced himself as Mr. Willem Botha and handed a card to Mrs. van Warmelo, the card of her friend Mrs. Pieter Maritz Botha, on which were written the following words, "You may trust the bearer as you would myself."

No other introduction was necessary.

Mrs. P.M. Botha, sister of Sir David Graaf, whose striking personality and unique experiences throughout the war would alone fill a big book, was one of Mrs. van Warmelo's dearest friends.

Any one coming from her to Harmony could depend upon a hearty welcome.

Mrs. van Warmelo looked at her visitor with her keen and searching eyes.

He was short of stature and carried a little walking-stick for support, and his eyes, when they looked into yours, were shrewd, humorous, and true as steel.

A *great* little man he was, and is today, God bless him!

I stretch out my hands to him across these pages and clasp his in the sympathy and understanding of what we went through together. True as steel! Yes, that describes him well, for in all his dealings he was a noble friend, an honourable foe.

Fate had been hard on him in leaving him a helpless prisoner in the hands of his enemies when his whole heart was with his brothers in the field, but Providence was kind in giving him the power and opportunity he required for serving land and people under circumstances as unique as they were dangerous and difficult.

From him Mrs. van Warmelo learnt of the existence of the Secret Committee.

No names were mentioned to her, but the general outline of their work was described, and her assistance was invited in that branch of the work which included the sending of dispatches to the President.

Her fame as an exceedingly clever "smuggler" had evidently spread, and if the plan of the White Envelope had been known to her visitor at the time, he would no doubt have been even more satisfied with the result of the visit.

******

That the committee in Pretoria formed only a very small part of the scheme of espionage all over South Africa I am well aware, but it is with this particular committee that we have to do, and a detailed account of the work carried out by them will give the reader some idea of the system generally employed by the Boers.

Not with the foolhardy young spy who came into the capital to buy a pound of sweets or a box of cigarettes, not with the reckless youth who came in to spend a few days with his friend and to escort his sweetheart to church on Sunday night, thereby increasing the difficulties and danger of detection for his more earnest fellow-countrymen, are we concerned in this book.

These escapades were of such frequent occurrence, and were so well known to many people in town, that it would have been dangerous in the extreme to use them for serious purposes.

From the earliest days of the occupation Pretoria was always full of spies, and the English were aware of it, but, do what they would, they could not prevent it.

Although we always knew how things were going in the field, I do not for a moment believe that the accounts of British reverses brought unofficially in to town by the spies were always reliable, nor do I sanction the reckless coming and going of irresponsible men. Alas, no! too bitter have been the experiences of disastrous results brought about by their thoughtlessness.

The van Warmelos were warned from the beginning against having dealings with them if they really wished to be of service to their people, to which warning they owed their safety and the privilege of being able to help their countrymen till the end of the war. General Emmet, as prisoner in the Rest Camp, also sent a warning, saying that General Botha had instructed him to tell Mrs. van Warmelo that her name was known on commando.

As time went on, Pretoria was being shut in more completely every day. Blockhouses rose on every side; on the hills which lie around the town searchlights played from commanding positions over many miles of country, making darkest night as clear as noonday; barbed-wire fences enclosed the entire capital, and outposts were on guard night and day—with no avail!

The spies glided in and out like serpents in the night, and some idea of the hardships and perils they went through in order to achieve their purpose will be given in this true story of the great Boer war, some idea of the dangers to which their assistants in town were exposed, and the part played by women and girls in the scheme of espionage.

I believe the events related here to be tame in comparison with some of the risks incurred and heroism displayed by other Boer women all over South Africa, but we must confine ourselves strictly to Hansie's diary, as it was written from day to day, before time could obliterate the smallest detail from her memory.

Hansie's diary with all the bitterness left out; Hansie's diary without its sighs and tears, its ever-changing moods, and deep emotions; Hansie's diary, shorn of all that makes it human, natural, and real,—surely what is left of it must be tame and totally unworthy of the original!

And yet it needs must be!

This book must be a calm, dispassionate review of the past, a temperate recital of historical events as they took place, and, as facts speak largely for themselves, I leave the details to be filled in by the reader's imagination.

CHAPTER 15

The Formation of the National Scouts Corps

If what theosophists say be true, that thoughts are living forces, then it seems to me that the subtle power and influence of a national maxim must be far-reaching and powerful in its effect on the national mind.

Of this we had ample proof as the war proceeded.

With "*Might is right*" working ceaselessly in a hundred thousand brains, some people in South Africa and England began to believe that might *was* right, and with "All is fair in love and war" held up by the united force of a million minds, is it to be wondered at that anything and everything seemed justified under martial law? And yet, when we come to think of it, how pernicious and demoralising the effect of such maxims must be on the public in general and the uneducated mind in particular. Under its influence a nation may become, in times of war, dishonourable and treacherous, may be dragged from one abyss of degradation to another, deeper than the last, until all self-respect is gone and the voice of conscience is silenced for ever.

Well may we guard against this growing evil in South Africa! Well may we keep our national mottoes pure!

I do believe that the Dutch South African saying, "*Geduld en moed, alles sal reg kom*" ("*Patience and courage, everything will right itself*"), is responsible to a great extent for the South African indifference to duty. It was first spoken by President Brand, of the Orange Free State, no doubt in all thoughtlessness of what it might lead to, for no one could have foreseen that the first part, "*Geduld en moed,*" would fall into disuse and be forgotten, because these good qualities do not come easily to men, and the second, "*Alles sal reg kom,*" would be made an excuse for a sort of lazy optimism, by which anything could be justified which comes easiest to us at the moment.

"*Alles sal reg kom*," yes, but not if we shirk our responsibilities. "*Alles sal reg kom*" if we are true, staunch, and honourable, if with perseverance and patient endurance we fulfil our duty when its demands upon us are most exacting and difficult.

Rightly interpreted, this popular saying would have been a strong support to the Boers at a time when they were assailed by the fiercest temptation, and this brings us to the subject with which this short chapter deals.

We were frequently told during the war that it was Lord Kitchener's policy to procure the services of as many members of the opposing forces as could be persuaded, for material considerations, to take up arms against their fellow countrymen, a policy which he had often employed in other countries and to which he owed much of his success. This may or may not have been the case in previous wars in which he had taken a leading part, but in the great South African war this policy was crowned with undoubted success, in the formation of the National Scouts Corps.

The thought has occurred to me that the words "National Scout" may convey nothing to my English reader.

Would to God that it conveyed nothing to us either!

It will be necessary to explain. The first downward step to becoming a National Scout was the voluntary surrendering of arms to the enemy, to become a "handsupper," as the *burghers* were called, who laid down their arms while the Boer leaders were still in the field.

There were three kinds of handsuppers; first, men who, through a mistaken sense of duty, surrendered themselves to the enemy, in order to bring the war to a speedy termination and so to save the women and children from further suffering; second, the men who, wearied of the strife, became hopeless and despondent and only longed for peace, indifferent as to who should prove to be the victor in the field; and third, the men who, through their lust for gain, fell an easy prey to the temptations offered them in gold and spoil by the enemy, surrendering their trusty Mausers in exchange for the Lee Metfords of the enemy, with whom they thereafter stood, side by side, in infernal warfare against kith and kin. To the latter class of handsuppers the National Scouts, better known throughout the war as "Judas-Boers," belonged. In most cases they were first employed by the enemy as "Cattle Rangers," to gather in the livestock from the farms and protect them from recapture by the Boer commandos. The next step downwards followed as a matter of course, active service against their brother *burghers*.

A few months after the occupation of Pretoria the first public meeting was held in the Rex Bar, now known as the Lyceum Theatre, on Church Square ("under the Oaks"), for the purpose of recruiting National Scouts from the ranks of the *burghers* in Pretoria. Many prominent men attended this meeting, which, it will be remembered, was presided over by a distinguished British officer. These men went, not to become members of the National Scouts Corps, but to ask a certain question when the right moment arrived—and then they rose with one accord. "What about our oath of neutrality?" They were told that the oath of neutrality need not disturb anyone who wished to join the ranks of the enemy; it would be nullified by the oath of allegiance, and was declared to be "a mere formality." The noblest motives for uniting their strength to that of the enemy, in the endeavour "to restore peace to the land," were laid before the *burghers* of the Transvaal. Not only would the helpless inmates of the concentration camps be spared further suffering, but the deplorable loss of life of men on both sides in the field would cease.

Then too, the pay was a consideration not to be despised in days of so much hardship and privation. Large sums were paid for the capture of each brother *burgher*, and so liberal a share in the plunder brought home by them that there are, at the present time, well-to-do farmers, poor before the war, now flourishing and well known in their districts as successful "pocket patriots."[1]

The National Scouts became a strong and well-organised body of men, versed in all the arts of Boer warfare, familiar with the country—a dangerous and treacherous addition to the difficulties with which the faithful *burghers* were beset.

It must be clearly understood that there can be no comparison between the act of the men who, when condemned to death, saved themselves by turning king's evidence and the treachery of the men who, voluntarily and for greed of gold, took up arms against their fellow-countrymen. Under the impulse of fear men may be guilty of a crime for which they may have to do penance with lifelong remorse, and for these we may feel pity, even if we do not understand and cannot enter into the cowardly weakness by which they were driven to betray their comrades. But in the case of the National Scouts there were no extenuating circumstances except perhaps that the greater

---

1. "*Zak-patriotten.*"

responsibility rested on the men who paid in dross for the dishonour of their fellow-creatures.

It was the public recruiting of National Scouts from amongst the burghers who had taken the oath of neutrality that first induced the Boers who remained true to their cause to use their influence in bringing the war to an end. But they determined to assist their fellow-countrymen, not the enemy, and when the call came from the field they were found ready to depart for active service or willing to devote themselves to secret service in the towns, as the case may be. I may say here that the appointment of the Secret Committee did not at any time bear an official character.

Although the Boer leaders knew of its existence and made use of information conveyed through the members, they did not approve of the work of espionage being carried on in the towns, because of the great danger to which it exposed the women and the needless risks incurred by the men.

The Secret Service of the Boers was not confined to the *burghers*. In every department of importance there were British subjects in the employment of the Boers, especially in that part connected with the registration of names of the men who joined the National Scouts.

From every part of the Transvaal the names and addresses of Boers joining the English were sent to British headquarters in Pretoria, these lists being again conveyed to Captain Naudé, who passed them on to Boer head-quarters in the field.

There was no break in this part of the Boer espionage until the war came to an end.

In the Burgher Camps Department, as the headquarters of the concentration camps in Pretoria were called, there were men at work for us too, men who by smuggling through statistics of the high mortality and other facts connected with the camps, strengthened the hands of the pro-Boers in England and acquainted the world with the real state of affairs even before the Blue books could appear.

Towards the latter end of the war thousands of *burghers* had succumbed to their temptations, and the appalling increase of the Scouts Corps preyed on the minds of the Boer leaders more than any other calamity. Everything that ingenuity could devise was tried to stop the *burghers* from sinking deeper into degradation, members of the Scouts Corps, when captured by the Boers, being executed without mercy and their fate made known far and wide.

Hell was indeed let loose in South Africa and every man's hand was turned against his brother. The worst passions of mankind rose to the surface, were deliberately played upon, making havoc of every tradition of country and race.

In the towns, where the renegades felt themselves comparatively safe under the protection of the British troops, their work was carried on quite openly. It would not be possible to describe the feelings of the faithful Boers when they contemplated this hideous aspect of the war.

Many futile efforts were made to stem the tide of crime, but it was a woman in Pretoria who devised a plan which would undoubtedly have struck terror to the hearts of many waverers had it been put to practice by the Boer leaders, after she had successfully carried it out.

At her instance a trusted mechanic, working secretly at dead of night, made half a dozen tiny branding-irons in the form of a cross, to be used for branding the traitors between the eyes, when captured red-handed. This drastic measure was, however, not resorted to.

Chapter 16

A Consignment of Explosives

The following story was related to Hansie by her mother soon after her return from the Irene Camp, and must be repeated here for its connection with subsequent events.

One afternoon in June Mrs. van Warmelo had been visited by a young friend, Miss F., with a man whom she introduced as her brother, an unexpected arrival from Europe.

"Indeed!" Mrs. van Warmelo exclaimed. "What a delightful surprise it must have been to you!"

"Yes, but he is leaving again very, very soon. In fact"—here Miss F.'s manner became mysterious—"he is here on a mission and we shall see very little of him."

Mrs. van Warmelo expressed her regret at this, and the conversation naturally turned to the general topic, the war.

Leading questions were put to Mrs. van Warmelo, and she felt that her assistance was required for some purpose or other; but being too discreet to invite her visitors' confidence, she waited.

After beating about the bush a good deal, Miss F. remarked:

"You know the Zoutpansberg District very well, do you not?"

"Yes," Mrs. van Warmelo answered; "we lived there formerly."

"Then you will perhaps know trustworthy people in Pietersburg, people on whom one can thoroughly rely in these days."

Mrs. van Warmelo answered hesitatingly:

"Yes—there is one, at least, on whom I can depend."

"Would there be much risk and difficulty in communicating with General Botha through such a person?" Miss F. inquired.

"General Botha!" Mrs. van Warmelo exclaimed. "But he is not in the north. He is on the High Veld, somewhere south-east of Transvaal, and much easier to communicate with than if he had been in Zoutpansberg."

"How could one get a message through to him?" Miss F. asked, and her hostess decided to beat about the bush no longer.

"Do you not think it would be better to trust me and tell me what you wish to do? I would be better able to answer and help you."

Miss F. then turned to her brother and said:

"Mrs. van Warmelo is quite right. Tell her everything." Upon which the young man explained that he had been sent out on a secret mission connected with a consignment of dynamite which lay buried on the eastern frontier. News had been received in Europe that there was a dearth of explosives and, consequently, a temporary cessation of adventures on the railway lines, and it was for the purpose of communicating the fact that this consignment had arrived that he had travelled to Pretoria via the East Coast and over Durban. How to get into touch with some reliable person in Pretoria who was in direct communication with the Boer forces had been his greatest problem, and he was grateful indeed for Mrs. van Warmelo's guarded promise of assistance.

"I cannot tell you anything now," she said, "but if you will leave the matter in my hands I promise that you will hear from me tomorrow morning."

Mr. F. then told her that he had brought with him a small quantity of the dynamite, made up into two separate parcels, non-explosive apart, but dangerous when mixed together in a certain way. He had been deputed to instruct the Boers how to mix these ingredients.

He had with him, too, a large prospecting hammer, the long handle of which was bound with leather and closely studded with nails. But the handle was *hollow* and contained a number of detonators, to be sent out to the Boers for blowing up trains and for damaging the railway lines and bridges. One other article of interest he had brought with him, a huge Parisian hat for his sister, and he told Mrs. van Warmelo how the polite inspector of goods on the frontier had held the lovely headpiece up, admiring the pink roses nestling in black lace and chiffon, and little dreaming that he was handling many yards of dynamite fuse.

"A lovely hat!" he exclaimed when he put it back into the box, without having noticed the *weight*, which alone would have betrayed it to any one familiar with ladies' headgear.

Early next morning Mrs. van Warmelo sallied forth to the house of her confederate, Mr. Willem Botha, at the other end of the town.

He listened to her story attentively and said, "There are spies in town at this very moment, and they are leaving for the general's commando tonight."

This was good news indeed, and Mrs. van Warmelo immediately made an appointment with Mr. Botha to meet Mr. F. at Harmony that afternoon.

On her way home she called at Miss F.'s house, informing her of the appointment.

That afternoon at Harmony a map was closely studied by the two men and the exact spot pointed out where the dynamite lay buried, while Mrs. van Warmelo packed the detonators one by one in cotton wool in a small box, which was conveyed to Mr. Hattingh's house, where the spies were being harboured. In the meantime the entire crown and brim of the lovely Parisian hat had been unpicked, and that night the dynamite fuse, wound closely round the body of a spy, went out to the commandos, with the small box of detonators.

Soon after this Mr. F. returned to Europe as he had come, *via* Natal and Delagoa Bay, well satisfied that his mission should have been accomplished with so much ease.

What became of the sample of dynamite my reader will see in the next chapter.

Chapter 17

The First Interview With Spies, Introducing Two Heroes

Among other things, Mr. Willem Botha warned his friends at Harmony against having a single incriminating document in the house.

"Detection means death for all concerned," he said one day, "but without written evidence the worst the enemy can do is to send you out of the country or to a concentration camp. Destroy every paper of a dangerous nature you may have, as I have done, and then you need never feel anxious."

This wise counsel was all very well, but Hansie had a mania for "collecting," and she could not make up her mind to destroy what might become a valuable relic of the war.

She therefore had her diaries and white envelopes removed to some safe hiding-place and began a new book for future use.

In this book, in everyday pen and ink, she entered the ordinary events of the day, but in another she wrote in lemon-juice her adventures with the spies and all information of an incriminating character. Both books lay open on her writing-table—the "White Diary," as she called it, with its clean and spotless pages, with only here and there an almost invisible mark to show how far she had got, and the misleading record in pen and ink to throw the English off their guard in the event of an unexpected search of the house.

The white diary gave a sense of security and satisfaction at the thought of the secrets it contained for future reference, and it was only after eight years that portions of the writing became visible to the naked eye.

A few hours' exposure to the sun's rays, and the application of a hot iron here and there, made it sufficiently legible to be rewritten word for word, and it is to the existence of this diary that we owe our accurate information of what otherwise would have been lost for ever.

I may add here that it was only the re-reading of the White Diary after so many years, and the surprising amount of half-forgotten information Hansie found in it, that suggested the idea to her mind of publishing its contents in the form of a story.

It was on the morning of July 17th, 1901, that Mr. Botha was seen coming up the garden path between the rows of orange trees at Harmony, with his jauntiest air, by which it was evident that he was the bearer of news from the front. Briefly he informed our heroines that two spies had come in the previous night and wished to see Mrs. van Warmelo about certain communications sent out by her to General Botha a few weeks back. They were staying with Mrs. Joubert, widow of the late Commandant-General P.J. Joubert, and were leaving again the next night with dispatches.

In the interview with them at 9 o'clock the next morning Hansie made her first acquaintance with Captain Naudé, who plays the principal part in the story here recorded, and whose courage and resource gave him an unquestioned position of leadership.

Good reader, do you know what it means to be an unwilling captive in the hands of your enemy for more than a year, and then to find yourself in the presence of men, healthy, brown, and hearty, *your own men*, straight from the glorious freedom of their life in the *veld*? Can you realise the sensation of shaking hands with them for the first time and the atmosphere of wholesome unrestraint and unconscious dignity which greeted you in their presence? Well, I do, and it would be useless trying to tell any one what it is like, for those who know will never forget, and those who don't will never understand.

In Mrs. Joubert's drawing-room they were waiting for their visitors next day, Captain Naudé and his private secretary, Mr. Greyling—the former a tall, fair man, slightly built and boyish-looking and with a noble, intelligent face, the latter a mere youth, but evidently shrewd and brave.

The first eager questions naturally were for news of Fritz, the youngest of the van Warmelos and the last remaining in the field since the capture of his brother Dietlof in April of that year.

Mr. Greyling said that he had seen Fritz a few weeks back in perfect health and in the best of spirits, but barefoot and in rags. His trousers were so tattered that he might as well have been without, and Mr. Greyling had provided him with another pair. With unkempt beard

W.J. Botha

and long hair he seemed to justify the jest about a "gorilla" war with which some of our enemies amused themselves.

When the merriment occasioned by this description of the young warrior had subsided, the conversation turned on more serious matters.

The captain had with him a full report of the last conference held by the generals, and a copy of the resolution passed by them and President Steyn, a unanimous determination to stand together until their independence had been secured. What the ultimate destination of these documents was I am not at liberty to say, but copies of them were despatched, smuggled through in one way or another to President Kruger.

Captain Naudé also brought greetings from General Botha and told Mrs. van Warmelo how pleased the general had been with the news she had sent him on a previous occasion.

In order to explain the nature of the business which had brought the captain into Pretoria again, it will be necessary to turn our attention for a moment to the matters referred to in the previous chapter in connection with which he had once more risked the dangers of a visit to the capital.

"Yes," in answer to his inquiries, "the dynamite has arrived and is at Delagoa Bay. A sample will be brought to this house today, with instructions for mixing it."

This was glad news for the two men, and Hansie soon after took her leave, promising to come back in the course of the morning with the dynamite.

Her manner was rather mysterious, and she took some unnecessary turns, to make sure of not being followed, before she reached the house where the dangerous article had been hidden. There a brown-paper parcel was handed to her with a brief, "Read the instructions and destroy them," and she was left alone in a quiet drawing-room.

On opening the parcel she found a small bottle of yellowish powder, ostensibly a remedy for colic, to be used in the way prescribed, and a pot of paste purporting to be an excellent salve for chapped hands. The two, when mixed together in a certain way, made up one pound of dynamite and had passed safely through the hands of the inspector of goods on the frontier.

As Hansie was cycling back to Mrs. Joubert's house with her precious parcel, she had to pass the Military Governor's offices on Church Square, and the thought occurred to her that this was a fitting opportunity to interview General Maxwell regarding her tour of inspection to the concentration camps, and at the same time to procure a permit for the Vocal Society to hold a charity concert.

"Why not go in now?" she thought. "There is some fun in going to see the governor with one pound of dynamite in one's hands, and it would save me the trouble of coming into town again. Another thing: if I *am* being watched or followed, I am sure there can be nothing like a visit to Government Buildings to disarm the most suspicious."

Arrived at the governor's office, she noticed with some amusement that the urchin at the door wrote on the card, under her name, "Nature of business: permission *to have a consort.*" (This was indeed to come later!)

The German Consul was engaged with General Maxwell and Hansie had a long time to wait, and when at last she was shown in she found the affable governor in a very bad temper and his A.D.C., Major Hoskins, looking anything but comfortable.

The former shook hands and greeted her with a curt, "Well, what is the matter with you now?"

"That is very unkind of you, General," she said.

"Why?" he demanded.

"Oh, because it sounds as if I trouble you every day."

"Well," he answered, smiling slightly, "what can I do for you?"

"That's better, thank you," exclaimed Hansie cheerfully, and straightway plunged into business.

With her mind dwelling on explosives and Secret Service men, she reminded him of a promise he had given her soon after her return from the Irene Camp, that she should visit all the camps in the Transvaal and write reports for him, to be sent to London if necessary, for publication in the Blue books.

"I have come to arrange with you about my tour," she said.

"Yes," he answered. "I have thought about it and will give you the necessary permits and every facility. You will travel at government expense, and I will do all I can to make your way easy, on one condition. You must promise to give me a full and true report of things exactly as you find them."

Hansie was deeply touched by his confidence in her truth, which she knew was not misplaced, and gladly gave the promise he asked from her.

"What you are undertaking," he continued, "will not only be difficult, but dangerous. The accommodation in the camps will probably be very bad, and what would you think of a charge of dynamite under your train?"

Hansie glanced down at the parcel on her lap and said something about thinking she would risk it.

The conversation was taking an unexpected turn, and she longed to get away, but the governor still had much to say to her.

"You can safely visit all the camps except those in the north, in the Zoutpansberg and Waterberg districts, and the one in Potchefstroom." ("Boers ahead!" was Hansie's mental comment.) "And I don't think you ought to go alone. Have you thought of anyone who could accompany you?"

"Yes," Hansie replied. "A friend of mine, Mrs. Stiemens, who nursed with me at Irene, would like to go with me. She is the right woman for such an undertaking, strong and healthy and very cheerful."

This suggestion meeting with the governor's approval, it was arranged that they should visit the camp at Middelburg first, and while they were preparing for the tour he would notify their visit to the various *commandants* and arrange about the permits.

Permission to hold a concert was instantly granted, and she was on the point of leaving, when he asked her whether she had heard of President Steyn's narrow escape.

Yes, she had heard something, but would like to know more about it.

With evident enjoyment he proceeded to relate how the president had slept in Reitz, a small, deserted village in the Free State, with twenty-seven men, how they had stabled their horses and made themselves generally comfortable for the night, how they were surrounded and surprised by the English, who took all their horses before the alarm could be given, how the president escaped on a small pony, which was standing unnoticed in the back yard, and how all the other men were captured, General Cronjé (the second), General Wessels, General Fraser, and many other well-known and prominent men. The President must have fled in the open in nothing but a shirt, because all his clothes and even his boots were left behind. In his pockets were many valuable letters and documents.

Altogether this event must have given the English great joy, but I think they forgot it in their chagrin at the president's escape, for when Hansie openly rejoiced and blessed the "small unnoticed pony," expressing her great admiration for the brave president, the governor suddenly turned crusty again and said he could not understand how anyone could admire a man who had been the ruin of his country.

"Poor old general!" Hansie mused as she cycled slowly up to Mrs. Joubert's house, where the spies were waiting for her. "I have never known him so quarrelsome and unkind. I wonder what it could have been! The German Consul's visit or the president's escape? What a mercy that he knew nothing of———" She cycled faster, suddenly remembering that it was late and there was still much to do before the two men could begin their perilous journey that night.

After she had handed the parcel over to them, with verbal instructions for its use, she bade them goodbye and went home to lunch.

That evening Mrs. van Warmelo took important documents, of which we speak later, and European newspaper cuttings to the captain, with some money for her tattered son, and a letter for him in a disguised hand. No names were mentioned, and in the event of the spies falling into the hands of the enemy, nothing found on them could have incriminated anyone.

They were about to leave when she arrived at Mrs. Joubert's house.

Their preparations were conducted in perfect silence, except for an occasional whispered command, while outside, guard was kept by an alert figure, slender and upright, the figure of the aged hostess of the spies, who, it is said, was never visible to the spies and never slept by day or night as long as these men were being sheltered under her roof.

A brave and dauntless woman she was, knowing no fear for herself, but filled with concern for the fate of the men whose capture meant certain death, for it was whispered in town that on the head of Koos Naudé, captain of the Secret Service, a price of £1,000 had been fixed.

The men left Pretoria that night for the "nest" of the spies in the Skurvebergen, west from Pretoria, and from there they proceeded to where they expected to find the generals.

CHAPTER 18

The Case of Spoelstra

There were so many events of importance during the month of July 1901 that there is great difficulty in choosing the right material from Hansie's diary.

No wonder that that period seems to have been in a state of chaos, for the things to which we attached the greatest importance "ended in smoke," and seemingly small incidents assumed gigantic proportions before the glorious spring broke over the country.

Hansie was busy preparing for her tour of inspection through the camps, though to tell the truth she rather dreaded it, because she was far from strong, but she realised that this was an opportunity not to be despised.

General Maxwell frequently impressed it on her that she was the only exception, that no one else who had applied for leave to visit the camps had been granted permits—it was against the regulations, and he was only sending her because he knew he could depend upon her. He wanted to know *the truth*, and she, with her knowledge of the country and people, would be better able to draw up reports than any one else he knew.

Very flattering, but Hansie's heart sank when she thought of Irene.

What awaited her on this tour?

July 27th, when she paid him her last visit in connection with her passports, he asked her, as she was on the point of leaving him, whether she did not think the Boers ought to surrender now.

Now, Hansie had firmly made up her mind not to be drawn into argument with him again, but this question took her so much by surprise that she flared out with:

"Don't you think the English ought to give in? Why should the

Boers give in? We are fighting for our own, and England is fighting for what belongs to another. Why should England not give in?"

With some asperity he answered:

"I suppose it is a question of '*Eendracht maakt Macht*,' or whatever you call it."

"*Eendracht maakt Macht?*" she exclaimed. "I really fail to see the connection."

"Well," he answered, "isn't Might *Right* all the world over?"

"No, indeed!" she cried vehemently. "Might is right in England, and your motto is an apt one, but in South Africa might is *not* right. *Our* motto, '*Eendracht maakt Macht*,' means 'Unity is Strength.'"

The general seemed much surprised and did not look pleased at her assurance that he had been misinformed as to the correct translation—he had been told on "good authority" that the Boer motto was the same as the English.

"If might had been right," she continued, "the war would have been over long ago—our poor little forces would have been crushed—but unity is glorious strength, an *inspired* strength."

Alas, alas, that she was so soon to find out how a want of unity can bring disaster and defeat!

"It is very stupid to argue with him. Surely he cannot expect to find my views changing on account of the duration of the war!"

Now, whether this unfortunate conversation had anything to do with the next developments I do not know. I do not *think* so, for the governor was a broadminded and just man, not to be deterred from his purpose by any small consideration, but the fact remains that Hansie received a curt note from him four days later, informing her that he had changed his mind about allowing her to inspect the camps, and that all her permits had been cancelled. No word of apology or regret, but a curt request to return to him the passports and letters of introduction she had received from him.

"Serves you right," her mother said, "for showing your enemy your hand."

"Oh no," Hansie said, "I am positive that has nothing to do with it; in fact, I don't believe General Maxwell is responsible for this at all. He is acting under orders, and if I am not mistaken Lord Kitchener is at the bottom of it. *He* has put down that awful foot of his, mother, and there is nothing more to be done."

"Perhaps"—Mrs. van Warmelo looked grave—"perhaps they have found out something. I have often wondered at finding myself still at large after the commotion made about the petitions and the report of the consuls. I can't forget how critical things seemed to me when three consuls came to Harmony late at night, while you were at Irene, to warn me that the whole detective force was on the track of the petitioners. Poor Mr. Cinatti was frightfully excited and said that it was his duty to see that his petitioners' names did not become known. He warned me that everything would be done to find us out, traps would be set for us, and he advised me, if ever any one came to Harmony and said that my name had been revealed, I was to say No! No!! No!!! and he danced about the room, striking his left hand with his clenched right fist at every 'No!'"

Hansie laughed and said, "There is no fear of your being found out. The petitioners won't talk of that, you may be quite sure, and all the consuls are to be trusted."

"What are you going to do about this?" her mother asked, touching the general's note.

"Oh, I am going to wait a few days to make him 'feel bad' and then, I suppose, I must return my passports to him."

She waited three days, and then the general's behaviour strengthened her in her belief that he was not to blame for the shabby way in which he had treated her.

He was most penitent, begged her to forgive him for having caused her so much inconvenience, and said he had been "very weak" in entertaining the idea of her visiting the camps.

They talked about certain improvements which Hansie had suggested, and on which she had intended to lay much stress in her reports.

He promised that everything in his power would be done to arrest the high mortality, and, encouraged by his sympathetic attitude, she pleaded for "poor Middelburg."

"I have just been told that there were 503 deaths in that camp during last month (July). Can that be possible?"

"I am afraid it is only too true," he answered, sighing heavily. "The people on the High Veld are very badly off during this bitter weather."

"Will you allow me to send the warm clothing and blankets which I intended to distribute in the camps?" she asked.

"Certainly, the more the better. Every facility will be afforded you in this."

Hansie felt happier after this conversation with the governor, more convinced that something would be done to alleviate the sufferings in the camps.

✳✳✳✳✳✳

Now, if our heroine had been allowed to carry out her tour of inspection, she would have been out of "mischief's way" for many months, and much of what I am about to relate would not have taken place at all.

"Fair play is bonny play," and a breach of faith is bound, at some time or other, to be followed by undesirable consequences.

Hansie made up her mind to serve her country in another, perhaps better way, and in this she was assisted by the resistless hand of Fate, as we shall see in the following chapters.

That she was never "caught" is a marvel indeed, for she was most reckless of danger.

There were a number of intimate and trusted friends with whom she came into frequent contact, but who had no idea of the work which was being carried on at Harmony.

To these friends, however, she went with her "reliable war news" (more especially news brought into town by the spies, of the Boer victories) when anything of importance became known, and in time her friends found out that her news could always be depended upon as reliable indeed, although they had no inkling of the source whence it had been derived. There was danger of her becoming altogether too "cocksure," when she was one day pulled up sharply by the following occurrence:

Captain Naudé was in town again, was, if I remember rightly, under her very roof, when she visited a man for whom she entertained feelings of great affection and esteem, with the object of gladdening his heart with news of a particularly gratifying nature from the front.

He listened attentively, he asked a number of questions, nodding with the greatest satisfaction at her direct and definite replies.

"I must go," Hansie exclaimed suddenly, "I only came in for a few moments. We have to see some friends off tonight."

"Ah! Just wait a minute, please, will you?"

He hastened from the room, returning shortly with a parcel which he placed in her hands without a word.

"What is this?" she asked curiously.

"Five pounds of the best Boer tobacco."

"For me?" in amazement.

He approached her and whispered in her ear:

"For the spy!"

Hansie fled from that house, laughing as she went, and patting her parcel of tobacco rapturously.

"Oh, mother, wasn't it funny of him?"

"Yes, but when will you learn to be more careful? Hansie, you are frightfully reckless. You will not listen to reason, I suppose, until we find ourselves across the border and Harmony confiscated!"

The captain was delighted with the present and willingly added the extra five pounds weight to his cumbrous and heavy burdens.

★★★★★★

Somebody, leaving the country for Holland, offered to take documents and letters from the van Warmelos to the President on condition that they could guarantee that he would not be "found out."

This offer came at a most opportune moment, for there was information of the greatest importance to be sent to Mr. W.T. Stead.

For some weeks past Mrs. van Warmelo had been anxious to smuggle through to him copies of the two petitions to the consuls and a copy of their report on the concentration camps. For this the White Envelope was not considered satisfactory enough—the documents were too bulky and the post during those days not to be depended upon.

The information, therefore, was written on tissue paper (the usual method) and packed in a small bottle of Dr. Williams's Pink Pills, to be handed to a relative of Mrs. van Warmelo's in Holland, with instructions that he should read the contents and forward them without delay to Mr. Stead for publication in the *Review of Reviews*.

The "medicine" was faithfully delivered in Holland, but alas! the recipient, with unheard-of presumption, after having read the documents, decided in his own mind that they were not of sufficient importance to be published in London and quietly kept them to himself!

Kept them to himself, at a time when their publication to the world would have been of inestimable value to the Boers and would perhaps have saved thousands of lives!

Of course this breach of trust was not known at Harmony for many months—not, in fact, until so long after it took place that the war was drawing to a close, and it was too late to repeat the attempt.

When one thinks that but for one man's indifference to duty the report of the consuls would have been published in London at a time when all England was shaken with the revelations made by Miss Hobhouse and the agitation of the pro-Boers was at its height, then one cannot help realising the futility of fighting against Fate.

Not yet had the time of salvation arrived for the victims of the concentration camps—not yet—not until the toll of life had been paid to the uttermost.

Other schemes for supplying that section of the British public, desirous of being acquainted with *the truth*, with trustworthy information from South Africa, met with greater success, and I relate the following instance for the sake of the interesting circumstances connected with it, not for its own sake, for obvious reasons.

Many of my readers will remember the case of Mr. Spoelstra, a Hollander, which caused such a commotion in the Transvaal during the war.

He wrote a long letter for publication in Holland on the hardships and ill-treatment to which the Boer women were subjected in transit from their farms to the concentration camps, by the soldiers (chiefly, I may mention here, the Canadian Scouts and Australian Bushrangers, who were, however, all regarded as British soldiers, these distinctions not being sufficiently clear to the average South African).

This lengthy document Spoelstra confided to the care of a man who was about to leave for Holland.

On the borders of Natal, the man, on being cross-questioned by the inspector of goods, became so confused and agitated that he brought suspicion on himself, with the result that he was detained while his luggage was thoroughly overhauled.

The unfortunate letter was found, Spoelstra was arrested and immediately imprisoned in the Pretoria Jail.

The Dutch Consul, Mr. Domela Nieuwenhuis, on being appealed to, insisted on a public trial, which was granted after some delay, Spoelstra being allowed three days in which to procure his witnesses, *in Pretoria* and in the small camp in one of the suburbs, *not* in Irene.

Notwithstanding the shortness of the time and the restrictions placed upon him, he succeeded in getting nearly thirty women to give evidence on his behalf, and at his trial, which was publicly held, revelations of a very startling nature were made.

The greatest indignation was felt and freely expressed by the Dutch community when, in spite of having proved his accusations beyond a doubt, Spoelstra was fined £100 and sentenced to one year's imprisonment.

The fine was immediately paid by his friends.

Now, there was a brave Englishwoman, Mrs. Bodde, married to a Hollander, who was shortly leaving for England, who offered her services to Mrs. van Warmelo if the latter wished to make the circumstances of the case known to Mr. Stead. This was an exceedingly plucky thing to do, for the examinations on the frontier were much more severe than usual, after the discovery of Spoelstra's letter. Mrs. van Warmelo therefore promised to take extra precautions in concealing the articles she wished to send. After a great deal of trouble she succeeded in getting a full report of the Spoelstra trial, sixty large pages of closely typed evidence on tissue paper, and with this valuable material to dispose of Mrs. van Warmelo realised that it would be necessary to exert the utmost ingenuity.

She asked her friend Mrs. Bodde whether she would be taking a lunch-basket.

Certainly she would.

"Well," Mrs. van Warmelo said, "I will give you something for your lunch-basket, if you will promise not to open it until you get to London."

She promised, and Mrs. van Warmelo bought a tin of cocoa, a one-pound tin, unfastened the paper wrapper carefully, then damped the paper round the lid until it could be folded back without being damaged, removed the lid and pulled out the paper bag containing the cocoa. This bag she unfastened *at the bottom*, shook out fully two-thirds of the cocoa and filled up the empty space with the tightly rolled packet containing the documents, replacing the whole in the tin, cocoa side up, of course, and pasting down the paper wrapper over the lid to make it look like new.

Although there was very little cocoa in the tin, it was found to weigh exactly one pound as before.

Arrangements were then made with Mrs. Bodde for her future correspondence on the subject with Mrs. van Warmelo, and in due time the latter received a note from Mrs. Bodde announcing her safe arrival in London and saying that her friend Mrs. Brown (Mr. Stead) had received her (the documents) with open arms. She was not going to live in Mrs. Brown's house as she had intended (the documents would not be published in the *Review of Reviews*), but she was going into a house of her own (they would appear in pamphlet form).

This was good news indeed, and now my readers know how it came about that the sensational Spoelstra case was published in London in pamphlet form (in three successive pamphlets, for the evidence was found to be too bulky for one) during the war. The first pamphlet reached Harmony in safety through the post, the second and third, though duly dispatched, failed to reach their destination, but nobody at Harmony minded. The great object had been achieved.

Hansie, going to the post one day, took out of her letter-box a small flat book, addressed to "Mrs. Wentworth, Box 56."

She was about to throw it back into the post office, with "*not 56*" scribbled on it, when her eyes fell on the English postmark, Tunbridge Wells, and she stayed her hand in time.

Tunbridge Wells was the address of the brave Englishwoman, the great pro-Boer, and the package when opened was found to contain a copy of Methuen's *Peace or War in South Africa*, which was first "devoured" at Harmony and by other people in Pretoria and was then sent out to the commandos by the spies, to be read and reread by the *burghers* until there was nothing left of it except a few tattered pages.

Soon after the publication of the Spoelstra case there was some excitement in Pretoria about the appearance in the *Westminster Gazette* of a long article on the Irene Concentration Camp. The writer, who gave each detail with great accuracy, seemed to have personal knowledge and experience of the camp, and it was not surprising that Hansie should have been taxed with it on every side.

The consuls spoke to her direct, advising her to be more careful of her facts, and Mr. Cinatti, when she assured him of her innocence (?), said with huge delight, in his funny, broken English:

"Never mind, my dear little sing, you need not confess to *us*—but are you good at guessing riddles?"

"Not particularly."

"Well, dis one won't trouble you much. What is dis? It is small and oblong and white, and it was laid by a hen?"

"An egg," Hansie answered innocently.

He shouted with laughter.

"Are you sure?"

"Of course."

"Well, we are just as sure dat Miss van Warmelo wrote dat article. And if you want to see your work in print I'll bring it round dis very afternoon."

"I should like very much to see it," she replied.

That afternoon, just before Mr. Cinatti was expected, Gentleman Jim killed a big snake in his room, and Hansie, thinking to give her funny friend a fright for misdoubting her word, "arranged" the corpse on the steps of the front verandah, hiding the mutilated head under the leaves of the violet plants.

But the Consul came late, and other visitors before him heralded their arrival by shrieks and jumps, to the great delight of the mischievous girl.

"You are a very pranky little sing," Mr. Cinatti said, flourishing the *Westminster Gazette* before her eyes, "and den you want us not to believe dat you wrote dis."

And indeed, when Hansie glanced through the article, she found it difficult to maintain that she had not written it, for there were all her "pet" cases of overcrowding and underfeeding, her statistics, and the very terms she was in the habit of using when speaking of the volunteer nurses. She called them a "set of agitators," in sarcastic imitation of the *commandant's* favourite expression.

The only explanation to the affair could be that Mr. Stead, or perhaps Mrs. Bodde, had made use of the facts contained in one of Hansie's smuggled letters, and in that case she could naturally be held responsible. She was advised by loving friends to keep her boxes ready packed for a speedy departure, "for when the warning comes you will not be allowed much time to pack."

But she disregarded all warnings, except to take extra precautions for the safety of her diary.

Gentleman Jim's Room.

CHAPTER 19

Diamond Cut Diamond!

It would be a simple matter for me to fill this volume many times by relating the thrilling experiences and adventures of people unknown to me personally and yet known sufficiently by intimate friends who guarantee their truth and veracity, but this is not my intention in writing this book.

A brief outline, however, of the history of one of the principal members of the Secret Committee, during the war, will not be out of place here, because of his close connection with the "Petticoat Commando."

Mr. C.P. Hattingh, head keeper of the Government Buildings under the South African Republic and deacon of the Dutch Reformed Church under the Reverend Mr. Bosman, played the part of an honourable and staunch burgher throughout the war, and rendered countless services to destitute women and children, in addition to his strenuous labours on the Secret Service.

On the morning of June 5th, 1900, when it became evident beyond doubt that the British would enter Pretoria that day, he removed the Transvaal flag from Government Buildings and took it to his house for safe keeping.

To his surprise he was not asked at any time by the military what had become of the government flag, and he was able to keep it in safety until his position on the Committee became precarious and made it dangerous for him to preserve this precious relic of the past at his own house any longer.

He therefore secretly conveyed it to the house of a friend, Mr. Isaac Haarhoff, whose wife carefully concealed it until the war was over, and then handed it to him again. He gave it to General Botha, who presented it to the Pretoria Museum, where it is now preserved and exhibited as a priceless national memento.

Mr. Hattingh took the oath of neutrality with the other *burghers* in Pretoria and maintained his post in the Government Buildings for one month after the occupation of the capital. He was then asked either to take the oath of allegiance or resign from his post.

He chose the latter alternative, although he had a wife and family to support and knew not how, in time of war, he would find the means to do so.

After some deliberation he decided to begin a private bakery in a small building behind his house, and then began what proved to be a desperate struggle for existence.

With Boer meal at £8 per bag and flour at £5 per hundred pounds, the unfortunate man tried to make a small profit on the tiny sixpenny loaves. There was no question of engaging hired help, and he was obliged to work almost day and night in order to make the business pay. Sometimes he had neither sleep nor rest for thirty hours at a stretch except while partaking of his frugal fare. When flour became even more scarce he had to augment his supply by mixing it with mealie meal, ground sweet-potatoes, and barley, until, in fact, only sufficient flour was used to keep the loaves from falling to pieces.

By hard work he was not only able to pay his way, but assisted relatives and friends in a similar predicament.

As one of the deacons of the church, he came into constant touch with the wives and families of fighting *burghers*, brought into town from their devastated homes, and it was a common sight to see a row of these unfortunates standing in his backyard, holding dishes and buckets containing their rations of meal and flour, which they implored him to take in exchange for his ready-baked loaves, because there was a dearth of fuel.

Although their rations consisted of what had perhaps once been flour, but was now a black and lumpy composition, evil-smelling and swarming with vermin, the good man never disappointed his petitioners.

His fame as a philanthropist spread, and the rows of women in his back-yard increased. While engaged in serving them he listened to their tales of hardship and privation, watched their suffering faces, made mental notes of the harrowing details of each case.

There was an epidemic of "black measles" going through the town at the time in the overcrowded quarters of the "Boer refugees," as they were called. Scarcely a mother appealed to him who had not lost one or more children, in many cases all she possessed, within a few weeks.

Now, Mr. Hattingh would no doubt have concerned himself with the peaceful occupation of his bakery until the end of the war (for he had his hands more than full), had his compassionate heart not been wrung beyond endurance by the scenes he was forced to witness every day. His conscience smote him and he reproached himself with being in town when duty should have called him to the side of his fellow-countrymen, struggling against such fearful odds in their efforts to preserve their independence.

Bitterness filled his soul.

What religious and conscientious scruples he still had against violating his oath of neutrality he laid before his most trusted friends, to be met with the same answer everywhere, "The oath of neutrality is null and void, a mere formality," as the enemy had declared in connection with the recruiting of National Scouts from the ranks of the Transvaal *burghers*.

At this critical moment it was not to be wondered at that he should have accepted Captain Naudé's appointment of him on the Secret Committee, not only without hesitation, but in a spirit of intense satisfaction.

Henceforth the mind of the baker dwelt with ceaseless activity on the problems of the Boer espionage, while his busy fingers plied the brown and white loaves of bread.

Inspired by patriotism, driven by love and compassion, he became in time the most resourceful, the most ingenious, and the most trusted of Boer spies.

One evening, soon after dusk, while he was engaged in his bakery, he heard a timid knock at the door, which he opened, fully expecting to see a customer.

To his surprise he found there a Boer with a long, unkempt beard—a *"backvelder*," or, as we call it, a *"takhaar*," of the most pronounced type.

The man withdrew into the shadows as the door opened, and with great apparent timidity showed as little of himself as possible.

Mr. Hattingh asked him to come in, and he ventured forward with shrinking hesitation.

"What can I do for you?" Mr. Hattingh asked.

"Take me in," the man answered breathlessly. "Harbour me. I am a Boer spy, straight from the commandos."

Mr. Hattingh betrayed the greatest amazement, as if he had never heard of the possibility of such a thing.

"A Boer spy!" he exclaimed. "How did you come in?"

The man described the route he had taken, and in an instant Mr. Hattingh, with his intimate knowledge of the actual route employed by Boers, realised that the man before him was not from the field at all, but a National Scout, employed by the British to betray the loyal Boers—a "trap," in fact, such as were in constant use against their brother burghers.

Mr. Hattingh asked him a few more leading questions to satisfy himself of the true nature of the man's errand, and then, as if suddenly recalled to himself, broke out in evident agitation:

"But I cannot harbour you, my good fellow. I am *neutral*."

"Surely you would not have the heart to see me fall into the hands of the enemy!" the man exclaimed.

"I am very sorry," Mr. Hattingh replied, "but I dare not take you in."

"Tell me some news, then," he implored. "Our men are getting hopeless and desperate, and when we bring them news from town it gives them new courage to continue the war."

"I know of no news to tell you. I am *neutral*," Mr. Hattingh answered firmly, and the man left him with his mission unaccomplished.

Unseen himself, Mr. Hattingh watched him depart, and saw him getting into a cab, which was evidently waiting for him in the neighbourhood, and drive rapidly away.

Mr. Hattingh immediately went to his neighbour, Mr. Isaac Haarhoff, and told him what had happened.

"What do you think I ought to do? I am under suspicion without a doubt."

"Report the matter to the authorities at once," Mr. Haarhoff answered, and our friend accepted the advice with alacrity.

He mounted his bicycle and rode with all speed to the nearest Charge Office, reporting that a Boer spy had been to his house for refuge that evening.

"Why did you not bring him with you?" the officer inquired.

"I did not know what to do," Mr. Hattingh began, when another official made his appearance and asked what the matter was.

The first related what had occurred, and Mr. Hattingh, keenly watching the two men, saw the significant glances they exchanged, and caught the whispered:

"It is all right."

"No, old man," he thought, "it is all wrong, and you have been my dupe."

The men then turned to him, telling him that if he were visited by a spy again he was to take him in and report him at the Charge Office.

"Right," he replied. "I will do so." And on his homeward way he congratulated himself with the thought that he had no doubt been entered on the lists as a "faithful British subject."

This incident was followed, as far as he was concerned, by far-reaching consequences. Not only was he left with his family in the undisturbed security of his home-life after that, but he was able to carry on his work on the Committee in perfect safety, and when eventually the darkness closed over him in his prisoner's cell, he felt assured that this would count in favour of his wife and family.

Many were the men led by him through the streets of Pretoria to the spot where the *burghers* awaited them, countless and valuable the services rendered to the Boer commandos, innumerable the acts of kindness and charity performed by this brave *burgher* of Transvaal.

Mr. Colin Logan, who gave up an excellent position in the bank, was one of the men escorted out by him in order to join the Boer forces.

Riding slowly on his bicycle, with Mr. Logan walking beside him, they passed through a group of military tents, almost touching the soldiers as they sat around their camp-fires.

Not a shadow of suspicion could be roused by their calm behaviour, and they reached the *burghers* without any difficulty.

While they were exchanging a few words of greeting, the sudden, furious barking of the dogs at the Lunatic Asylum, not far from them, warned them of danger, and, taking a hasty leave, the *burghers* disappeared noiselessly into the darkness, and Mr. Hattingh literally tore home across the *veld* on his bicycle, clearing holes and jumping over stones in his mad career. He was able to reach his home just in time to be under shelter when the "curfew" rang 10 o'clock, the hour at which all respectable citizens, carrying residential passes, were supposed to be indoors.

What eventually became of Mr. Hattingh and the other members of the committee we shall see as our story proceeds.

CHAPTER 20

Thanksgiving and Humiliation

The documents sent out to General Botha, and referred to in Chapter 15, were connected with the report of the consuls, but the very first thing sent to the commandos by Mrs. van Warmelo was a copy of the first petition, tightly packed in a walnut, one of a handful which she gave the spy, with instructions not to eat any of them on the road.

He also took a verbal message to the effect that though the condition of the camps was bad, everything was being done in town to bring about the necessary improvements. Influential people were at work to make everything public in Europe, and the men in the field were urged to be brave and steadfast and of good cheer.

On July 29th Harmony was visited again by Mr. Willem Botha, bringing with him information of a disquieting nature.

In some mysterious way he had received a piece of paper from Mr. Gordon Fraser, brother-in-law to President Steyn, and prisoner of war in the Rest Camp in Pretoria, on which, in a disguised hand, was written a message imploring the Secret Service men to warn President Steyn and General de Wet that a certain man amongst them, a prominent official, was a traitor in their midst, paid by the enemy to betray their plans before they could be carried out.

This information made the conspirators very anxious, for it being full moon, there was no prospect of spies coming into town, and in the meantime incalculable mischief could be done. Neither was it possible to send anyone out who had not been before and was ignorant of the route. The matter had therefore to be left until the next suitable opportunity came and Mr. Botha went home with a heavy heart.

Unlike his usual prudent self, Mr. Botha did not immediately destroy the slip of paper on which the warning was written, but folded it carefully and placed it between the tattered leaves of an old hymn-book.

How he paid for this small indiscretion, the only one of which he was guilty, with days of anxiety and despair, and very nearly with his life, we shall see as our story develops!

******

In the early days of August the troops encamped around Harmony could, if they had used their sixth sense, have divined an air of suppressed excitement about the place.

Expectation of some sort evidently charged the atmosphere. Visitors were, in fact, expected, for Captain Naudé and his secretary had arranged to come in for the report of the consul, just before the new moon made its appearance, and now a faint crescent of silver in the heavens warned our heroines that their time was at hand.

Harmony had been chosen as a place of refuge, as the safest spot in all Pretoria, with so many troops around it!

For several nights in succession a fire was kept going in the kitchen until a late hour, and a plentiful supply of hot water kept in readiness for the warm baths which the visitors would so sorely need after their difficult and perilous journey.

Still they did not come, but on the morning of August 4th Mr. Botha paid an early visit, bringing with him the news that on the previous night five spies had reached the town in safety.

He did not tell where they were being harboured, it being one of the laws of the Secret Committee that names were not to be used needlessly, and that the people working for the committee were not even to know about one another.

So rigorously was this law enforced that from beginning to end the van Warmelos had dealings with Mr. Botha only, and did not see the four other members of the committee, nor even hear their names until——

The five spies had not come in as easily as usual. They had persistently been followed by the searchlights as they neared the town, but they were able to get through the barbed-wire enclosure in safety and had then separated and gone to their various homes, unobserved as they thought.

But one of them, a young man whom we shall call Harry, who was destined to play such a terrible part in the history of the Boer Secret Service, was followed home by three detectives, two of whom stationed themselves at the front door and the third at the back.

Fortunately when Harry became aware of his danger, he rushed out at the back.

The detective, whose name was Moodie, shouted, "Hands up, or I fire," but the young man drew his revolver with lightning-like rapidity and, firing twice, escaped from town under cover of the darkness.

The reported death of the detective caused a great sensation in the town next day, and it was not until many months after that we learned of the fate of the unfortunate man, not death, but mutilation worse than death—a ghastly wound below the heart and an amputated leg.

This event caused the British to enforce a stricter vigilance, and many houses were searched for the other spies, but without success.

The excitement in town did not abate for some time, and wherever Hansie went she was told what had taken place by people who would have been surprised indeed to hear that she was in possession of all the details, and even of documents brought in from General Kemp by those very spies.

The instructions were to see that the information contained in those documents reached the consuls without their knowing how and when they had been brought into town, and for this purpose several copies had been typed and were slipped under the doors of the different Consulates while the inmates were asleep.

Any day between August 5th and 10th Captain Naudé said he would come, and each evening found Harmony prepared to receive him, but on the 9th Mr. Botha brought a note from the gallant captain saying that he would be unable to partake of Mrs. van Warmelo's hospitality that month. A woman, whose name was unknown, had conveyed this letter to the Secret Committee. It contained no particular news except that August 8th had been celebrated as a day of thanksgiving for our victories, and the 9th, the very day on which the intimation was received in town, would be a day of humiliation for our many sins.

When this became known to the "inner circle," private prayer-meetings were immediately held in different houses in the town, while the men in the field held their day of humiliation under the open sky. In this way we worked together and supported one another spiritually, morally, and practically, in spite of searchlights and barbed-wire fences.

This was the first news received of the captain's safe return to the commandos after that eventful visit in July, and his friends were thankful to receive it. Another source of thankfulness was the fact that he was not coming in that month, for the enemy was on the *qui vive* for more spies, and consequently the dangers were multiplying for the Boers. The reckless coming in and going out of irresponsible men became a source of real danger to the people who harboured them, and on August 12th Mr. Botha came again to warn Mrs. van Warmelo against having dealings with any spies except those sent by the Secret Committee.

"You will only find yourselves in jail or over the border," he said, "which would not be so bad if that were all, but it would ruin our chances of assisting the generals."

He then reported that a young spy had come in on Saturday night and that he had been taken to Mrs. General Joubert's house the next morning while she was in church. The good lady was anything but pleased, on her return home, to find him there, for she had a houseful of people, and she was obliged to stow him into a tiny room, where he sat as still as a mouse, until he went back to commando. Not very cheerful for him, but a good lesson for the future!

******

Five or six men who tried to escape from town were captured near the Magaliesbergen and placed in the Rest Camp, so Dame Rumour said at the time, but the truth of the story, briefly related, ran thus:

I have mentioned the nest of the spies in the Skurvebergen not far from Pretoria in the western direction.

This "nest" had been surprised and taken possession of by the English while five of the spies were in Pretoria, and they, cut off from their own people as they were, were unable to escape.

One or two attempts were made, but the men were fired on and they had to abandon the idea for the present.

The curious part of this story is that these men (one can hardly call them spies) were Pretoria men who had escaped to the Skurvebergen for the first time only three weeks previously, and had gone backwards and forwards several times with small necessaries. One of the five, a man whose name I cannot mention here, for the sake of what is to follow, had been so often, and was so much at home both in Pretoria and the Skurvebergen, that his dearest friends did not know to which part of the country he really belonged!

Well, he was in a nice predicament now!

The house in which he was being harboured, with one of his friends, was unfortunately suspect. He could not remain there, neither could he escape from town.

Someone came to Harmony in great distress. What was to be done with those two men? To what place of refuge could they be moved that night? The visitor looked imploringly at Mrs. van Warmelo as if he expected her to offer Harmony, but she, mindful of Mr. Botha's warning, did nothing of the kind.

"Death is staring them in the face," the visitor continued. "I don't know what to do!"

Hansie, who knew the visitor well and trusted him implicitly, then pleaded with her mother—to no avail, Mrs. van Warmelo remaining firmly obdurate, and saying distinctly, for the edification of her visitor, "I have never harboured a spy, and I hope I never shall."

When the good man had departed, in sore disappointment, Hansie grumbled a good deal and said it was all very fine to assist these Secret Service men when there was no danger in doing so, but her mother took no notice of her for the rest of the day, and subsequent events proved that she had acted wisely in refusing to harbour men unknown to her.

What became of them at the time she did not know, and a few weeks elapsed before the crushing sequel to this escapade became known.

Chapter 21

Flippie and Co.

"Was there no fear of betrayal through the servants at Harmony?" I have often been asked since the war, and this reminds me that a short introduction to the other inmates of the property will be necessary for the reader's benefit and understanding.

The lower portion of Harmony, through which the Aapies River runs, was occupied by Italian gardeners, who employed a varying number of *kaffir* labourers in the extensive fruit and vegetable gardens.

The upper part, on which the house stood, was entirely under Mrs. van Warmelo's management. No white servants were kept, the domestic staff consisting of native gardeners, a stable-boy, and a house-boy, neither was there a single female domestic, either white or black, on the place.

One day a small white son of the soil presented himself and asked for work.

Mrs. van Warmelo looked him up and down and said she did not farm with children.

"What is your name?" Hansie asked.

There was no answer, and then she noticed that the little stranger was staring straight in front of him, while two great tears rolled slowly down his cheeks.

This touched her, and she repeated her question persuasively.

"Flippie," he answered brokenly.

"Where is your mother?"

"Dead."

"And your father?"

"Fighting, with five sons."

Then Hansie felt inclined to take him in her arms and kiss him for his dead mother and brave father and brothers.

She turned to her mother and whispered:

"Let Flippie stay. Make some agreement with him and let us try him as errand-boy or general help in the house and garden."

Mrs. van Warmelo nodded and turned again to him. The conversation which passed between them is not recorded in Hansie's diary, but Flippie stayed, and within a week the Harmonites wondered how they had managed to exist without him for so long.

He was as sharp as a needle, and, though only thirteen years of age, he proved to be a perfect "man" of business, rising early every day to go to the morning market and gardening with surprising energy and ambition.

This pleased Mrs. van Warmelo so much that she gave him a plot of ground to cultivate for himself, and he immediately set to work to plant vegetables, spending every spare moment of the day in *his* garden.

When Hansie laughingly said that she hoped to be his first customer, he protested vehemently against the idea of selling anything to her, and time showed that he meant to keep his word.

All he had was given away with large-hearted generosity and when he had nothing more to give, he *took* all he required from other people!

Yes, I am afraid Flippie's ideas of honesty were curious in the extreme. He had no idea of "mine and thine," as we say in Dutch.[1]

Arguments were of no avail, for Flippie was the scornfullest little boy I ever came across and knew everything better than his superiors.

Hansie set to work to study him, but found it necessary to reconstruct her ideas of him every day. Flippie baffled her at every turn.

One day she thought he would turn out to be a genius, the next she declared positively that he would come to the gallows, and the third she wondered helplessly whether he could by any chance do both.

Flippie could lie and deceive with the most angelic face and could melt into tears on the least provocation or whenever it suited his book to do so.

A phrenologist would have delighted in the study of that remarkable head.

The forehead receded and went on receding until there was noth-

---

1. *Mÿn en dÿn.*

ing left of it but a great lump at the back of the head, and the little nose tilted up at one in the most impertinent manner, which was given the lie to by the drooping corners of the sensitive mouth. What delighted one most was the sunny temperament, the ringing, infectious laugh, the cheery whistle.

Surely Flippie was the merriest and one of the most lovable little souls one could find anywhere, and his ruling virtue always seemed to be his unswerving loyalty and constant fidelity.

His heart seemed to be torn between his sense of duty to the fearful and wonderful old grandmother, who had taken the place of his dead mother in what bringing-up he ever had, and his sense of gratitude to his protectors at Harmony.

My story would not be complete without a short sketch of this grandmother, for she played a part of some importance in the events recorded here, and was at all times a sore trial to the inmates of Harmony.

We have no proof, but we *think* that Flippie's grandmother had a hand in the undoing of the security and peace which reigned supreme at Harmony before she came upon the scene.

Not that she ever lived on the property; no, her home was a small tent, one of a number which had been erected some little distance to the south of Harmony on Avondale, on the property of Mr. Christian Joubert, on the way to the "Fountains."

These tents were largely occupied by "handsuppers" and their families, amongst whom were found a few Judas-Boers—Boers of the most dangerous type. That the life of the loyal Boers in their midst was anything but a bed of roses can very well be imagined, and we know that bitterness and strife reigned supreme, for it was an open secret that renegades, hirelings of the enemy, held their dreaded sway over the inmates of that small colony.

Flippie and his grandmother did not belong to that degraded set, but the one was a thoughtless child and the other an exceedingly suspicious and inquisitive old woman, and that they were both used as unsuspecting tools by their more designing fellows I have not a shadow of doubt.

Mrs. van Warmelo and Hansie soon gave the old granny the name of "Um-Ah," for her tongue had been paralysed by a "stroke" twenty years back, and "Um-Ah," was all she was ever heard to say. It stood for yes and no and for every imaginable question, being only varied by the tone of voice in which it was said. Sometimes, when she became excited or impatient, it was fired off four or five times in quick succession.

This formidable old dame ruled Flippie with a rod of iron, appropriating the whole of his small salary every month and refusing to give him so much as a sixpence. When Mrs. van Warmelo found this out she stealthily added half a crown to his earnings for his own use, and this the generous lad regularly spent on sweets, cakes, and ginger-beer for his granny!

Even the chocolates and other good things to which kind-hearted soldiers treated him were laid as "trophies of the war" at his granny's feet, after he had vainly tried to induce Hansie to partake of them.

"Um-Ah" had an inconvenient way of dropping in at Harmony at all hours of the day, ostensibly to see if Flippie was doing his work well, but in reality to keep a watchful eye on the other inmates. She seemed to be always looking for something, and the time was soon to come when this unpleasant propensity should become a source of real danger to the van Warmelos.

✶✶✶✶✶✶

Besides Flippie, there were two other permanent members on the domestic staff—a gigantic native named Paulus, and a young Zulu who went by the name of "Gentleman Jim" on account of his dandified appearance and the aristocratic "drawl" affected by him. American darkies say, "Dere's some folk dat is slow but shua, and some dar is dat's *jes' slow!*" Well, Gentleman Jim was "jes' slow." He was the only one on the premises who steadfastly refused to speak one word of Dutch, although he perfectly understood everything said to him.

The result was that the dialogues carried on between mistresses and servant were in Dutch on one side and in English on the other, it being one of the rules at Harmony to address all natives either in their own tongue or in Dutch, never in English.

I may say here that even at the present time it is customary with many Dutch South Africans to employ no English-speaking natives, but rather to engage the "raw" material, *i.e.* those speaking neither Dutch nor English, because they are, in nine cases out of ten, still unspoilt by civilisation and have lost none of the awe and respect with which they, in their native state, regard the white man.

Gentleman Jim was the only exception ever known at Harmony, and there was no lack of respect in *his* manner; on the contrary, the flourish with which he took off his hat and his slow and dignified, "Good morning, little missie," were well worth seeing and a constant source of amusement to all.

Paulus, that magnificent specimen of manhood in its natural state, was by no means the least remarkable of the trio, and there was something tragic too about his rugged personality.

He had been taken by the English in the neighbourhood of Pretoria and brought into town on the false suspicion of having been employed by the Boers as a spy.

There being nothing found against him in proof of this, he was set free in town and allowed to seek employment, but, though he pleaded hard, he could not obtain permission to return to his home, where wife and children had been left in complete uncertainty as to his fate.

This native was a converted heathen, semi-civilised, but with the noblest instincts within him developed on natural lines to a remarkable degree. I have often longed to meet the missionary in whose hands the moulding of this rare product of nature had been carried out with so much success. Patience, faith, devotion, and an awe amounting to veneration for his white mistresses were among the most striking qualities Paulus possessed.

There were hundreds of his stamp on the farms all over the country, natives brought up by the Dutch farmers and trained as useful servants in their homes and in the fields, but it was rare indeed for one of them to find his way into the towns. Fate had been unkind in separating him from his dear ones for so many months, and Paulus went through days of melancholy and despair.

One day, when Hansie heard him sigh more heavily than usual, she asked:

"Are you thinking of your wife and children, Paulus?"

"Oh yes, Nonnie, I am always thinking of them, but I was thinking also how sad it was to forget all my learning. I was getting on so well with my reading and writing, and now I find it so hard to go on by myself."

"Oh, if that is all, Paulus," Hansie said cheerfully, "I can help you a lot. Bring me your books this evening and let me hear you read."

The poor fellow's look of gratitude was touching to behold. He needed no second invitation, and appeared that evening in his Sunday suit, with a new shirt on, and his hands and face scrubbed with soap and water until they shone like polished ebony.

A Dutch Bible, a book of hymns and psalms, and a small spelling-book were all he possessed, but Hansie found him further advanced than she had expected, and wonderfully intelligent, and she soon added a few simple reading-books to his small store.

Now and then she instructed him for a short hour, and it was a pleasure to see the change which came over him within a few weeks. Learning became the joy of his life, and in his ambition to get on he forgot much of his anxiety and distress at the enforced separation from his wife and children.

One evening when Hansie had gone into the kitchen to look over his work, there was a sudden fumbling at the door and "Gentleman Jim" stumbled in with a campstool under one arm and a slate and Bible, an English one, under the other.

"Coming to learn too, little missie," he said, grinning from ear to ear and settling himself comfortably on the stool.

Paulus bent over his writing and said never a word. Hansie nodded uncomfortably.

That this self-invited pupil was unwelcome was, but he himself seemed serenely unconscious of the fact.

There was no love lost between Paulus and "Gentleman Jim"—not that there had ever been an open rupture, but Paulus despised the dandified Zulu, and "Jim" looked down (figuratively speaking, for he was quite a foot shorter in stature) on Paulus's rugged simplicity.

They systematically ignored one another, and were only heard to exchange brief sentences, in English from Jim and in Dutch from Paulus, when necessity compelled them to address one another, for Jim could speak no Sesuto and Paulus knew neither Zulu nor English.

Their antipathy to one another was so marked, in fact, that "Gentleman Jim" refused to have his meals with Paulus and had built a small kitchen apart for himself, under one of the big willows. On this occasion Hansie did not feel pleased at "Jim's" appearance either, for it was one thing to teach the self-contained and reverent Sesuto, and quite another to instruct the flippant "Gentleman Jim."

But Hansie did not know what to say and asked Jim to let her hear him read. He began laboriously, floundering hopelessly over the long words.

"Fruits, meat *and* repentance,"[2] he read with painful uncertainty, when Hansie interrupted him with a laugh:

"That will do, Jim; you are wonderful, and you need not come again."

✶✶✶✶✶✶

---

2. "Fruits meet for repentance."

Other natives on the premises were of the shiftless, wandering type, changing hands continually, and many were the instances of their simplicity, not to say rank stupidity.

On one occasion a "raw" *kaffir*, on being ordered to take a heavily laden wheelbarrow from one part of the garden to the other, was found half an hour later, still in the same place, vainly trying to place the wheelbarrow on his head!

I believe it was the same native who, when told to empty the contents of a waste-paper basket on a burning heap of rubbish in the garden, returned without the basket, and when asked what he had done with it, pointed, with an air of injured surprise, to its smouldering remains on the heap of rubbish.

Indeed, the patience of the housewife was often sorely tried. A relative of Mrs. van Warmelo's coming into the kitchen one morning, found one of these new "hands" before the stove in a sea of hot water, desperately trying to fill a small kettle *by the spout*, from a large one!

Chapter 22

The Secret Railway Timetable

Thank God for the early rains!

After the long winter months, dry and dusty, terrific storms pass over the country, torrents of rain, lashing hailstones. The beautiful world is washed clean, and everywhere the moist brown earth gives promise of a plentiful supply of fresh young grass, which means food for the weary underfed horses on commando, and new life, new hopes to the men.

Only the middle of August and already the first summer rains are falling!

Thank God again!

The cruel strain of anxious thought for our heroes in the field can be relaxed for a moment, and we turn our energies with redoubled vigour and strengthened faith to the task at our hand. Heaven knows that we shall require all the courage we possess to face the impending disasters, of which the shadows have already fallen on our hearts.

★★★★★★

One morning the disconcerting news reached Harmony that Mrs. Naudé's house had been surrounded by armed soldiers at break of day and that she had been taken away with her child, in a waggon, no one knew where.

The empty house was being closely watched.

Did the enemy really think that the sagacious captain of the Secret Service would walk into the trap some fine evening, there to meet with certain destruction? Evidently, for the house was guarded night and day.

★★★★★★

August 5th brought new sensation and fresh material for thought and conversation.

There had been a brief lull in the adventures, and all were of opinion that as long as this spell of vigilance lasted no spies would enter the town. It therefore came as a surprise when our little friend with the walking-stick was to be seen coming up the garden path of Harmony, wearing that air of happy mystery so familiar to his fellow-workers.

The spies had come at last, not the captain himself, but his secretary, Mr. Greyling, with two other men named Nel and Els, on an important and extremely dangerous mission.

They had arrived too late to be brought out to Harmony, but they were staying with Mrs. Joubert, and, if they were successful in obtaining the help they required, their intention was to leave again that night.

At this point in the visitor's narrative, Hansie, who had been engaged in making butter, came in with an expectant look. Mr. Botha motioned her to draw nearer, and in hurried whispers, although there was no one in the room but themselves, told them that these men had been sent to procure a copy of the secret railway timetable, an official book containing full detailed information of the military trains, provision and ammunition—trains, in fact, laden with clothing and everything required by the military. The women looked at one another and smiled at the audacity of the request. They had never heard of such a timetable and might as well have been asked to send the moon to the front.

But their visitor was very grave.

This was no child's play, but a very serious matter, for a great deal depended on the securing of that book.

The horses on commando were in a very poor condition after the hard winter, and the men had no clothes to speak of. So it was absolutely necessary that they should have their stock reinforced by the capture of some of the enemy's trains.

Mrs. van Warmelo promised to do her best, but gave her visitor little hope of success.

Soon after he left, a carriage drove up with Mrs. Joubert, her son "Jannie," and her married daughter, Mrs. Malan.

Their mission was the same as Mr. Botha's, the secret timetable, and Mr. Jannie, as he drew Hansie aside, urged her to do all in her power to procure a copy of this valuable book. The same ground was gone over, with the same result, "We can but try." That whole morning was spent in seeing different people, trusted friends, on the subject, and everywhere Hansie and her mother were met with the same objections.

Most people had never heard of this timetable, and those who knew of its existence, were convinced that it would be quite impossible to get a sight of it, as it was in the hands of officials only.

The afternoon again was spent in roaming disconsolately about the streets of Pretoria, weary and discouraged.

Suddenly Hansie exclaimed:

"Oh mamma, how stupid we have been! Why, we never thought of D. He is the only one who can help us. Let us go to him."

Mrs. van Warmelo's tired face beamed at her daughter.

"*Of course*, but I dare not go to him direct—that would be indiscreet indeed. Let us send some one for him."

"F.?" Hansie suggested.

"Yes, he would do."

They were walking rapidly to an office on Church Square, when they met the very man they were in search of.

"This is wonderful!" Hansie exclaimed. "We were just going to ask F. to call on you, as we have a great request to make."

Talking in rapid whispers, the trio walked across the Square. The man's face was inscrutable at first, but his curt and business-like way soon gave place to a look of thoughtful contemplation.

"This is about the most unheard-of request that has ever been made to me. I know the book exists, but I have never seen it—I shall have to think about this. When must you have it?"

"Before six o'clock this evening," Hansie answered.

"Will you leave me now?" he said. "I must think. If by any chance I am able to procure a copy, you will find it under your front door between 5 and 6 o'clock."

Well satisfied, the two ladies proceeded on their way home, when they were met by Consul Nieuwenhuis, who invited them to have tea with him at Frascati's.

Hansie looked at her mother.

"I think we have earned it—don't you?"

Mrs. van Warmelo nodded and laughed.

Arrived at Frascati's they found a regular gathering of the consuls, gaily chatting while they partook of the good things set before them.

"Oh, mother!" Hansie said regretfully, when they had parted from their friends. "What a pity we could not tell them anything! How they would have enjoyed sharing our sensations! I can tear the very hair out of my head at having to keep all these adventures to myself!"

They then went to Mrs. Joubert's house to tell the spies that there was just a chance that one of the people they had seen that day would get the timetable for them.

Mrs. van Warmelo, with her usual prudent forethought, asked to see Mr. Greyling only, knowing that it was safer to deal with one man than with several, so she was shown into the drawing-room while he was being brought from some unknown back region, with much caution and bolting of doors and drawing of blinds. It was amusing, when he entered the room, to see him going straight up to Mrs. Joubert and shaking her heartily by the hand. As a matter of fact, these enterprising young men enjoyed her hospitality, slept under her roof, and partook of the food she secretly prepared for them without ever setting eyes on their hostess.

She was not supposed to know of their existence, and as she was close and silent as the grave, no one ever got anything in the way of information out of her.

It was good to see Mr. Greyling again.

He said that Captain Naudé was with General Botha near the Middelburg line and had been prevented from coming into town that month.

Very little fighting was being done on account of the poor condition of their horses after the severe winter. The men were in splendid health, and the same spirit of determination and courage which had always characterised them possessed them still.

Mr. Greyling and his comrades had come in under some difficulties. They had been escorted on horseback as far as Eerste Fabrieken on the North-east Railway, when they had nearly run into the enemy's lines. They altered their course and rode to Irene, hiding themselves and fastening their horses in a clump of thorn trees, where they remained until nightfall.

On their way to Pretoria in the darkness, Mr. Greyling's horse fell into a hole, throwing him out of the saddle, but his foot caught in the stirrup and he was dragged about forty yards, bruising his head and severely wrenching his ankle. Although by no means fit for the journey, he was determined to go back that night, because the friends who were waiting for him with his horse did so at the utmost risk of their lives. The best news he brought was that the Boers had retaken the Skurvebergen and that it was again the centre of the Secret Service. Three of the Boers had fallen there during the fight.

Although he fully appreciated the obstacles in the way of procuring a timetable, he said he felt he could hardly go back to the commandos without it. His instructions had been very explicit.

Whether she found the timetable at Harmony or not, Hansie promised to come back that evening, with the European and Colonial newspaper-cuttings, so eagerly sought after by the men on commando.

Arrived at Harmony at about 5.15, Hansie could conceal her impatience no longer, but, running up the garden-path, she threw open the front door with a flourish, and behold, a small flat parcel on the floor, a book wrapped carelessly in a bit of white paper! The secret timetable!

She only had it in her hands for a moment, but one thing she will ever remember, the slate-coloured cover and the thick red letters heavily scored:

For the use of officers and officials only.

The excited women looked at it as if fascinated, turning the leaves over slowly and murmuring blessings on *his* head.

"Look here," Mrs. van Warmelo whispered, "here we have the meanings of the different signals, and here the different engine-whistles are explained. Every 'toot' has a meaning, Hansie———" But Hansie had flown to her room to don her cycling dress, and was soon on her way, guarded by her faithful dog. On reaching her destination she was again shown into the drawing-room, but Mrs. Joubert came to her and asked in a whisper whether she would not like to go to *the* room.

Need I say that she jumped at the suggestion?

Away with caution, to the winds with prudence and reflection! Was not the mother safe at Harmony and her wise counsels forgotten?

Hansie was led silently through mysterious corridors into the open backyard, by a mute figure in black.

This figure pointed to a door and disappeared, and at the same time another figure rose from Hansie knew not where, and stood sentinel over the gate leading into the street.

She ran up the steps and rapped smartly at the door, turning the handle after a moment and walking in, to the evident consternation of the three young men inside. There was a general scuffle, followed by a laugh of relief, when her figure became visible through the heavy clouds of smoke which filled the room.

Mr. Greyling came forward to meet her and introduced the other men, who shook her hand until it ached.

It was quite evident that the sight of a young lady was a wonderful and most welcome thing to them.

Hansie took Mr. Greyling aside and handed him the packet with strict injunctions not to mention her name on commando, for it was a well-known fact that there were traitors in the field, who lost no opportunity of conveying information to the British. She did not tell him how the book had come into her possession, although his surprise and curiosity were plainly visible, and the worst that could have happened, had he fallen into the hands of the enemy and turned king's evidence, would have been the betrayal of her name.

The other men were clamouring for a hearing, so she turned to them and inspected the huge brown-paper parcels containing clothing, etc., to which they drew her attention and which they were about to convey to the commandos.

One of them, with a look of comical despair, was shaking his head, while he counted the parcels on his fingers. The other showed Hansie how impossible it was for him to fasten his coat and waistcoat, for he had on three woollen shirts and three pairs of trousers, of different sizes. So had the other two, and Hansie could not refrain from expressing her amazement at their being so heavily laden on an expedition so perilous.

But, in high spirits, they laughed at her fears.

They had done the same thing before. One said it was his seventh visit, another said it was his third, and they so evidently enjoyed their adventures that one felt they were to be envied rather than pitied.

They parted in fun and high good-humour, but Hansie's heart was wrung with many a pang, and many a deep and earnest prayer for their protection was sent up by her that night.

"I wish you could have seen that room, mother," Hansie exclaimed as they sat in their cosy dining-room, discussing the events of the day. "It was filled with so much smoke that I could hardly breathe, and it was littered with papers and cups and plates. They wanted me to sit down and chat with them."

"I am surprised you did not," her mother retorted.

"Well, you see, I had no lamp and I was afraid I should be arrested, and besides, you would have been terrified to death, thinking I was in the hands of the English with that precious timetable."

Chapter 23

System Employed by the Secret Committee

Mr. Willem Bosch, a cripple, unable to take active work upon himself, acted as Secretary to the Committee, Mr. Els was old and infirm, and Mr. Botha, as we have heard, had been struck by lightning and was frequently prostrate with headaches of an intensely severe nature.

But for these infirmities these men would have been on commando with their brother *burghers*.

The wider circle of conspirators consisted of ten or twelve men and women, who carried out the instructions of the committee, but in no case attended their meetings or conferred with them in the presence of the spies from the field.

Their work chiefly consisted in finding out men anxious to escape from town and ignorant of the way to go about it—an exceedingly difficult and dangerous task, with so many National Scouts and other traitors in their midst.

In order to protect themselves from the danger of being led into a trap, the following precautions were taken by the committee and strictly carried out by their fellow-workers:

When a man was found anxious to join the Boers, he was instructed, under the most binding injunctions to secrecy, to keep himself in readiness to depart at a given moment, on the shortest possible notice. The arrival of an escort from commando was then awaited.

They did not have long to wait, as two or three times a week, without fail, a small escort of armed men was to be found at a certain spot in the vicinity of the capital, while one of their number was sent into town to inform the committee of the fact.

The fugitive was then instructed to walk slowly in a certain street, from one point to another at a given hour. Here he was met by a man unknown to him, usually one of the four, who signed to him to follow him.

He was not allowed to speak to or follow his leader too closely. It was not known to him beforehand whether his destination lay north, south, east, or west. He had but to follow and to find himself, as darkness fell, in the hands of the armed *burghers*.

The men in town were unarmed. It was one of the first rules of the committee that no spy entering the town should carry arms of any description, this rule having been made to safeguard them from death in the event of their being taken by the enemy.

Too often was this precaution disregarded by young and hot-headed spies, who took the risk upon themselves, preferring death to falling into the hands of the English.

Captain Naudé's case was recognised by the committee as an exception when once it became known to them that a heavy price had been set on his head.

Incidentally I may remark here that this sum was known, during the early part of the war, to be £500 and that it was gradually increased to £1,500, as the captain became more notorious for the daring nature of his enterprises. He was told by an English officer, after the war, that the British had spent over £9,000 in the vain attempt to capture him. This statement may, or may not, have been correct, but certain it is that nothing was left undone to put an end to his activities, numbers of men and women being employed, under liberal payment, to trap him when he visited Pretoria.

In the field, too, his life was known to be even more precarious than in town, for many were the hirelings surrounding him, watching their chances to capture him and hand him, dead or living, into the power of his foes.

It was therefore an understood thing that Captain Naudé should at all times be armed, heavily armed, in the field and when he came to town.

Not so the Secret Committee. What might be his only safeguard would, in the event of their arrest, prove to be their undoing, and this they fully realised as they remonstrated, not once, but many times, with the young spies who worked for them.

The violation of this rule, which they wished to see enforced so rigorously, was sometimes followed by most terrible consequences.

That this brave band of earnest men should have continued their work so long, beset, as they were, with a thousand dangers and difficulties, is a marvel indeed. With so much treachery in the air, it is a wonder to us still that they were able to carry out their daring enterprise with so much success and to escape detection for so long.

But they were prudent and cautious, they knew and trusted one another, and they observed, with conscientious thoroughness, the unwritten motto of the committee:

"*Think quickly, act firmly, calmly, prudently, without fear. Speak as little as possible.*"

Terrible were the experiences of some of the men on their secret visits to the town.

Captain Naudé, arriving one night at the house of his friend Mr. Hattingh (the spies naturally did not take shelter in their own homes), was informed that his mother lay dangerously ill in her house close by. It was feared that she would not recover. In the shadows which enveloped her she seemed to have forgotten all about the war, and her only cry was for him, her son.

What was he to do? His mother was surrounded by nurses, and the house was filled with relatives and friends.

As captain of the Secret Service, his name was too well known. He could not show himself at such a time, when he had every reason to believe that the enemy was watching him with extra vigilance.

The next news, while he was still in hopeless deliberation, was that his mother had passed away.

It needs a strong man's most powerful self-control to "act firmly, calmly, prudently," at such a time, and yet even then he restrained the impulse to go to her.

Of what avail to kiss that icy brow?

Next day, from his hiding-place behind the window curtain, he watched his mother's funeral procession, passing by.

His comrade, Johannes Coetzee, nicknamed Baden-Powell, the man who had left the town with him on his second expedition, once had a miraculous escape from death.

He was leaving for commando with a bag containing clothes, a number of Mauser cartridges which the committee in town had collected by degrees, when he was taken prisoner by the enemy just as he was nearing the wire enclosure.

He was immediately taken to the *commandant*, who examined the bundle containing the contraband articles, and ordered him to be escorted to another department. Of his guilt, proof positive had been found, but this fact was not conveyed to the armed soldier who was about to escort him to his doom.

On their way, he knew not where, Coetzee pleaded with the guard to release him.

"I have been taken under false pretences," he said. "I am innocent, an employee at the Lunatic Asylum. If you will escort me over the railway line, I will pay you."

"How much money have you?" the man asked.

Coetzee took some silver from his pocket, counted it and said:

"I have only thirteen shillings."

"That will do," his guard replied, and conducted him in safety to the asylum, in the vicinity of which he found his tethered horse, still waiting for his return, the soldier himself holding his horse and assisting him to mount with the bag containing the ammunition.

Disregard for wise counsel from older men, head-strong self-will, and a sheer indifference to death and danger were the causes of much disaster in those days.

On the other hand, recklessness and the very disregard for death mentioned above brought more than one man safely through the fierce fires of adversity, as we shall see in the tragic and stirring events to be recorded in this and the next chapter.

One there was amongst the spies, noted for his extraordinary bravery, a hero of the rarest type, of whom we can only speak with bated breath and thrilling hearts. In the brief record of his heroic life—and still more heroic death—we have a rich inheritance.

Adolph Krause was his name, a man still young, a married man. He was a German by birth, but a full *burgher* of the State for which he sacrificed his noble life.

The first time Krause had left the capital he had been escorted out, with eight other Germans, by Mr. Willem Botha, while Captain Naudé conducted seven or eight young Boers to the freedom of the *veld*.

There had been no adventures then.

Subsequently, in and out he came and went, with the greatest regularity, and as often as twice a week he would leave the town with large numbers of Boers and Germans, eager to join the *burgher* forces in the field. His services became more and more valuable.

One evening when, after two days' rest in town, he was again preparing to depart for the commandos, his friend Willem Botha called to escort him through the town, as had been previously arranged.

Mr. Botha's house was in Proes Street between van der Walt and Market Streets, while not far away his trusted friend and confederate Mr. Hocke lived, a man who rendered such innumerable services to the Boers that his name must not be forgotten here.

These two men met at Mr. Krause's house and found him ready to depart.

Although a man of slender build, he had now attained to such gigantic proportions that his friends could scarce believe their eyes, and, incredible as it may seem, the following is a full and accurate description of what he had about his person that memorable night:

Two pairs of trousers; two shirts; two full Mauser *bandoliers* over his shoulders and crossed over his breast; a woollen jersey; a thick coat; a long Mauser gun thrust into one trouser-leg; a German revolver belonging to Mr. Hocke; his own revolver, and a bag of about two feet in length, containing Mauser ammunition, which had been buried by Mrs. Botha and was now going "to the front"; boots, soap, washing soda, cotton, and a number of other small articles, which had been ordered by the women on commando—that unknown band of heroic women, fleeing north, south, east, and west with their men, for whom they cooked and sewed and prayed throughout the long years of the war.

Krause had been "shopping" in town for these brave sisters in the field, and I am sure his thoughts that night were not of fear for the perils he was about to face, but of satisfaction and pleasurable anticipation of the joy his arrival at commando would occasion the women at the front.

Would that one of their undaunted band could be induced to give the world a record of their unique and altogether wonderful experiences of the war!

Mr. Krause's slight form was now twice, perhaps nearly thrice its usual size, and his friends, when they looked at him, laughed in incredulous amazement.

"Oh, man, what would I not give to possess a photo of you as you are dressed tonight!" Mr. Botha exclaimed between his fits of laughter.

It was now 7 o'clock and nearly dark.

The two guards, walking up and down the street on their accustomed beat, had just withdrawn; 7 o'clock was their dinner hour, this the plotters knew.

In a moment, Krause, with the bag over his shoulder and one leg of necessity held very straight, limped out into the open street, "Oom Willie" (Botha) following and crossing to the other side.

Close to a street lamp, at the corner of Market Street, Krause suddenly saw a soldier walking on ahead, upon which he immediately turned down into Market Street, with the evident intention of pursuing his way along Vermeulen Street. This his friend quite understood as, ever on the opposite side of the street, he watched and followed Krause in his course.

Again a soldier appears on the scene, this time walking *towards* them in Vermeulen Street. No time to turn back now; forward, boldly forward—the fugitive has been observed.

Under one of the lamps the watcher on the other side sees to his horror that one of the bandoliers has pushed its way up to the neck and is showing plainly above the collar of the coat.

The British guard observes this too, for he turns under the lamp and watches the retreating form intently. Just a moment, and he raises his whistle to his lips, giving forth the shrill alarm.

The game is up. Mr. Botha, unarmed, can be of no assistance to his friend, who now must fight his way alone from death and danger. The Mauser gun, which has been impeding his every movement, is whipped out of the trouser-leg as he flies, weapon conspicuously in hand, through the well-lit streets of Pretoria, until, making a sudden dive, he disappears between the wires of a fence, into the seclusion of a peaceful private garden. There is no time to think. He rushes through the garden from one side to another, out into the next street, and so on; block after block he takes, until he finds himself alone in a quiet street, far from the scene of danger, and while his enemies are surrounding and searching the block into which he first had disappeared, he is many miles away, plodding weary and heavy-laden to friends and liberty.

Only half satisfied as to his comrade's escape, Mr. Botha returned home in sore distress that night to watch and await developments, and it was not until Krause surprised him later with another and wholly unexpected visit that he learnt the sequel and happy ending of that memorable flight.

CHAPTER 24

The Death of Adolph Krause

Uninterrupted communication had once more been established between the conspirators, and all was going well.

So it seemed!

But the Prince of Darkness was at work. And with him an accursed band of Judas-Boers.

How can I tell the tale? How force into the background of my mind and soul the unspeakable horror with which all my being is filled when I contemplate this aspect of the war, in order to collect my thoughts sufficiently to find the words I need?

That week the town was full of spies.

Captain Naudé had come in on Thursday night and was to leave again on Saturday night. Another spy, young Delport, a brave and reckless youth, was also in the capital, "recruiting" men to take out with him to commando.

That Saturday night, as Mr. Botha was on the point of leaving his home for the captain's place of refuge, from where he had to "see him off," as arranged, Mrs. Krause arrived at his house in some agitation and said that her husband had just come in and wished to see Mr. Botha. Krause was suffering from an exceedingly painful whitlow in the thumb of his left hand, she said, and he had come to see a doctor and to have the whitlow cut. She implored Mr. Botha and his neighbour Mr. Hocke to come without delay, and to be present when the operation had to be performed.

With all the speed he could Mr. Botha hurried to the house in which Captain Naudé was waiting, explained the case of Krause to him and took a warm and hearty leave, kneeling with him for a few moments first, as was his wont, in earnest prayer to God for the protection of the traveller.

He then called for Mr. Hocke, and the two men hurried to Mr. Krause's house in Prinsloo Street, where they found the doctor (a man initiated in all the mysteries of Boer espionage and a trusted friend) on the point of performing the small, though painful operation.

When it was over, Mr. Botha, prompted Heaven only knows by what foreshadowing of disaster, gave his friend a serious lecture on the dangers of his recklessness.

"How can you go about the town so much in broad daylight, whenever you come in?" he asked. "Always on that bicycle of yours! Surely you must know that you expose yourself to untold dangers!"

"Oh, I could not always stay indoors! The house is far too close," the patient exclaimed, nursing his lacerated thumb.

Mr. Botha urged him to leave on Sunday night, not to remain longer than was necessary, and to take with him a young German, who had been wounded and was now convalescent, after having been concealed and nursed for many months by trusty friends in town.

And another warning he impressed upon him with unusual earnestness:

"Whatever you do, Krause, don't associate yourself with the party leaving under young Delport's guidance. I fear that there is something terribly wrong. He is going out with far too large a number, fifty men in all, he told me yesterday, and something warns me that amongst the men there are detectives on the English side. Delport is young and very reckless, and the thought of the great number going out with him this time has made me more anxious than I can say."

Krause produced his revolver from an inside pocket, and declared that before he surrendered himself a prisoner more than one British soldier would be killed or wounded by him.

With a heavy heart and many sad forebodings, Mr. Botha left him. For he remembered, with increasing anxiety, a visit he had had from Delport, when the latter had asked for his assistance in getting his men—fifty, as he had said—safely through the town.

Mr. Botha had refused at the time, pretending that he had never taken part in such proceedings, and warning the young man that the game he was about to play was hazardous in the extreme.

"If you *must* go out with those men, leave on Monday night, when the others have escaped in safety," was his last advice to Delport.

Unfortunately, Fate decreed that Krause and Delport should meet accidentally on Sunday morning, the day after Mr. Botha's warning to Krause.

ADOLPH KRAUSE.

Together the two men, flinging caution to the winds, or perhaps in their enthusiasm entirely forgetting the wise counsel of their friend, laid their heads together, and agreed to meet at a certain point that night, Krause with the wounded German and two or three of his most faithful friends, and Delport with his party of fifty men.

As Mr. Botha, with strange intuition, had predicted, there were dastardly traitors in that group of fifty men—Judas-Boers—who, under the pretence of seeking an opportunity of joining the *burgher* forces, had persuaded Delport to allow them to accompany him. That *he* was innocent in this black crime of hideous treachery, no one who knew him ever had a doubt.

At the appointed place the two men met. Farther on they were joined by the wounded German and his comrades; still farther, beyond the boundary of the town, under a cluster of trees, well known to them as a secret trysting-place, the large party had assembled one by one and was awaiting the arrival of its leaders.

The latter, seeing in the distance a group of moving figures which they took to be their friends, walked boldly and serenely forward—to find themselves a moment later in a most deadly trap!

The conflict must have been a desperate one!

He who played so brave a part in it, Krause, the only armed man on his side, shot down his opponents one by one, until they closed on him, and then, overpowered by the fearful odds and battered beyond recognition by heavy blows from the butt-ends of their guns, he was at last pinioned to the ground by his infuriated captors.

Three men were taken, Krause, Venter (a mere boy, the son of a widow in Pretoria), and one other—who must be nameless here.

Of the rest some fled into the open *veld*, while others, hopelessly ignorant of their surroundings or of the route to take, wisely returned to town under cover of the darkness of the night.

With one exception. Fritz W., the wounded German, lost his way and was unable to go back to town before the curfew-bell, the hour at which every resident was supposed to be indoors.

Finding himself near a small camp of soldiers in the vicinity of the Pretoria West Station, he cautiously crept into one of the tents, where he found a solitary soldier, sound asleep. Without a moment's hesitation, he stretched himself down on the ground beside him, thinking over the tragic events of that awful Sunday evening and dozing off at intervals, from sheer exhaustion of mind and body.

During the night another soldier, evidently returning from duty as guard or outpost, entered the tent and lay beside him on the other side.

So he spent the night between two British soldiers, and with the first approach of dawn he cautiously and stealthily extricated himself from his perilous position and made his way to town.

✶✶✶✶✶✶

Three or four days after the perfidious betrayal of the Secret Service men the committee was staggered with the tidings of the execution of their comrades, Krause and Venter, in the prison-yard of the old Pretoria jail.

The third, the nameless one, had, it was said, saved himself by turning king's evidence.

Of their last days on earth nothing will ever be known, but those of us blessed or cursed with the divine and cruel gift of imagination see in our mind's eye two men in prison-cells in solitary confinement, one a broken-hearted husband, the other the beloved son of a widowed mother.

Wounded and suffering they lie on their last bed of pain. Friendless and alone they await the untimely end of their brief but glorious career. Longing, with all the weakness of the human heart, for one last look of love, one reassuring clasp from a tender woman's hand, they prepare themselves to meet the death they have faced so often and so manfully in their heroic struggle for liberty and independence.

Fear? Despair?

No—a thousand times, No!

Could there have been fear or despair in the hearts of those two men, with the knowledge beating in their brains that they held their lives in their own hands, that one word from them of information against their fellow-workers could avert their doom, and that they, and they alone, could save themselves at the sacrifice of honour and fidelity?

How in the end they met their fate we do not know—we can but dimly guess.

The painful task of acquainting Mrs. Krause with the fate of her husband fell to the lot of Mr. Botha and Mr. Hocke.

As she would probably be destitute, the two men decided to collect a sum of money before approaching her with their evil tidings, and this they had to do by stealth, in order not to bring suspicion on themselves.

They were successful in obtaining over £34 for the bereaved wife in a very short time, from friends and sympathisers as poor as they themselves, and later, from the same source, in the same unostentatious way, a far larger amount was collected in order to send the widow to her relatives in Germany.

These details, mundane though they may appear after the stirring acts of heroism described above, are significant of greater things—self-sacrificing generosity, unswerving loyalty, and a compassionate desire to atone, in some practical and helpful way, for their share in the disaster brought on innocent and helpless womanhood.

CHAPTER 25

The Shoemaker at Work

That the inborn sense of humour of the Dutch South African race should have been stunted in its growth, if not completely crushed, by the horrors of the war, would be small cause for surprise to most people who have given the matter a thought. But to those of us acquainted with the facts, an entirely different and wholly comprehensible aspect of the case has been made manifest.

The blessed gift of humour is only sharpened by the hard realities of life, can never be appreciated to the full in the calm and shallow waters of prosperity.

Of this we had innumerable proofs during those tempestuous days, and certain it is that the memory of a harmless joke, enjoyed under circumstances of unusual stress and trouble, grows sweeter and is strengthened as the years go by.

For dry humour and keen enjoyment of the ludicrous, our friend Mr. W. Botha could not easily be surpassed; and I advise you, good reader, if you have the chance, to induce him to tell you the following story in his own words, and to watch the flicker of amusement in his eye.

★★★★★★

Four of Captain Naudé's spies are in town again, resting, shopping, and exchanging items of war experiences with their friends and relatives.

Countless parcels have arrived from various stores of note in town, and four big bags, full to bursting, are arrayed against the wall for transportation "to the front" at 7 o'clock that night.

But what is this? Another bag? Impossible! There are but four men going out and each one has his load, quite as much as he can carry already.

What does it contain? A beautiful brand-new saddle, the property of an English officer, which Willie Els, son of the Committee member, has determined shall on no account be left behind.

Expostulations from the older men are all in vain.

The saddle, with the four other bags, is put into Delport's cab, which is waiting at the door, and, after many fond farewells, the young men drive off in the direction of the Pretoria Lunatic Asylum.

At this time there is no better spot for exit from the capital, but in order to reach it one point of extreme danger has to be passed—the point at which a British officer, with five-and-twenty mounted men, is stationed, in command of a searchlight apparatus for scouring the surrounding country.

The dangerous spot has been frequently passed in safety by these very spies.

Tonight they pass again in unobserved security, but alas! when they have crossed the railway line, immediately opposite the asylum, where they are in the habit of alighting with their parcels, they find to their distress that, try as they will, they cannot carry more than the four bags allotted to them in the first instance.

The bag containing the precious saddle must go back to town.

Oh, the pity of it!

The critical spot must be passed again, and, as ill-luck would have it, the British officer hails the passing cab and is about to get in, when his eye falls on the bag.

"What is this?" he asks the driver.

No concealment possible now!

"A saddle, sir."

"A saddle! Whose, and where are you taking it?"

"From Mr. Botha to Mr. Els in town. On my way I was stopped and asked to take some passengers to the asylum, which I have just done. I was going to Mr. Botha when you stopped me."

The officer looks doubtful, feels the bag all over and, taking a notebook from his pocket, enters all the details of this most suspicious-looking affair, the number of the cab, the name and address of the driver, the names and full addresses of the two men who have been mentioned.

Then he gets in and peremptorily orders the cabman to drive to such-and-such an hotel in the centre of the town.

With a throb of relief Delport deposits his fare at the hotel and, whipping up his horses, drives at the utmost speed to Mr. Els' house, to warn him of the danger he is in.

Mr. and Mrs. Botha have just retired for the night, when they are aroused by a hurried knock at the front door. They admit two girls, one of them the daughter of Mrs. Els, the other a sister to Mrs. Naudé, both extremely agitated.

Miss Els speaks first:

"Oom Willie, you must please come to our house at once. My father is very ill."

Oom Willie's heart sinks into his slippers.

This, the long-expected sign that their game is up, has come at last.

He hastens to the home of his friend.

When he learns the truth the case does not seem so hopeless after all and he feels his courage returning.

"We must think of some plan with which to meet the police when they come. Quick! There is not a moment to lose. They may be here at any minute."

In an incredibly short time the officer's new saddle is buried in a bag of coal, which is again sewn up and thrown into the back-yard, while an old and worthless saddle is produced, Heaven only knows from where, cut up into pieces and placed in a large basin of water on the dining-room table.

"Now, Oom Gerrie," Mr. Botha says, as soon as he can find his breath, "you are a shoemaker by trade, and this old saddle has been sent to you by me to make shoes for my children."

"But you have not got any! and I have never made a shoe in my life!"

"Well, then, for my nieces and nephews. Never mind about your ignorance. When any one comes in, remember you are just on the point of beginning your work. I shall send you an old last when I get home."

A pocket-knife, a hammer, and a few nails scattered on the table complete the shoemaker's outfit, and there he sits, with trembling hands and spectacles on nose, far into the night, for does he not expect the dreaded knock at his front door before the dawn of another day?

Next morning Oom Willie raps smartly at the door and walks in unceremoniously, to find Oom Gerrie just about to begin his work, as with shaking hand he adjusts his spectacles.

"How is trade this morning?" he asks, with a jolly laugh, as he settles himself on a chair to watch his friend's discomfiture. But Oom

Gerrie is not pleased at all. The trade is getting on Oom Gerrie's nerves, and he takes no part in the hilarity around him.

Two days pass, three, four, and no English officer appears, no search is made for contraband of war in Oom Gerrie's house; but every time the door is opened or a footstep heard on the verandah, Oom Gerrie may be found with one hand plunged in a basin of water, while with the other he adjusts his spectacles.

Poor Oom Gerrie!

He gives up his trade in despair at last, for after all it does not pay, but as long as the old man lives he will be forced to listen to the question:

"How is the boot-making trade?"

CHAPTER 26

Bitten by Our Own Dogs

The events about to be recorded in this chapter have just reminded me of an incident which took place immediately after the occupation of the capital.

An old *kaffir*, who had been with the English just before Pretoria was taken, told Mrs. van Warmelo that three Boer men had ridden out on bicycles to the English lines, and held consultation with them— traitors evidently, in secret understanding with the enemy, to whom they took information of some sort.

The old *kaffir* wound up his remarks by saying:

"Missis, you are bitten by your own dogs."

How true this was, was soon to be brought home to us in the most forcible way; but before we go on to the next developments in our story I must not forget to tell you, good reader, that the three spies from whom Hansie parted on the evening of August 15th had quite an escape as they left the town.

They were driven in a cab, with their numerous parcels, as far as the wire enclosure, by a friend who always escorted them through the most dangerous parts of the town.

This friend, a young Mr. van der Westhuizen, played an important but unobtrusive *rôle* in the history of the men with whom we are concerned.

When Hansie met him first he was in the Pretoria hospital with a badly wounded arm, of which some of the muscles had been completely severed. As he never recovered the entire use of that arm, he was detained in Pretoria with other men unable to escape, and, carrying his left arm in a sling, he was made use of by the Secret Committee and by Mrs. Joubert, who employed him as her coachman.

He carried a residential pass, which he produced on every imaginable occasion, and was able to render untold services to the spies by conveying them with their parcels to the wire fence. But on this occasion they nearly got into serious trouble, for, just as the cab was nearing the enclosure, a searchlight from one of the forts was turned full on them. In consternation, one of the men ordered the driver to turn to the left, another to the right, but with great presence of mind he ignored them both, and drove straight on, thus disarming a group of soldiers, standing near, of any suspicions they might have had at seeing a cab so near the fence at night.

Fortunately, the light was soon turned in another direction.

The spies descended with their parcels, and were shortly in the deep furrow along which they had to creep to reach the wire fence, cautiously wending their way to friends and liberty, when some one came running after them, shouting to them to stop.

It was van der Westhuizen with a parcel they had left in the cab.

In this way the three men left the town with the railway timetable, not to come in again until September 10th.

My readers will remember the five men who were cut off from their refuge in the Skurvebergen some time back, and one of whom Mrs. van Warmelo had refused to harbour.

I shall not name them, for I do not feel myself justified in damning the reputation of the Boer traitors for ever by publishing their names, but the events I am about to relate cannot be excluded without changing the entire character of this story.

These men had been concealed by other friends, and when the scare was over they escaped from Pretoria to the commandos. They had nearly been forgotten when news reached the capital of their capture by the enemy, five of them in all, and of their imprisonment in jail.

While their life hung in the balance a time of nervous dread, not to be forgotten, was passed through, for they would either be shot as spies or they could save themselves by betraying their friends.

The suspense was soon over.

One of them—the very one, in fact, who had been refused admittance to Harmony through Mrs. van Warmelo's prudence, turned king's evidence and, to save his own precious skin, revealed the names of the good friends who had sheltered him at their own peril.

Rumour said that two of the betrayed would be shot on the evidence he gave against them.

Not only the names of his friends in town did he betray, but he also told the authorities how and when and where the spies came in, the names of the men who worked with him on commando, and the families who harboured them in town.

More than eighty people were incriminated.

On every side whole families were arrested, the men being put into jail, while their women and children were sent away to concentration camps.

My readers must understand that this was an entirely different set of people, not known to those at Harmony, and with whom they had had no dealings. It was no credit to Hansie that she and her mother were not on the list of the betrayed. She remembered with humility and shame her unreasonable fit of temper when her mother refused to harbour the traitor, and determined to give ear to her wise counsel in future.

They and their friends were in no way affected by his treachery, except in so far that it cast a gloom over them and made them realise that the Boers would not be able to hold out much longer against the machinations of these traitors of their own flesh and blood. Another matter for grave concern was the thought that Captain Naudé might attempt to pass through his usual route, not knowing that the enemy had been informed of it, and run straight into the traps prepared for him.

How to get out a warning to the Skurvebergen in time was the problem before them now.

Hansie spent the next few days in flying about on her bicycle to find out if any one in the "inner circle" had been arrested.

Thank God, no. Mr. Willem Botha was at home, the Jouberts were still in undisturbed security, all the other members of the Secret Committee were safe.

They congratulated themselves and one another on their escape, and Mr. Botha, visiting at Harmony a few days later, once more impressed on them the danger of coming into contact with any spies other than those they knew and trusted.

And again he warned them to keep no papers in the house—"for," he continued, "we must always bear in mind that we can never be sure we have not been betrayed. Our names may be on the black list already, and the enemy may only be waiting to catch us red-handed. No one is safe, and no one ought to *feel* safe."

There was a moment's pause, and then he went on, with evident reluctance: "I have good reason for warning you again. I do not wish to alarm you, but only last night, as I was walking in the moonlight with my wife, we passed a man I know well, with a girl on his arm. The moon was shining very brightly, and, as they passed me, I distinctly heard him say, 'This man has also been given away.'"

Hansie felt a thrill of acute anxiety for her friend. The two women looked at one another.

They tried to console themselves with the thought that the man might have mistaken Mr. Botha for someone else. There was nothing to do but wait, but the suspense and uncertainty were very hard to bear, and long were the discussions over every imaginable possibility.

They knew that the traitor was acquainted with the captain of the Secret Service and his private secretary Mr. Greyling. Did he also know the names of the members of the committee? Did Greyling confide the secret of the timetable to him? These young men were reckless. Death was their daily bread, and caution was a thing unknown to them.

Wonderful developments could be expected within the next few days.

The lowering clouds of adversity gathered closely, surely, mercilessly, around our friends.

Clasp that hand again, and once again, in mute farewell. Look deep into those steadfast eyes. It may be for the last time for many long, relentless years; it may be for the last time—on earth!

CHAPTER 27

The Betrayal of the Secret Committee

It was only a few days after the van Warmelos had parted from Mr. Botha that Mr. J. Joubert arrived at Harmony with the tidings that four men had again entered the town that night. One of them was a lad of nineteen, young Erasmus, whose parents had been killed by lightning when he was a child, and to whom Mrs. Joubert had been a second mother.

When he arrived at their home that night they were very angry with him, and demanded what he meant by coming into the very heart of danger.

He meekly answered that he had merely come to see how they were all getting on, and to spend a few days at home, casually remarking that there was a dearth of horse-shoe nails on commando, and that he had been ordered to bring some out.

He and his comrades knew nothing of the recent betrayal, and it was their good fortune that they had used an entirely different route, coming through Skinner's Court. They had not seen a single guard.

Besides the horse-shoe nails, there was the usual demand for clothing and European and Colonial newspapers.

Mrs. van Warmelo immediately made a parcel of the cuttings which she and her friends had been collecting for some time past, and wrote a tiny note to Mr. Greyling, warning him and his fellows against coming in through the usual way, which was now guarded, and informing him that his name had been betrayed. This note was hidden in a match-box with a double false bottom, covered with matches, and given to Erasmus to be handed to Greyling.

Since the revelations made, it was not safe to see the spies, nor was it known by whom the match-box had been sent.

After all, in spite of Mrs. Joubert's vexation with the reckless youth, she was thankful to know that someone was going out to Skurveberg with a warning to the Secret Service.

Erasmus had to leave without the horse-shoe nails, because, though J. Joubert hunted all over the town, he could not procure enough to send out.

The stores sold them only to the military and blacksmiths, and the latter were curious to know why he did not bring his horses to them to be shod.

Mother and daughter were there at 5.30 p.m., with their parcels, and at 6 p.m. the spies were to leave, Mrs. Malan and van der Westhuizen driving out with them as far as they could.

That was a real danger, compared with which all other risks were as nothing, to drive through the streets of Pretoria with spies, at a time when everyone was liable to be stopped to produce residential passes and to show permits for horses and carriages.

But, indeed, those women were not to be intimidated by anything!

We have now come to a morning into which many events of disastrous importance were crowded, the fateful September 9th. Before breakfast, an agitated girl, unknown at Harmony, arrived with the intelligence that Mr. Willem Botha had been arrested at 8 o'clock the night before.

No other names were mentioned then, but it was felt instinctively that the entire Secret Committee had been betrayed and arrested, and the news, when it reached Harmony during the course of the day, found mother and daughter to some extent prepared. The shock, nevertheless, was so great, so crushing, that it took them some time to recover sufficiently to form a plan of action.

Hansie hastily swallowed some food and was preparing to go to town, when her mother asked her what she meant to do, whether she had thought of anything, or if it was advisable to show herself at all just then.

"I don't know what I am going to do *afterwards*, mother," she said, "but I am going straight to Mrs. Botha now."

"Hansie!" exclaimed Mrs. van Warmelo in consternation, "you will do nothing of the kind. Their house will be watched, and you will be followed home. You can do nothing to help that poor woman now, and to be seen with her would be an unpardonable and unnecessary risk."

But Hansie had made up her mind, and nothing could persuade her that it was not her duty to stand by her friend in her hour of need. There was good reason, too, for her anxiety.

After thirteen years of happy, though childless married life, Mr. and Mrs. Botha's home was about to be blessed with an infant child, and it was the thought of the expectant mother's anguish and despair that took Hansie to her side.

"Well" (Mrs. van Warmelo was secretly pleased with her daughter's behaviour), "if you are determined to expose yourself to this danger, I think I had better begin to pack at once, for we shall certainly be sent away."

"All right, mother," Hansie laughed; "pack away, and I'll come home as soon as I can to help you."

She took tender leave of her mother, cheering her with hopeful words and whistling gaily to Carlo to come and protect her on her adventurous expedition.

No one could have been more surprised to see Hansie than Mrs. Botha. She stared as if she could not believe her eyes, and then fell sobbing on her young friend's shoulder.

"How could you risk it to come here?" she exclaimed.

"No one else has been near me, and I am deserted by all my friends since——" here she fell a-weeping again, and clung to Hansie for support.

As soon as she could speak, she gave an account of all that had taken place.

She and her husband were sitting under the verandah the night before, talking about the miserable business of the spy's infidelity and its disastrous results to so many people in town. Mr. Botha was just saying that, in the event of his arrest, his wife need have no fear of his betraying a friend, and that the English might shoot him, but they would not get a shred of information out of him, when two detectives on bicycles rode up and dismounted at the steps.

Mrs. Botha just had time to whisper hurriedly to her husband that she would rather see him dead than have him come back to her a traitor, when the detectives, producing a warrant for his arrest, approached him.

He gave himself up quietly; there was nothing else for him to do. He was unarmed, for it was one of the first rules of the Committee and practically their only safeguard in the event of an arrest, to carry on their work without weapons of any sort.

The house was thoroughly searched for spies and all books and papers were taken away, but, thanks to Mr. Botha's prudence and foresight, not a single incriminating document was found.

The remembrance of this was a source of great comfort to his wife, for, without proofs, his life was safe, although he would probably be sent as prisoner of war to one of the distant islands.

Mrs. Botha was a brave and true woman. She did not think of herself at all, but she was so much concerned for Hansie's safety that she urged her to go home at once and not to come again. The first part of her injunctions Hansie obeyed, but she refused to promise not to be seen at that house again.

It was being closely watched, there was no doubt of that, and on getting into a cab she soon became aware of being followed by two men on bicycles.

This was rather exciting, and Hansie actually enjoyed the chase. Instead of urging her cabby to whip up his horses, she gave him instructions to go as slowly as possible, well knowing that it would be more difficult for anyone on a bicycle to follow a crawling cab unnoticed than to pursue a more swiftly moving vehicle.

When she reached Harmony and paid her fare she saw, out of the corner of her eye, that the men dismounted before the War Office.

"Were you followed home?" was her mother's first question.

"Yes, indeed," she replied, laughing; "they are near our gate at this very moment, and I can just imagine them going to the sergeant-major presently, asking questions about the people living here. And I am quite sure his answer will be, 'Bless you, no. Those two ladies are quiet and well-behaved, and you don't suppose they could be carrying on any of *that* business under my very nose!'"

Hansie's diaries had all been removed to an office in town and placed in a *safe* safe. All safes were *not* "safe" in those days, but this one belonged to a man who was known as a model of good behaviour throughout the war. White envelopes, diaries, copies of official dispatches from the field, all had been removed from Harmony, except the "White Diary" which lay open on her writing-table, and to which we owe a detailed account of the stirring events of September 1901.

What it naturally did not contain was accurate information of the arrest of the other committee members and their subsequent experiences.

Trusted friends were beyond her reach, and she had to content herself with what information she could gather from men "about the town," but this information, verified by what she was told by the men concerned long after the war was over, will give the reader a fair idea of the events of this period.

Not only Mr. Botha, but all the members of the Secret Committee had been arrested that night, and two days later the staggering tidings came of Mr. Jannie Joubert's removal to the Rest Camp, where "political prisoners" were detained.

Now indeed fears of a speedy raid on Harmony were justified.

Their fellow-conspirators were all in the hand of the enemy, and although they trusted them implicitly, and knew there was no one amongst them base enough to betray his friends, they had no reason to think that the people who had betrayed the others would spare them.

One revelation after the other was made that day, and Hansie learnt from someone, who said he was in possession of all the facts, that, despicable though the treacherous spy's behaviour had been, he was not responsible for the exposure of the Secret Service Committee.

Alas, no! the appearance of another traitor in our midst has to be recorded here.

One of the young spies in the service of the committee had been taken by the enemy, how and where I am not at liberty to say, but there were circumstances connected with his capture, and facts known to the enemy of the hazardous part he had played on previous occasions, which made it clear from the beginning that he would be convicted.

Someone who was allowed to visit him regularly in his cell told me that he stood his trial bravely and steadfastly refused to betray a single name to save himself. Threats and persuasions were of no avail.

On Saturday night in his cell his death sentence was read to him.

The execution was to take place on Sunday morning at 6 o'clock, he was told.

Incidentally his jailers informed him that there was still a chance for him if he would give the authorities the names of some of the people in town who were in communication with the Boers in the field.

He was then left to his pleasant reflections.

Reader, we must not be too harsh in our judgment of him. He was only a boy, not yet twenty years of age, and we shall never know what anguish of mind he endured that night.

When day broke he was in no way fit for the harrowing scene awaiting him. His father, his sister, and his *fiancée* were admitted to his cell at the fateful hour that morning, to take their last leave of him.

They clung to him, sobbing, wailing, and imploring him to give the names of his fellow-conspirators. What arguments were brought to bear upon him we shall never know.

He yielded, and in that Godforsaken cell on Sunday morning he gave the names required of him, the five members of the Secret Committee and other names familiar to us all, Jannie Joubert, Franz Smit, Liebenberg, etc.

Ah, if he had been executed that day, how his memory would have been revered by his friends and respected by his foes! But what was he now?—a traitor, oh God! a traitor to his land and people!

And a coward too, base and craven-hearted, shielding his miserable life with dishonour and treachery.

That the enemy would not have shot him in any case, because of his youth, makes no difference to the blackness of his deed, except perhaps to add to the bitterness of his remorse when afterwards he was apprised of this fact.[1]

The death sentence was commuted, and instead he was sentenced to several years' hard labour; he was, in fact, still "doing time" in Pretoria and Johannesburg two years after peace had been declared.

Of the women who were the cause of his downfall I can only say that they were never in any way connected with the "Petticoat Commando."

******

When the news of Jannie Joubert's arrest became known, Mrs. van Warmelo positively forbade her daughter to go to Mrs. Joubert's house.

There was nothing to be done, and although they had every reason to believe that their names were on the list of the betrayed, nothing could be gained by exposing themselves to unnecessary danger.

It was told Hansie, the day after the last sweeping arrests had been made, that Mrs. Joubert's carriage had been standing before the Military Governor's office for some time.

This information brought the reality of the situation vividly to her mind.

What was the old lady doing there? Pleading for her son? Was there

---

[1] The writer was misinformed on this point. After the age of fourteen, boys are liable to be executed.

no way of helping her? These questions preyed on Hansie's mind, until she obtained permission from her mother to visit Mr. Jannie's sister, Mrs. Malan.

Mrs. Malan was in bed with influenza, she said, but it was quite evident that acute distress of mind had a large share in her indisposition.

On Sunday night, after the fateful morning of the last betrayal, the Jouberts were surprised by a visit from the provost-marshal himself, accompanied by another officer.

They asked permission to search the house for the ammunition which they knew to be concealed there. Ammunition! Jannie said he knew of none, except a boxful of cartridges standing in the loft. They had been found lying about the house and were stowed away when the English had taken possession of Pretoria. He took the officers up to the loft and showed them the box, but they were not satisfied, and ordered him to appear before the provost-marshal the next day, to give a satisfactory explanation.

A search was also made for documents, but nothing was found except an old heliographic chart which his father, Commandant-General Joubert, had used long ago in *kaffir* wars.

Jannie Joubert went the following day to give an account of himself, and the next thing his mother heard was that he had been arrested and removed to the Rest Camp. (*Arrest* Camp, some people called it!)

He was very independent and refused to take the oath of neutrality, which, strange to say, he had hitherto avoided, and it would certainly not have been to his taste had he known that his mother had been to the military governor to intercede for him.

The result of that interview was not satisfactory. He would only be released on signing parole.

This, Mrs. Malan thought, he would certainly refuse to do.

"We were treated with marked kindness," she continued, "and this may be taken as proof that the English are not aware of the *real* facts."

The two women laughed in mutual understanding of their conspiracies.

"Still this leniency may be only a blind, Hansie. It is painful not to know *how much* the enemy knows."

"What will you do if Captain Naudé and Mr. Greyling come in tonight?" Hansie asked.

"Shelter them, of course!" was the undaunted reply.

******

That night as Hansie lay on her sleepless pillow, she felt as if all the batteries of the gold mines were thumping on her heart.

Mrs. Malan's last words to her rang continually in her ears:

"Willie Botha will be executed without a doubt."

But before day dawned Hansie's heart was at rest and she slept, for she had solved the problem in her mind.

She would go to General Maxwell and plead with him for the life of her friend.

He was human and tender-hearted, that she knew, and she would tell him how an innocent young life hung in the balance, how the lives of both mother and child would be imperilled if such a cruel fate befell the father. If her pleadings were of no avail, she would offer to give, in exchange for his life, the name of one well known to her as a dangerous enemy to the English.

And when she had made sure of his release, hers would be the name she would reveal.

During the dark days which followed Hansie found her strong support in the thought of this resolve.

Chapter 28

Hansie Earning the Vote

Events moved quickly in those days.

The conspirators had hardly had time to recover from the shock of the recent arrests, they were just beginning to wonder what would happen if their unsuspecting friends from commando walked into the pitfalls prepared for them, racking their brains for plans to avert such a catastrophe, when the very thing they feared took place.

Instead of the familiar figure of Willie Botha coming up the garden path with news, Mrs. Malan drove up with Jannie Joubert's *fiancée*, Miss Malan.

Their appearance at Harmony brought all that had happened most forcibly to the minds of the stricken inmates, filling them with the sense of acute loss; and when they heard what their visitors had to tell, four women more forlorn would have been hard to find.

In short sentences Mrs. Malan told how four young men, all ignorant of the fate of their fellows in town, had tried to come in from the High Veld, bearing with them dispatches from Captain Naudé to the president and to the committee of spies in town.

These men had gone to and fro for months without a single encounter with outpost or guard, but on this occasion, when they reached the wire enclosure, they were unexpectedly met by a storm of bullets.

One of them, as he stooped to get through the fence, felt the hot air of a bullet passing under his nose.

He hastily gave the order to retreat over the "*koppies*" and across the railway line, thus entering Pretoria on the opposite side.

When they met again, before entering the town, one of them was missing!

Young Els had disappeared, and no one knew whether he had been shot or taken, or whether he had fallen into some hole and perhaps been so severely injured that he could not follow them. His comrades were in deep distress. To go back and search for him was impossible, so they entered the town at the utmost peril of their lives. Torn and bleeding, they slunk through the streets of Pretoria, avoiding the light of the electric lamps, and concealing themselves behind trees at the sight of every man in khaki, until they reached Mrs. Malan's house.

Their guardian angels must have kept them from going to Mrs. Joubert's house, as usual, that night.

Imagine their surprise and horror when they heard of the betrayal of the committee, for the warning sent out to Skurveberg did not reach them, they having come from the High Veld.

The news of Jannie's arrest and of Mrs. Joubert's house having been searched, and now being so closely watched that they could not possibly take shelter there, came as a crushing blow.

True to her word, Mrs. Malan determined to shelter them that night, but the house being too dangerous a hiding-place, they were stowed away in Mr. David Malan's waggon-house, closely packed in one small waggon, and there they still lay when the van Warmelos heard of their arrival.

From the bosom of her dress Miss Malan produced the dispatches and a number of private letters.

The dispatch to the President Hansie offered to send by the first opportunity, without telling her friends that it would go by the very next mail per White Envelope. This was a secret she naturally could not divulge to her most trusted fellow-workers, although she could guarantee that the work would be carried out, and they had enough confidence in her to leave the matter in her hands.

The letter from the captain to the committee was left at Harmony to be read and destroyed. Needless to say, Hansie, with her mania for collecting war-curios, made a full copy of both letter and dispatch in lemon-juice before regretfully consigning them to the flames. It was hard to destroy original documents for which such risks had been run!

What was most disconcerting was to hear that the authorities, evidently aware that the men had come through in spite of having been fired upon, were searching for them in town. It was imperative that they should leave that day, or at least as soon as night fell, for the risk they ran was very great.

Hansie promised to think of some way of helping them to escape safely, and said she would see them in the afternoon.

The feeling of responsibility on her young shoulders was very great. There was no one to turn to, no man to whom this dangerous mission could be entrusted, except one, her young friend, F.

She thought of him and wondered whether she could confide to him a scheme which had been slowly forming in her mind.

That afternoon she was on the point of leaving for Mrs. Malan's house, with a packet of letters and newspapers, when two lady callers arrived at Harmony brimming with the news that the town was in a great state of excitement. Armed soldiers were patrolling the streets, men were stopped to show their residential passes, and every cab and carriage was held up for inspection.

The general opinion was that there were spies in town, for the lower part of the town and west of Market Street were cut off by a patrol, while a systematic search of the private houses was being carried on.

Hansie chafed at the delay, listening with impatience to their excited talk, and wondering what they would say if they knew that she was on the point of going to those spies with the parcel in her hands.

By a happy coincidence, when the callers had taken their departure, another visitor arrived—F., the very man she wished to see.

But he, too, was full of the excitement in town and did not notice the unusual anxiety in Hansie's manner.

"General Botha has come in 'to negotiate,'" he said. "The town is alive with soldiers, but there must be something else brewing at the same time, for every house is being searched, and a cordon has been drawn round some parts of the town. It is impossible for any one to get through from one place to another beyond Market Street."

Hansie's heart sank for a moment.

Then she said: "I have to go to town at once, F.; will you come with me? I have a great deal to tell you and we can talk as we go along. You remember you once said that I must come to you if ever I got into any trouble. Well, I am in serious trouble now—not for myself—but, tell me, have you your residential pass with you?"

He produced it.

She continued: "Then we are safe for the present. Let us sit in the Park while I tell you in what way I want you to help me."

They found a secluded spot under one of the trees in Burgher's Park, and there Hansie took him into her confidence, unfolding her plan to him.

"If, as you say, F., a cordon is being drawn around the houses that have already been searched, those three men may be cut off at any moment. They cannot wait where they are at present, no more can they show themselves on the streets without residential passes. If you can help me to borrow three passes for them, I myself will walk with them as far as the wire enclosure and bring the passes back to you."

F. whistled, called her "plucky," but thought the whole thing far too risky.

"You would all be taken near the wire fence," he said, "and what about the men who would be without their passes while you had them?"

"They must not show themselves," she said.

"And if they are found in their homes?"

"Oh!" she cried impatiently, "they must be willing to risk something too."

"Have you thought of any one?" he asked.

"Yes, I have thought of D. and G., if you will bring them to me. Fetch them, F. I'll go and tell the men to wait for the passes. You will find me at your gate."

"But then you would have only two passes, Hansie."

She looked earnestly into his eyes, and he turned away without a word.

He went off in one direction and Hansie in another, and when she reached Mrs. Malan's house she was told that the three men had decided to risk the dangers of the street and to leave immediately. In this they were impelled, not so much by the consideration of their own safety, as the thought of the perils to which they exposed the Malans by remaining in their house. When Hansie told them she was procuring residential passes for them, they held a short consultation and eventually decided to wait another half-hour. With passes in their pockets they would be comparatively safe.

Promising to come back immediately, Hansie rushed to F.'s rooms, where she met him coming through the gate with D. and G.

"F.," she whispered, "be quick. They are on the point of leaving."

He drew her aside and said: "I am very sorry, Hansie. The fellows refuse to lend you their passes."

"Refuse!" she echoed in miserable incredulity. "Refuse! oh Heaven, and this means life or death to those men! They *cannot* appear on the streets tonight without passes."

"It is a great thing to ask, Hansie. You cannot blame them."

"F., I must once again remind you of your promise. Help me now. I am not pleading for myself."

He drew his residential pass from his pocket and placed it in her hand, motioning her to go. She gave him a quick look of gratitude, but returned the pass with the words, "No good to me unless I have three. Think of something else."

He called to the two other young fellows who were standing moodily apart and ordered them to think.

They thought. Perhaps they would have been standing there thinking still, if F. had not suddenly burst out with:

"Look here, you fellows, it is not safe to stand out here like this, and we are losing time. Let us go into my room and talk this thing over."

They walked rapidly towards the house, where a number of bachelors lived together, and reached the room unobserved.

F. drew the blinds, locked the door, and placed Hansie in an easy chair, while he and D. rummaged in a writing-table for some papers. G. sat on the bed with his long legs stretched out in front of him.

The two young men were whispering together, bending eagerly over some papers they had found.

"This one will do," Hansie heard F. say, "but it will take some time."

"Don't you think I ought to go and tell the men to wait?" she asked.

"No, better not be seen walking in and out here. We will make haste!"

Ah, why did Hansie not obey the warning voice within, and go?

For the next ten minutes nothing was said. The men cut and glued and typed without a word, and the result, when it was placed in Hansie's hands, was a document exceedingly well-planned and put together.

This was what she read:

Military Governor's Office,
Pretoria.
Special Pass
for J. W. Venter, G. Vermaak, and L. Erasmus to be out until midnight, on Secret Service.
Signed by Major J. Weston,
Assistant Military Governor.

What puzzled her at first sight was the small official crown above, undoubtedly authentic, and the unmistakable signature of the major below; but on closer inspection, she observed that the part containing the original letter had been cut away from the centre, the top part with the heading and the bottom part with the signature being pasted down on the blank page underneath.

On the middle part of the blank sheet the "Special Pass" was typed, and the whole when completed, with the date plainly typed underneath, looked like a single sheet of paper folded in three.

Hansie shook hands with them all, and asking G. to go to Harmony to reassure her mother, she sped on her way to Mrs. Malan's house.

F. called out after her, "If you come back this way, Hansie, I'll wait for you and see you home."

"All right, thank you," the answer came.

It was now past 6 o'clock and nearly dark. Every one else was at supper, and Hansie flew through the deserted streets with apprehension at her heart.

She was met at the gate by Mrs. Malan, wringing her hands and crying out:

"Oh, where have you been so long? Why did you not come sooner? *They've gone!*"

Then Hansie felt inclined to lie down and die.

Fortunately there was no time for that.

There was still something to be done, and, with the precious paper clasped to her heart, she could at least pursue the men. Perhaps she could overtake them before evil should befall them.

"What direction did they take, and how many of them are there?" she asked.

"Four," Mrs. Malan answered. "One has a residential pass. If they are held up, the other three will escape while he pretends to be searching for it. Go over the Sunnyside bridge and call 'Jasper' when you see four men——"

Without waiting to hear more, Hansie turned and ran, stopping only a moment at F.'s gate to call out his name. She did not wait to see whether he had heard, but ran again, and he, sauntering towards the gate a moment later on the look-out for her, saw her flying form just disappearing in the darkness.

"Something has evidently gone wrong," he muttered, and he, too, in his turn began to run, pursuing the figure of the girl as she sped after the Secret Service men.

She did not stop when he caught up with her, pulling her arm through his, but ran on, telling him in brief sentences what had happened.

Every few yards she called, "Jasper! Jasper!" in the vain hope that this might bring the fugitives forward, should they have concealed themselves behind the trees along the road.

Poor Hansie was becoming thoroughly exhausted, when suddenly, as they neared the Sunnyside bridge, four men under the electric light became plainly visible.

"You must run again, Hansie," F. said, and putting his arm around her, he literally carried her along.

Alas! the figures proved to be four *kaffirs* coming *towards* them, and, with a broken sob, Hansie realised that all their efforts were in vain.

It was no use running now.

Sunnyside was badly lit, and one could barely see two yards ahead, so the plotters walked slowly to Harmony, encouraging one another with the thought that the men must already be beyond the outskirts of the town.

"We have heard no shots, and that is a good sign," Hansie said, "for the men were armed, and in the event of a surprise they meant to fight for their lives."

CHAPTER 29

A War-Baby and a Curious Christening

As far as was known, no men were arrested that night.

The man who had escorted the spies through Sunnyside and over the railway line, the dauntless van der Westhuizen with the bandaged arm, had left them not far from the wire enclosure, and had then waited some time, listening for sounds of commotion.

As no shots had broken the stillness of the night, he had every reason to believe that they had escaped with their lives.

✶✶✶✶✶✶

For some weeks there was a "lull in spies." But there was no lack of other sensations, for September 1901 will ever be remembered as one of the most trying months throughout the year of the war.

It reminded one of that September month before war was declared, when the air was filled with the sweet, penetrating odour of orange-blossoms and many hearts were torn with the agony of suspense and a feeling of impending disaster.

Again the orange trees were in full bloom, bringing back to one's senses the remembrance of past suffering, and the full realisation of present horror and unrest.

The great weeping-willows were showing their first mysterious tinge of pale yellowish green, and Hansie, watching them, wondered what developments would have taken place before those overhanging branches would be crowned with the full beauty of midsummer. September 1901 was a month of proclamations and peace negotiations, all of which "ended in smoke."

After General Botha's visit to Pretoria the Boers concentrated their forces around the capital, strong commandos under General Botha, de la Rey, Beyers, and Viljoen. It was said that there were quite 6,000 troops in town awaiting developments, and Hansie coming home one evening, surprised her mother by saying that "Khaki was in the deuce of a funk!"

Her mother remonstrated with her, expressing her strong disapproval of such language, but Hansie only laughed.

"I was told so in town, mother. The enemy seems to expect our people to sweep through the town, if only to release our prisoners. How I wish they would come and carry off some of our splendid men in the jail and Rest Camp!"

The fate of the committee men had not yet been decided.

As they were kept in solitary confinement and naturally not allowed to hold communication with any of their friends, nothing was known at the time of the troubles undergone by them, and it was some years after the war before Hansie came into full possession of the facts.

Ten men in all had been taken that night, the five members of the committee and five other men in their service, and they were kept separate, not being allowed to see one another during the sixteen days of their imprisonment in the Pretoria jail.

Now, the remarkable part about this story is, that though nothing had been arranged between these men in the event of an arrest, no line of action agreed upon by them by which they could safely guard themselves and their friends, they one and all adopted the same policy under the severe cross-questioning to which they were subjected in their cells.

My readers must understand that trials under martial law are not necessarily conducted with the ordinary formalities of a court of justice; in fact, in the case of these men it cannot be said that there was a trial at all, for they were cross-questioned in their cells apart, and without witnesses.

They never saw the light of day except for a ten-minutes' exercise in the prison-yard every morning; and, on comparing notes afterwards, they found that they had been subjected to the same treatment undergone by the unfortunate men who had turned king's evidence and who had been the cause of their undoing. To some of them the death sentence was read at night, with a promise of pardon if they betrayed the names of their fellow-conspirators in town, and sometimes they were visited in their cells by officers who informed them that one or other of their fellow-prisoners had "given away the show."

"You may safely speak out now, for we know everything. So-and-so has turned king's evidence." But these brave men saw through the ruse, and steadfastly refused to sell their honour for their lives. With one accord they answered, "So-and-so may have given you information, but *I* know nothing."

They were subjected to severe treatment, half-starved, threatened, told that they were condemned to death, and then severely left alone with the sword hanging over their heads—to no avail. Not a word of information was wrung from them, no murmur of complaint crossed their lips.

This lasted sixteen days, and during that time they suffered intensely, the food being unfit for consumption and their surroundings filthy beyond words. As I have said before, there were among their number men physically unfit for hardships like these.

Mr. Willem Botha was one of them, and as the days dragged on, the headaches with which he was afflicted became more frequent and increased in violence.

He feared that he would lose his reason and, in losing it, betray all to his jailers, and he was consumed with anxiety for his wife.

After the first shock of his arrest, he was suddenly overwhelmed with the recollection that he had forgotten to destroy the slip of paper on which the message concerning the Boer traitor in the Free State had been conveyed to him through a prisoner in the Rest Camp. He tried to remember what he had done with it, but in vain. Each day found him torn with anxiety, searching his memory for the threads of recollection, broken in the stress of the last stirring events before his arrest. Suddenly one day it flashed across his mind that he had pushed the slip of paper between the tattered leaves of an old hymn-book.

Bitterly he reproached himself with his unpardonable negligence. That slip of paper, containing injunctions to the committee to convey information of such a serious character to the Boer leaders, would be sufficient proof against him and his fellows. No other evidence would be required to bring them to their death, if it had fallen into the hands of the enemy.

The unfortunate man, in his prison cell, prayed for deliverance, not only for himself, but for the trusty comrades who would be exposed to such deadly peril by this, his one act of indiscretion.

The weary days dragged on.

Suffering, not to be described by words, was the daily portion of this man.

His fellow-prisoners shared the same fate, with one exception.

Mr. Hattingh in his prison cell, who had been taken in his deacon's frock-coat that Sunday night, reaped the rewards of the sagacity he had displayed on the occasion of the visit to his house of the Judas-Boer.

There was a marked difference in the treatment he received at the hands of his jailers. He was not once condemned to death, and he was hardly cross-questioned during the entire term of his imprisonment—better food, kinder treatment being accorded him than to any of his fellows, as he found on comparing notes with them afterwards.

It was quite evident that he was the only man about whose guilt the enemy was in a certain amount of doubt.

His family, too, was privileged, his wife being allowed a few days' grace to sell her household goods before she was conveyed to a camp with her children, while the families of the other men were instantly removed and their homes taken into possession by the English.

If the enemy had only known it, Mr. Hattingh, who was known for his uprightness and moral integrity, had no intention of perjuring himself in the witness-box, but had fully made up his mind to confess his complicity and to face his death like a man and a patriot.

There is no doubt that this brave man would have been endowed with the required courage to uphold his word when the hour came, but it is equally certain that no word of accusation in evidence against his fellow-conspirators would have been wrung from his lips.

When at the end of the sixteen days no proof of their guilt had been found, their captors, recognising and appreciating their staunch fidelity and unswerving loyalty, removed them from their cells in the dreary jail to the Rest Camp, where they were able to enjoy the privileges of the ordinary prisoners of war, and refreshing intercourse with their brothers from the field.

But before they were admitted to the Rest Camp they were brought one by one into the presence of a British officer, who pompously read their sentence to them.

How the other men passed through their interview with him I do not know, but Mr. Hattingh's story, told in his own words, runs thus:

After a few questions had been put, the British officer said to him:

"You have been found guilty of high treason, but Lord Kitchener has been kind enough to commute your sentence to banishment as prisoner of war."

"But how could you find me guilty?" Mr. Hattingh asked. "I have never been tried."

"Be silent," the officer commanded sternly. "You have nothing to say."

Mr. Hattingh says he was only too glad to "be silent," and betook himself to the Rest Camp with alacrity.

During the weeks of their imprisonment in the jail those at Harmony were not living in a bed of roses.

Of Willie Botha's loyalty they never had a doubt, but the other men were unknown to them, and they knew that all were aware of the part played by them in the Secret Service. And even if they were not betrayed by one of the prisoners, it was a mystery that they had not been betrayed *with* them.

Many of their friends, the families of the men in jail, had been sent to camps or across the border, and no one was more surprised at finding themselves still in Pretoria than Mrs. van Warmelo and her daughter.

They felt the strain, the uncertainty of their position keenly, and throughout those weeks they were obliged to conceal from their good friends, the Consuls and their families, the danger to which they were exposed and the intense anxiety with which they were filled, not only on their own account, but for those brave men in the Pretoria jail.

Towards the end of September, when the prisoners had been removed to the Rest Camp, a baby-girl was born in Willie Botha's house.

The mother had been left undisturbed in her home, a consideration for which she and all who were concerned for her were devoutly grateful, and now she had passed through the portals of Gethsemane and the wide gates of Eden, in the bitter-sweet experiences of motherhood.

The news of the birth of a daughter was duly conveyed to Willie Botha in the Rest Camp, with a request to the authorities to allow him to visit his wife and see his child before leaving South Africa's shores for Bermuda.

Permission was granted for a two-hours' visit.

An armed soldier escorted him to his home and sat outside, under the verandah, drinking coffee and enjoying the good things with which he had been provided, while, inside, his prisoner, speechless with emotion, knelt beside the mother's bed, showering kisses on the tiny feet of his infant daughter.

When the first greetings were over Mr. Botha said:

"Wife, what became of that old hymn-book which was standing on the shelf in the dining-room?"

"I don't know," she answered; "I suppose it was taken away by Elliot with all the other books and papers."

"Elliot!" he muttered between his teeth.

"Elliot, betrayer of friends, and Judas-Boer!"

This man had been intimately known to them all, had, in fact, for many months lived with his wife and family, as guest and friend, under the hospitable roof of Mr. and Mrs. Hattingh, at whose hands they received innumerable acts of love and kindness.

Elliot was the man by whom the members of the Secret Committee were arrested that Sunday night.

Verily it can be said of him—

"For it was not an enemy that reproached me; then I could have borne it; neither was it he that hated me that did magnify himself against me; then I would have hid myself from him. But it was thou, a man my equal, my guide, and my acquaintance. We took sweet counsel together, and walked unto the house of God in company."

The occasion of Willie Botha's visit having been made to serve at the same time as a christening, there were quiet, sacred rejoicings when the minister, who had in the meantime arrived, performed the ceremony.

As soon as the service was over Mr. Botha walked rapidly to the dining-room and glanced over the empty book-shelves. Nothing there!

He stood on tiptoe for a moment, surveying the topmost shelf, and was about to turn away disappointed, when his eye fell on the tattered psalm-book, lying unnoticed in a corner of the shelf.

He could hardly believe his eyes! He pounced on the book, turning over the pages in the greatest agitation and suspense.

The fateful slip of paper fell into his hands!

Triumphantly he marched back to his wife's bedroom and held the magic paper before her astonished eyes, telling her of the sleepless nights and days of suspense he had endured through it.

With unspeakable thankfulness in their hearts, they then and there reduced the fragment of paper to ashes, thanking God for His wonderful deliverance.

But the hour of parting was now at hand—and over this, good reader, we must draw the veil.

★★★★★★

On their way back to the Rest Camp the armed escort, becoming confidential, positively assured his charge that peace would be proclaimed before October 10th. The "Powers" had intervened, he said, and the English were leaving the country!

He was an Irishman.

Chapter 30

Forming a New Committee

Not until it became positively known at Harmony, towards the middle of October, that the members of the Secret Committee had been sent away to Bermuda, did Mrs. van Warmelo and Hansie breathe freely again.

The suspense of five full weeks was over at last, a suspense not to be described, and never to be forgotten by those who endured it.

It did not seem possible to grasp the fact that those brave men had escaped with their lives, and Hansie, looking up at the stars that night, felt that she had learnt something of unspeakable value in the relief and gratitude with which that period of concentrated suffering had been followed.

Carlo looked up at the stars too, for he invariably followed his young mistress's gaze, but on this occasion, seeing nothing unusual in that vast expanse, he stood up on his hind legs before her and gave a short bark of inquiry.

"They have gone, Carlo," she said. "I know you won't believe it, but they have really gone, and if 'Gentleman Jim' knew anything about this, he would surely say, 'I 'spose their time hadn't come yet, little missie.' That's it, Carlo. Their time had not come yet. But they have left things in a fearful muddle, and we will have to work as we never worked before. The first thing to be done to-morrow morning will be——"

She stopped suddenly—not even to her faithful Carlo could she confide the secret plan which she had made for reorganising and re-establishing on a safer footing the Secret Service of the Boers in town.

She would form a new committee, of five women this time, who would carry on the work on the same lines which had been adopted by the Secret Committee, and this plan, when she unfolded it to her mother that night, was received with warm approval.

The first and last meeting was held at Harmony on October 15th and was attended by Mrs. Malan, Mrs. Armstrong, Mrs. Honey, Mrs. van Warmelo, and Hansie, who was appointed secretary.

Bound together by the sacred oath of fidelity and secrecy, these five women vowed to serve their country and people, as an organised body of workers, as long as they had the power to do so.

On the occasion of his next visit to the capital Captain Naudé was to be informed of the formation of the new committee, but for the rest its very existence was to be kept a dead secret.

Mrs. van Warmelo told the members that she was in a position to communicate with the President in Holland by every mail, and that the methods employed by her would be revealed to them *after the war*. With this they expressed themselves satisfied, willingly leaving the matter of sending away dispatches from the field in Mrs. van Warmelo's capable hands.

It was felt that the greatest responsibility resting on them at the time was to have a suitable place of refuge ready to receive the captain when next he entered the town.

There was no house free from suspicion since the arrest of the committee, except—except—Harmony!

Harmony, surrounded as it was by British officers and their staffs, by British troops and Military Mounted Police—Harmony was at last chosen as the most suitable, the only spot in Pretoria in which the Captain of the Secret Service could be harboured with any degree of safety.

It was arranged that he would immediately be brought to Harmony when he came again, and in the meantime the committee would be on the look-out for an opportunity to send a warning and instructions out to him not to approach the houses hitherto frequented by him.

For many weeks no spies belonging to his set came into town. No war news of any description reached his friends, except one day the information, conveyed we know not how, of the safe arrival at the Skurvebergen of young Els, the spy who had been fired upon and was missing from his companions on that eventful September 12th. That this news gave his relatives and friends great joy and relief after the intense anxiety gone through on his account, my readers will readily understand.

★★★★★★

The discovery of the White Envelope was not always a source of unmixed satisfaction.

One of them, containing news of the betrayal and arrest of the committee, and sent to Alphen in the ordinary way, failed to reach its destination. This caused the senders so much anxiety that for some time they did not dare risk the sending of another. The letter might have fallen into the hands of the censors and the secret be discovered by them, in which event they were probably waiting quietly to catch up further information.

It may have been only a coincidence, but at this time the plotters at Harmony observed that the censorship on *their* post had been withdrawn altogether.

They knew only too well what this meant! And their hearts sank when they thought of the White Envelope!

It meant, good reader, that there was a most disquieting increase in the vigilance of the censor; it meant that their letters were opened *by steam*, to throw them off their guard, and to encourage them to write with greater frankness to their absent friends.

Mother and daughter felt the hair rising on their heads when they thought of one of their precious White Envelopes being subjected to a treatment of *steam* by the censor, and of his exultation on beholding the result.

As the days went by, their dread of him and his evil machinations increased, for hardly a letter reached them that did not betray traces of his handiwork—or unhandiwork, for he was not always judicious in the quantity of glue used by him in reclosing the envelopes. He should have been a little more economical in the use of government property if he really wished to hoodwink his enemies, and he would have saved Mrs. van Warmelo the trouble of damping the envelopes afterwards where they stuck, on the inside, to the letters.

While the steaming process was being carried on at the General Post Office, no White Envelopes were taken to the censor, but they were posted at Johannesburg by friends, and in this way the distant correspondents were warned of danger, until it became evident that the steam-censorship had been withdrawn and the old reassuring order of things been established once more.

A week or two later another White Envelope from Holland reached Harmony in safety, by which it was known that the secret was still undiscovered, but the fate of the missing envelope remained a mystery to the end, and was a constant reminder and warning to the conspirators to be careful in the use of their priceless secret.

I am sure the post office officials had plenty to do during the war, but there is no doubt that their labours were considerably lightened by the "smugglers" who chose to dispense with the services of the censors entirely. And then we must not forget the activities of the spies and of their fellow-workers in town.

Quite a large private postal service was carried on by them, as we all know, and every week, before the entry into Pretoria became so difficult and dangerous, hundreds of letters were carried backwards and forwards, to and from the commandos.

One man in town was in the habit of receiving great batches of these smuggled letters, which he distributed to the various addresses, until one day he was very nearly caught. He had just received a packet of communications "from the front" and had opened it on his writing-table in his quiet study, when the doors were opened unceremoniously and some officials entered with a warrant to search his house. Carpets were taken up, walls were tapped, furniture was overturned and examined, books were removed from their shelves and every cranny inspected with the greatest thoroughness, but the pile of letters lying open on his writing-table, over which they had found him bending when they entered the room, was passed over without so much as a glance.

This may sound a bit unreal, unlikely, but there are similar cases on record, which we know to be true beyond a doubt, and one of these I must relate, because it so closely concerned our friends at Harmony and so very nearly proved to be their undoing. They did not know it at the time, but were told by Mrs. Cloete, after the war, that she had sent all their uncensored, their "smuggled" letters, to her friend at Capetown, Mrs. Koopmans de Wet, with instructions to read and return them to her as soon as possible, which Mrs. Koopmans had done, with the alarming news that her house had been thoroughly searched for documents while the pile of letters was lying open on her writing-table.

The authorities must have been "struck blind," she had said, for though they had overhauled the place and had taken away with them every suspicious-looking document, they had passed and repassed the papers on her table without a word and with nothing more than a superficial glance.

This information had alarmed Mrs. Cloete so much that she had immediately packed every incriminating letter and all her White Envelopes into a tin, which she secretly buried, with the help of her German nurse, under one of the trees at Alphen.

And there they, or what is left of them after ten years, still lie, for the spot has never again been found, although every effort was made to do so.

Chapter 31

"Tea For Two"

It was at the time when the northern territories were being swept by the enemy for the first time that Mrs. van Warmelo heard that a relative of hers had been put over the border, and was staying with her husband at the Grand Hotel in Pretoria.

She therefore asked Hansie to call at the hotel to inquire whether she could be of any assistance to them in their trouble, and Hansie donned her prettiest frock that very afternoon on her "calling" expedition, Carlo walking with unusual sedateness by her side.

"We'll go and see General Maxwell too this afternoon, Carlo," she said, "and see whether we can get that permit. Always put on your best clothes when you go to the Military Governor, my boy. You'll find that Tommy Atkins never keeps you waiting then."

Arrived at the hotel, she suddenly remembered that she had forgotten her young relative's name, and did not know whom to ask for.

She was waited upon by a hall-porter, who watched her with a face of stolid patience while she searched her memory for the forgotten name.

At last she said: "The lady I want was a Miss Maré, but she has married an Englishman since last I saw her, and I have forgotten his name. Can you tell me whether there is a young couple with a baby, from Zoutpansberg, staying at the hotel?"

"I'll find out, miss."

He came back with the information that there were four young couples from Zoutpansberg, each with a baby.

Hansie wondered that he did not smile.

"Are they all in?" she asked.

"Some are in and some are out," he said.

Suddenly he seemed to wake up.

"Would it be any help if I told you their names?" he inquired.

"Yes, indeed," she exclaimed; "I would know the name at once if I heard it."

He brought her the book in which the names of visitors were entered, and read one name after the other slowly.

"That's it," Hansie said. "Knevitt! Is Mrs. Knevitt in?"

"No, miss, she is out, and I happen to know that she is leaving again soon. They only arrived yesterday. They were put over the border by the Boers."

"I don't understand," Hansie answered.

"Don't you see, miss? The Boers are still in possession of Pietersburg, and Mr. Knevitt, as a British subject, has been put over the border."

"Oh yes, I see. Well, will you please give these cards to Mrs. Knevitt when she comes in?"

Once on the street, Hansie again addressed herself to her faithful companion:

"It is not hard to believe that the world is turning round, Carlo, when one has to believe that Pretoria is the other side of one's own border. I wonder what our next sensation is to be."

She was soon to find out.

The military governor was engaged, and she was shown into the office of an under official, a tall, fair man whose name she did not catch.

She was politely asked to take a seat and the nature of her business inquired into.

The tall, fair man bent over some papers he had before him and toyed with a gold pencil, while she stated her case as clearly and concisely as she could.

He asked her a few questions, with long pauses in between, and again bent over his papers, making pencil marks and turning the pages over slowly.

The silvery chime of a tiny clock told the hour of five.

"You—er—will have some tea?"

"No, thank you," surprised.

A moment's silence, then he pressed an electric bell at his right hand.

An immaculate "Buttons" instantly appeared.

"Tea for two," the officer commanded, without raising his head.

Buttons disappeared, to return in an incredibly short time, bearing aloft a well-appointed *tête-à-tête*.

When he had withdrawn, the hospitable officer, of whom it could well be said that "he had a teapot in his soul," poured out two cups of tea with an abstracted air, pushed one towards Hansie with his right hand, while he slowly stirred his own with his left.

"Have some tea," he said persuasively.

There was no answer, and he again bent over the work with which he was occupied.

Hansie got up quietly and left the room, but she had not gone many yards in the long corridor before she became aware of hurried footsteps following.

It was the tall officer, very straight now, who called out to her:

"Stop, stop a moment. Where are you going?"

Without turning round she replied:

"To General Maxwell. He *never* keeps me waiting," and walked on rapidly.

"Don't go," he implored. "Come back to my office. I have your permits quite ready for you. I was busy with them all the time."

She turned round slowly and walked back with him to his office.

"Thank you *very* much," she said as she took the papers from his hand.

He opened the door for her with exaggerated courtesy, and she went on her way, brimming over with delight.

"I missed two teas this afternoon, but I got my permits and came off with flying colours," she confided to her dumb companion. "Let us go home and tell the mother all about it, Carlo mine."

CHAPTER 32

Kidnapping Mauser the Kitten

One afternoon when Mrs. van Warmelo and Hansie were returning home, as they passed the house occupied by one of the biggest "lords" in the British Army, they saw an exquisite black kitten sitting on the steps leading from the street to the garden.

Such a kitten! Coal black she was, except for a snowy shirt front and four dainty, snow-white paws.

A delicate ribbon of pale blue satin was fastened in a bow round her neck, and she blinked at the passers-by in friendly consciousness of her superior beauty.

"Oh, you darling!" Hansie exclaimed. "I wish you belonged to me!"

"She does," Mrs. van Warmelo answered, and stooping, she picked up the unresisting kitten and placed it in her daughter's arms.

It was done in a moment and was meant for a joke, but Hansie took the matter seriously and walked on, rapturously caressing her small "trophy of the war."

"Hansie, put that cat down," Mrs. van Warmelo said, looking anxiously up and down the street.

"No indeed, mother; you gave her to me."

"You know very well I did not mean you to keep her. I decline to have anything more to do with the matter."

She walked rapidly on and Hansie followed in some uncertainty, but holding on to her new-found treasure as if her life depended upon it.

Soon she caught up with her indignant parent and said in a conciliatory tone of voice:

"Surely, mother, you don't suppose I would steal a cat from any one else! But Lord —— is trying to take my country, why should I not take his cat?"

"Two wrongs never made one right," her mother answered, "but do as you please. You always do."

Hansie kept that kitten and, after Carlo, loved it better than any other pet, and even Mrs. van Warmelo relented as she watched the playful creature hiding in the shadows and springing out at every passer-by.

"What are you going to call her?" she asked her daughter.

"Oh, I don't know. Perhaps I'll go and ask Lord —— what *he* called her."

She stopped, observing her mother's frown, and then went on:

"We must think of a name, a nice, appropriate war name."

A few moments later the kitten crept into a corner, with a small mouse held firmly between her jaws.

"Oh, mother, look, she has caught a mouse already. She is going to be a splendid mouser. And oh, now I have a name for her. We'll call her '*Mauser*,' mother dear!"

So be it. "Mauser" is her name, and hereafter she may be seen invariably in Hansie's company, a welcome addition to the small, harmonious family.

Perched on Hansie's shoulder as she sat reading under the verandah, or purring round her as she lay under the trees, with Carlo watching by her side, Mauser was ever to be found where her young mistress was; and when the latter went to town she and Carlo were invariably escorted to the gate by the faithful Mauser, who again welcomed them on their return.

This kidnapping episode had taken place a few months after the British entry into Pretoria.

A full year had gone by; and Mauser, the kitten, had developed into a beautiful full-grown cat and was the mother of five mischievous little ones, grey-striped and very wild, for whom she had made a home in a deep hollow in the trunk of one of the big weeping-willows, the very tree under which "Gentleman Jim" had built his small kitchen of corrugated iron.

It is a stormy night in November 1901, a month remembered by all for the violence and frequency of its storms.

Hansie is bending over her diary, trying to make her entries between the crashes with which the house is shaken.

Her mother is lying on a couch near by; her tired eyes are closed, but she is not asleep. Who could sleep in such a storm?

Perhaps we may be allowed to look over the writer's shoulder.

Nov. 8th, Friday, 10 o'clock p.m.
And this terrific storm has been raging for hours! It seems incredible.
It was the same last night and the night before. As I write, the roar of thunder never once breaks off, peal after peal, crash after crash, vivid, dazzling flashes of lightning, torrents of rain mixed with hail, and a howling wind.
Such a night is never to be forgotten.
One is thrilled and impressed by its magnificence, by its awful grandeur and its majesty, and yet I think one would go mad if it continued for any length of time.
I feel as if *I* am going mad with the thought of our thousands and thousands of women and tender little children exposed to all this fury. . . .
Where is the God of pity tonight?
Surely not in our desolate land, not in our ruined homes—*not in South Africa!*
The fourth storm within a few hours, each more violent than the last, is just approaching, and this one threatens to surpass the others in unabated fury.
The Lord hath turned His face from us.
The hand of the Lord is laid heavily upon us. His ear is deaf to our cries and supplications. I cannot write, my soul is crushed by the sorrow, suffering, and sin around me . . . .
I feel better now, but the struggle has been great. . . .
At the front, fierce blows have been struck lately. Our men are fighting as they never fought before. . . .
How the storm rages on! In my sheltered home, safe from the fury of the elements, I think I suffer more than the women under canvas, for *their* sakes. . . .
The letter I have before me must be answered now. He asks me to bind myself to him definitely. . . .
I have decided to do so. It is a weighty step, and God knows. . .
But I have long prayed for guidance, and it seems to me clear enough that we are destined for one another.
So tonight, in this raging storm, with a heart filled with the desolation of land and people, the blackness of the present, the hopeless misery of the future, I am going to write the words

which will bind me for ever to L.E.B.

Strange betrothal! Strange sequel to a stormy life!

But perhaps—perhaps, the future holds something for me of calm and peace....

With throbbing brow she went out into the night to watch the storm, from a sheltered corner under the verandah.

Nothing fascinated her so much.

Suddenly a blinding flash, accompanied by a sound like the sharp cracking of a whip and instantly followed by a deafening roar of thunder, drove her to her mother's side.

"Are you all right, mother? That bolt fell very near. I thought it struck the house."

"It was frightfully close," Mrs. van Warmelo answered. "Come and sit beside me here. I am quite sure one of our big trees has been struck."

She was right, for walking through the demolished garden next morning, they came upon the spot where the bolt had fallen and found one of the gigantic willow trees furrowed from top to bottom, with the outer bark scorched and curled up like paper and the white bark showing underneath.

Jim was breaking down his little kitchen with all the speed he could.

"What are you doing, Jim?" Hansie asked.

"Jim's shifting," was the answer, soberly and sadly made.

"But the storm is over. All the danger is past. You can safely stay on now."

"No fear, little missie. The Big Baas was very cross last night, and when Him cross He don't care what He do. Jim want to live a little longer."

Hansie laughed.

"I wonder where Mauser could have been with her kittens last night!" she exclaimed, putting her hand into the deep hollow of the tree. "The nest is empty. Do you know, Jim?"

"No, little Missie. I 'spose Mauser's time had not come yet," he said, with stolid philosophy.

"I suppose not."

But alas, alas! Mauser's time was soon to come, for the soldiers, setting a strong trap to catch a wild cat which was nightly plundering them of their meat ration, caught Hansie's beloved Mauser instead, killing her instantly.

No reproaches from her mother were added to her keen remorse as she bent over the motherless kittens, whispering: "*I* will care for you, as *she* would have done; but oh, remember this, that honesty is the best policy, and all is *not* fair in love and war."

✶✶✶✶✶✶

Tragedy was in the air.

A bee-keeper came to Harmony one morning to help Mrs. van Warmelo to take out honey from the hives, and this disturbance, combined with the fact that the soldiers had unwisely set up a smithy near the beehives under the row of blue-gum trees dividing their camp from Harmony, enraged the bees so much with the noise and the smoke and heat of the smithy fires, that they attacked man and beast in vicious fury.

In a few moments all was confusion.

The servants rushed about frantically, in their endeavours to bring the fowls and calves under shelter in time.

The two women took refuge in the house, closing the doors and windows, while they watched the consternation and disorder in the camp.

Fortunately there was only one horse in the smithy at the time, a beautiful chestnut mare belonging to the Provost-Marshal, Major Poore, so Mrs. van Warmelo was told afterwards.

The soldiers seemed to lose their heads entirely. They ran away, not into their tents, but right away into the "*koppies*" on the other side of the railway line.

The bee-keeper cut the halter with which the unfortunate horse was tethered to a post, then he too took refuge.

What followed was pitiful to behold and will never be forgotten by the women, helplessly, and as if fascinated by the scene, watching from their windows.

The infuriated bees, deprived of all other living things on which to wreak their vengeance, turned, in their thousands, on the hapless mare, which stood unmoved, as horses do, when lashed by hail or panic-stricken under flames.

She made no attempt to save herself, but with bent head and ears laid flat she stood still under the furious attack of countless bees.

One or two of the men, wrapped up to the eyes in the coats and waistcoats of their comrades, cautiously approached the mare at their own great peril, and tried with all their strength to move her from

The Apiary, Harmony.

the scene.

In vain. As if rooted to the spot she stood, with her four feet planted firmly on the ground, and they desisted in despair, once more fleeing to the hills.

All day they sat upon the hillside, homeless, many of them hatless, until towards afternoon, when, the fury of the bees abating, they ventured a return to their tents.

The next day, when the dead mare had been removed for burial, a letter was brought to Mrs. van Warmelo from the Provost-Marshal, commanding the immediate removal of the beehives to some safer spot in the lower portion of Harmony.

This was done by degrees, little by little every night, in order to accustom the bees to the change gradually, and there was never any repetition of the attack.

Hansie, writing to her brother in his prison-fort at Ahmednagar, that his bees had put a valuable English horse out of action for ever, received in reply a postcard, with the single comment, "My brave bees!"

Chapter 33

The First Spies at Harmony

As we have said, the committee of women had decided on Harmony as the only safe spot for harbouring Captain Naudé on his next visit. It was still hemmed in by troops on every side, and, as the weeks went by, and the van Warmelos became *more* convinced that their name had not been betrayed with those of the Secret Committee, they settled down with a sense of peaceful security and prepared themselves once more for the reception of their friends.

Their wonderful "escape" was a topic of daily conversation, and they congratulated themselves over and over again with not even having been approached by the military and put on their best behaviour.

No promises had been given by them, and they felt free as the birds of the air to continue their work of outwitting the enemy, whenever occasion presented itself. But occasions were rare now.

As far as was known, there was no longer a spot in the fence-work around Pretoria through which a spy could enter unobserved, and no word or sign had been received from the brave captain for more than three months. By this they knew that he had been informed of the calamities which had befallen his friends in town.

Still they doubted not that he would at least make an attempt to come in again. His friends remembered his once having said that his keen enjoyment of the perils he underwent was only enhanced by the obstacles which lay in his way, and when the English thought they had made it quite impossible for any man to cross their lines, it would be his greatest pleasure to prove how much mistaken they were.

There was no vain boasting in the quiet and natural way in which he made these remarks, and they were remembered with a strong conviction that he would keep his word. But still it was realised that his greatest difficulty would not be so much his entrance into the town as his perplexity when once he found himself there.

He would not know where to go. His friends had been banished, their houses were occupied by the enemy, and as yet he did not know of the existence of the new committee. Sending out word to him was impossible.

No man could risk the unknown dangers of leaving the town under the present conditions to warn him; no one would know where to find the Secret Service Corps in the field. His friends decided to possess their souls in patience, trusting in the capabilities of the wily captain and knowing full well that if any one could find a way out, or in, he would.

He did not disappoint them, and they might have known that on this occasion everything he did would be exactly opposed to his former methods.

It was to be a time of surprises for everyone.

Hansie and her mother were just talking about the captain and regretting the appearance of the young moon—which meant under ordinary circumstances, *no* spies in town—and wondering how much longer they would be able to endure their suspense—wondering, too, how they would communicate with the commander in future and longing for reliable news from the field—when the unexpected happened.

At break of day December 17th three travellers entered the town, travel-stained, torn, and weary. They walked boldly through the streets of Pretoria in the dim light of a summer's dawn, and what their destination was we shall see presently.

The van Warmelos were having supper that night at 8 o'clock when the door opened unceremoniously and Flippie's shock head was thrust in.

"There are two ladies looking for Harmony," he said. "They are at the front gate and want to see you."

Hansie immediately went out and met two girls, strangers to her, coming up the garden-path.

"Good evening," she said. "Do you wish to see my mother?"

"Who are you?" was the somewhat unexpected but perfectly natural question.

"I am Miss van Warmelo. Do you want anyone here?"

"Yes," one of them replied in a hurried and mysterious way. "There are two men at your garden gate and they want to see Mrs. van Warmelo."

"Won't you ask them to come up to the house?" Hansie asked. "You can't very well expect my mother to——"

"Oh yes, she must," the other broke in hurriedly; "it is all right—she knows them. They will tell her themselves what they want."

"Wait here a moment. I will call my mother."

Hansie had some trouble in persuading her mother to leave the house.

"I am not going down to the gate to see any men," she said. "Let them come up to me."

"They won't, mother. It is no use. There is something behind this. They are either our own spies or the English are setting a trap for us. Be on your guard, but come out into the garden."

Sorely against her will Mrs. van Warmelo hurried out of the house, where she gave the girls a cool and haughty reception, saying:

"I don't understand this. Will you be good enough to ask your friends to come up to my house if they wish to speak to me?" And with that she turned back to the house alone.

Girl No. 1 said, "I think I had better go and fetch them, they are waiting near the wire fence," and walked rapidly down the path, while Hansie followed slowly with girl No. 2, asking many questions, but getting none but the most unsatisfactory replies.

When they reached the gate, girl No. 1 had disappeared altogether and there was no sign of the men. Hansie thought this very suspicious, and was about to turn to her companion with an impatient remark, when she suddenly said something about going to look for girl No. 1 and disappeared too, leaving Hansie standing alone at the gate with her troubled reflections.

Men and girls had now disappeared for good it seemed, and, after what seemed an endless time of waiting, she decided to go back to the house, when she was suddenly joined by her mother, now thoroughly alarmed.

"It must be a trap, dear mother," she whispered. "I can't make it out. Ah, here is some one coming at last"—but then her heart stood still, for a tall English officer, with helmet on and armed to the teeth, advanced, saluting the two ladies in the pale light of the young moon.

"Naudé," he whispered, stretching out his hands to them.

Captain Naudé in an English officer's uniform! Thank God, thank God!

In a moment all was happy confusion.

The captain introduced his corporal, Venter, warmly took leave of girls No. 1 and 2, thanking them gratefully for services rendered by them that night, and then the four people sauntered up to the house, talking loudly as they passed the sergeant-major's tin "villa" on the other side of the fence.

The glimpse Hansie caught of the good man, calmly sitting inside, smoking his pipe and reading, little dreaming that his arch enemies were within a stone's throw of his peaceful abode, added a delightful thrill to the sensations experienced by her that night.

Very little was said when once they got inside. The hostesses took in the condition of the starved and exhausted heroes at a glance and busied themselves with preparations for a feast, while the men stretched themselves on the sofas in the dining-room. When Mrs. van Warmelo had lit the fire in the kitchen and set the kettle on to boil, Hansie opened the windows of the drawing-room as wide as possible, lit the lamps and candles, and opening the piano, played some "loud music" for the edification of the sergeant-major.

"I've made him understand that we have visitors," she said, laughing, when she got back to the dining-room. "He will quite understand the all-pervading smell of coffee, even if he can't account for the ham and eggs at this time of night."

Home-made bread, butter, and preserves, rusks, cold plum-pudding, and fruit completed the repast—and how the men tucked in! They were so bruised and worn-out that they could hardly sit up straight to eat, and when they had each "forced a square meal into a round stomach" they once more stretched themselves out on the sofas, supremely content with their pipes.

Mother and daughter sat beside them talking until nearly midnight.

"Tell me" (Hansie began at the end)—"tell me where you disappeared to from our gate. I can't quite forgive you the nasty fright you gave us. You might have come straight up to the house."

"Well," Naudé answered, "I did not know whether you were still in town and alone at home, and we could not risk finding you with visitors. While we were at the gate some of the Military Mounted Police passed and we thought it safer to go for a walk. Unfortunately we walked right into their camp, and before we knew where we were, we were falling over their tent-ropes, and in our hurry to escape from them we found ourselves before the house of the military governor, where the sentinels on guard saluted me most respectfully. I can't tell you how glad we were to find you waiting for us when we came back to the gate." The diary shrinks from the attempt to describe the thrilling adventures these men had to relate, their hairbreadth escapes, their hardships, privations, and fatigue.

They sat talking with them far into the night, their hostesses hung on every word, their hearts full of admiration and respect for men so brave, so strong and calm, facing death a thousand times without flinching, looking their troubles philosophically in the face, trusting implicitly in their God.

The faith of Captain Naudé was sublime.

By degrees they got the story of their entering into the town from them.

It seemed that at this time Pretoria was so well guarded that it was almost impossible for the wiliest of spies to pass through the sentries unobserved, but, after much cautious inspection, one single unguarded spot had been found, the drift of the Aapies River, over which the S.E. railway bridge passed. This drift, which was about twenty feet wide, was so completely fenced in with a network of barbed wire that it was evidently not considered necessary to place sentinels there. By throwing over their parcels first and working away the ground for more than an hour under the barbed wire, the men were able to crawl and wriggle their way through the barrier.

They made it a rule never to clip the wires around the town, because this would betray the route used by them, but out in the *veld* no wire fences were spared.

When they had removed the worst traces of dust and dirt from their clothes they walked boldly through the streets, Naudé in the uniform of an English officer and Venter and Brenckmann, as his orderlies, dressed in khaki.

They were anxious to get under cover before the full light of day overtook them, but none of them knew where Harmony was, and they actually walked over the lower portion of Harmony's grounds, across the main road and over the Sunnyside bridge, hiding themselves in the thick poplar bushes beside the river. Here three *kaffir* police sprang up and saluted Naudé as he passed. But for his uniform, he and his men would have been lost.

After a short consultation it was decided that Brenckmann should risk walking through the town in daylight to his home in Arcadia and send some one in the evening to escort Naudé and Venter to Harmony.

The two men had a terrible day in the bush, lying as flat as possible in the choking heat, without food and nothing to drink but a little filthy water in a hole near by.

When night fell Brenckmann sent his sister, with one of Venter's, to their hiding-place, and then the search for Harmony began. It was the unsuspecting Flippie, lounging about the streets after his day's work was done, who gave the required information and volunteered to show them the way.

Before they retired for the night Naudé took Mrs. van Warmelo's hand, and, looking earnestly into her face, said:

"Do you know what it means to harbour me? There is a heavy price on my head, and in the event of an attack I do not mean to be taken alive. There will be a fight under your roof. I am well armed"— he tapped his revolvers significantly; "it means confiscation of your property and imprisonment for you and your daughter. Are you prepared for this? If not, say the word; it is not yet too late for us to seek refuge elsewhere."

"You are heartily welcome here," she replied, "and if it comes to fighting——"

"We have arms too," Hansie broke in, "a revolver and a pocket-pistol. It will not be the first time that Boer women have fought side by side with their men——" She stopped in some confusion, suddenly remembering General Maxwell and the permits he had given her.

"I fervently hope there will be no fighting," she continued. "I am sure there will not be. There are too many troops lying around Harmony, we shall never be suspected of harbouring spies; but if we should be surprised in the night, don't begin shooting at once. We have a hiding-place for you."

Mrs. van Warmelo led the way to her bedroom, where the men were to sleep, and, removing a rug from the floor beside the bed, she lifted two boards and disclosed an opening large enough for the body of a man to pass through.

"Put all your belongings in here and creep in at the first alarm," she said. "We will cover you up securely. Leave the matter in our hands."

"By the way," said the captain suddenly, "who is Flippie?"

She gave him a brief outline of Flippie's history and how he came to be at Harmony.

"Why do you ask?"

"Well, I should like to cultivate Flippie's acquaintance. I must find out what he thinks of how *we* come to be with you."

"Oh, Flippie is all right," she declared. "You can trust him with anything. But perhaps it will be safer for you to remain in hiding while you are with us, not to be seen even by the servants."

"We can arrange all that tomorrow," Captain Naudé answered. "I am sure you must be tired now, and perhaps you will not get much rest. There are many things to do and to discuss tomorrow. I must see several people and give you the reports for the president."

"Will you let me be your secretary?" Hansie asked. "I am secretary to the new committee."

"I shall be very glad if you will," Captain Naudé replied.

Chapter 34

The Captain's Visit

Needless to say, there was not much peace or rest for anyone that night.

Mrs. van Warmelo and Hansie kept guard all night in the dining-room. Every time Carlo barked outside they sprang up in alarm, their hearts throbbing, their breath held up in listening suspense, but nothing happened; and when day broke and the glorious sunlight flooded the garden, all their fears vanished, and they felt as if they had been harbouring spies all their lives.

They were up early, and as soon as their guests heard sounds of life about the house they cautiously emerged from their rooms, looking about them anxiously and inquiringly.

"Come in and have some coffee," Mrs. van Warmelo said warmly. "Did you have a good night? The servants are not in the house yet and you are safe for the present, but we must make our plans immediately. Are you going to be seen about the house or not?"

Captain Naudé then informed her that his orderly Venter wished to go home to his people in Arcadia towards evening, if she could lend him civilian clothing to wear, for once in the town the khaki was more of a danger than a safeguard to him, and Captain Naudé was in the same difficulty himself.

It would never do for him to be seen at Harmony in an English officer's uniform—"unless," he added inquiringly, "you are in the habit of entertaining the British military?"

"No, indeed we are not!" she exclaimed indignantly, and told him the story of the officers who had tried to visit her.

"Only one dear old colonel comes now," Hansie said, "but he has not been here for a long, long time. I would enjoy introducing you to him."

"Not in these clothes," Naudé replied. "An English colonel would know at once to whom they belonged. No; if I am to remain at Harmony as an ordinary visitor, you will have to provide me with ordinary clothes."

Mrs. van Warmelo promised to do that during the course of the day, and in the meantime it was decided to keep the men in the unused spare bedroom, out of sight of the prying eyes of servants and possible callers.

There their meals were served to them, the women washing up their dishes without a sound in the privacy of their own bedrooms, and at the same time doing all in their power to look and act as usual, showing themselves all over the house and garden, and busying themselves with the usual household duties.

"What did those two khaki women want with you last night, Miss Hansie?" the irrepressible Flippie asked as soon as he saw her that morning.

"Khaki women! What *do* you mean, Flippie?"

"They *were* khaki women," he said aggressively. "I saw two English officers with revolvers with them, and they were pretending they didn't belong to them. What did they want with Harmony?"

"I don't know them, Flippie. I never set eyes on them before. I am sure they were up to no good."

"But what did they say they wanted with Harmony?" he persisted.

"They told me they were looking for something else," Hansie answered lamely. "Have you fed the fowls, Flippie?"

"No, but I wonder—"

"Then go and do so at once," Hansie interrupted severely. "It is long past 6 o'clock."

He went unwillingly.

On comparing notes, she found that he had carried on the same conversation with her mother. There was no doubt that his suspicions had been thoroughly roused, and for the next few days they had their hands full, trying to keep his curiosity in check. Perhaps if they had taken Flippie into their confidence and trusted him with their secret, it would have saved them all the anxiety and unrest they had to pass through afterwards, but they acted for the best, and perhaps they would have been betrayed in any case.

What use to speculate now on what might have been?

Hansie's first duty that day was to go to town and inform the members of the Secret Committee of Naudé's arrival in Pretoria, and to procure clothing for Venter.

A friend of hers, whom she judged to be about the same size as Venter, gave her a splendid suit of clothes, nearly new, without asking many questions, and placed his further services at her disposal.

She then went to Venter's relatives in Arcadia and told them on no account to visit him at Harmony, as he was coming home to them that evening. Too many people knew about the spies at Harmony, and there was good reason for beginning to feel uncomfortable.

The women of the committee promised to call at Harmony that afternoon.

When Hansie arrived home she sewed on Venter's buttons, supplied him with studs and ties, a clean pocket-handkerchief, and a new hat.

I believe he had on clothing belonging to six different people when he sallied forth soon after sundown, and Mrs. van Warmelo was glad to see the last of him, for her cares and responsibilities were multiplying, and his presence in the house was one more.

The captain was still in his uniform, but he was provided with clean underclothing from the "boys'" wardrobes, and from that moment the unmistakable smell of commando no longer pervaded that home!

The rest of the morning was spent in making copies of the dispatches to the president and drawing up a list of the necessaries to be provided by the committee for the men to take out with them, and in the afternoon Harmony was besieged with a stream of callers.

Poor Hansie thought they would never end, and while she was entertaining them in the drawing-room her mother was keeping the others quiet in the dining-room—Mrs. Honey, Mrs. Armstrong, Mrs. Malan, and the two spies.

That night their sleep was deep and refreshing, for they were worn out in mind and body. There was only one man in the house, and they were getting used to his presence, and the thought of the secret hiding-place gave a sense of security.

They were up early again next morning, and, all the "business" transactions having been done the day before, they devoted themselves to the entertainment of their guest.

A more delightful day they never spent, and the memory of it clings to them still.

Captain Naudé was beginning to feel the restrictions of city hospitality, and, longing to get out into the big garden, where the early figs and apricots held their tempting sway, he asked Mrs. van Warmelo once more to provide him with a suit of civilian clothing.

He was taller and slighter of build than the "boys," but she gave him a suit belonging to the youngest son, Fritz, and from that moment he walked freely about the house and garden.

His helmet and uniform lay buried in the hiding-place under the floor, but his revolvers he kept on under his coat, in the leathern belt strapped around his waist. This fact was significant of the deadly peril in which they all were.

While the women were hastily getting through their household duties in order to have a long talk with him, he roamed about the garden and finally stretched himself out on the benches under the six weeping-willows at the foot of the orange avenue.

"Who dat lying under our trees, Miss Hansie?" "Gentleman Jim" inquired, from his perch in the mulberry tree behind the house.

"A friend of ours, Jim. He has been very ill in the hospital and has asked us to let him spend the day in our garden."

"Oh yes, I can see him's cloes much too big for him."

"Hand me that basket, Jim, if it is full," Hansie commanded. "Here is another; and when you have finished, make a big fire in the kitchen, because we must have a nice dinner today for the baas."

"All right, little missie," was the respectful answer.

"Gentleman Jim" was settled, and the same performance was gone through casually with Flippie and Paulus; but the three Italian gardeners and the eight or ten *kaffirs* employed by them were left to think what they pleased, and they went about their work without taking the slightest notice of Captain Naudé.

"The people in your hospital have nice ruddy complexions," Mrs. van Warmelo said laughingly, when Hansie told her what the captain was passing for; but the ruse answered, and, for the time at least, all suspicions were lulled to rest.

When they joined the captain in the garden later on they invited him to help them to gather strawberries for the people who were coming to see him again that afternoon. They were just engaged in the pleasant task, chatting gaily and feeling, oh, so safe, when Mrs. van Warmelo started violently.

The sergeant-major was standing on the other side of the fence, watching them intently.

Captain Naudé bent low over the strawberry plants and whispered:

"Don't move. Go on picking quietly. He will soon go away."

He did, apparently satisfied with the appearance of the stranger, but the ladies had been seized with a sudden nervousness and implored the captain to come into the house.

Mrs. van Warmelo pointed out to him a group of dense loquat trees, with dark-green, glossy foliage, a suitable place of refuge should he be compelled to flee from the house at night.

He was not a man of many words, but, once started, there was no difficulty in getting all the information they wanted out of him, and he answered their leading questions in a simple, straightforward way, his every word bearing the unmistakable stamp of truth.

I have avoided going into the details of the actual war as much as possible.

It has not been my intention to weary my reader with dry facts concerning battlefields, nor to give the war reports and war rumours, so often unreliable, with which Hansie's diary is filled, but the events connected with Captain Naudé's first visit to Harmony I wish to give in the smallest detail. Great historical truths stand out in bold relief against a background of minute details and the realistic description of the common life. This background Hansie's diary affords better than anything written from memory after many years could have done.

While the captain slept Hansie made her notes, and when he woke she was with him again for further news.

Her thirst for information was insatiable.

"I have been longing to ask you, captain, where you got your English uniform," Hansie said as they sat down in the dining-room with the great bowls of scarlet strawberries before them. "Tell us everything while we remove these stems."

"You have heard of the terrible battle we had at Bakenlaagte—when Colonel Benson fell, mortally wounded? I was there."

"Were you?" they exclaimed in breathless surprise.

"Yes, and the uniform lying buried under your floor I myself took from the dead body of Colonel Thorold after the battle."

By degrees a full description was given of that great British reverse on the High Veld and what took place after.

When the battle was over and Colonel Benson lay mortally wounded, surrounded by doctors and officers in high authority, Naudé advanced, and asked to be allowed to take his papers. The men protested, but Naudé ordered them all aside and gently removed every paper from his pockets. He had no important documents with him and the private papers were of course returned to the men in charge of the dying officer.

He expired soon afterwards and was mourned by the Boers as well as the English, for he was admired and respected by all for his courage and daring, and his fame as an honourable foe had spread throughout the Boer lines.

Many of them were heard to say that they had only meant to catch him and that they bitterly regretted his death.

It was one of the worst battles, under General Botha, Naudé had ever been in. About twelve Boers were killed instantly, and three wounded to death.

With the storming of the cannon, Boers and English were so close together that the one could hear what the other said, and Naudé's corporal, Venter, saw a poor soldier fall back mortally wounded, gasping out with his dying breath, "Oh, dear mother!"

God of pity! who will tell that bereaved parent that her son's last thoughts and words were for her alone?

It was terrible to hear the wounded and dying praying and calling to their God for help. Nationality, language, enmity, and bitter hatred were forgotten as side by side those mortal foes prepared to meet their God—*one God!*

Imploring one another for help, praying for one drop of water to alleviate their dying agonies—in vain!

Two cannon were taken by the Boers, one of which they destroyed at once, keeping the other for their future use.

When all was over General Botha spoke a few touching words to his men, thanking them for their bravery, and congratulating them on their success.

Unpleasant though it may be to think of, it is my duty to relate that, before burial, the soldiers were stripped of their clothes, and every Boer permitted to take what he required, but the bodies were treated with respect.

Naudé, for purposes of his own, chose the uniform of the dead Colonel Thorold, which had six bullet holes through it and was covered with bloodstains.

Revolvers, leggings, whistle, helmet, all was complete, even to the stars and crown on the colonel's shoulders.

Naudé felt himself rich indeed in the possession of articles which he knew would be invaluable to him on his next entry into Pretoria.

One of his men took Colonel Benson's uniform, but handed the crown to him (Naudé) at his request, and then the bodies were covered with blankets for a hurried burial.

Oh, cruel war when men slay one another!

"Oh, blest Red Cross, like an angel in the trail of the men who slay!"

There were about ten dead English *officers* on the field and nineteen wounded, of whom three or four died afterwards.

✶✶✶✶✶✶

"When did you see General Botha last?" Mrs. van Warmelo inquired.

"About three weeks ago, and then he was looking well and brown. He told me of a narrow escape he had had. He was completely surrounded and barely got off with his life. His hat was left behind, also his Bible and hymn-books. Lord Kitchener, courteously, and with a touch of humour, returned the books to him with a boy's hat which had been found on the field, thinking evidently that it belonged to the general's little son, who was known to go everywhere with him; but General Botha sent the hat back to Lord Kitchener with a message to the effect that it was not his son's, but had belonged to his '*achter-ryder*,' and thanking him for the books."[1]

"Tell us some of your own escapes," Hansie begged, "I am sure you have had many."

"So many that I have forgotten them nearly all," he answered, "but one I shall never forget."

He then related how he and twenty of his men had once been pursued for four hours by about one thousand English. The bullets fell like hail about them, and he was keeping the saddle he rode on, as a curiosity, because of the many bullet holes in it. Once a bullet passed between his coat and shirt along his stomach, the shock taking his breath away. He was sure he had been mortally wounded, but could not stop to find out, and the very recollection of it still caused him to experience the sensation of coming into close contact with death.

---

1. General Botha tells me that the hat which was returned to him by Lord Kitchener had first belonged to his little son, Louis, who had written his name in full, in blue pencil, on the inside of the crown, and had given it, when he had no more use for it, to his little native orderly.

CHAPTER 35

Memories Bitter-Sweet

The captain's visit was not an unmixed joy. Some bitter revelations were made, much pathos mixed with the humours of the situation and tragic experiences related by all—but on these I shall merely touch, as unavoidable and necessary for the completion of my story.

After the treachery of their own people and the arming of the natives, nothing troubled the men so much as the fact that the fighting burghers were, in some parts of the country, suffering from sore gums and showing signs of scurvy, caused by an unchanging diet of meat and mealies. The spies wanted to communicate this to some good, trustworthy doctor and to get medicine for them to take out to the commandos, but Mrs. van Warmelo told them that no medicine in the world could cure that. What they wanted was a change of diet—fresh milk, vegetables, fruit, and an abundant supply of lime-juice, etc.

Sending out lime-juice would be as absurd as impossible, for it would be as a drop in the ocean of want—and as it was, the men were handicapped by the two bottles of good French brandy which they were taking out for medicinal purposes. These could not be thrown across with the other parcels, but would have to be carried on their persons as they wriggled through the barbed wires across the *drift* of the Aapies River.

In some districts, where the destruction of farms had not yet been completed, the commando found a sufficient supply of fresh fruit and vegetables and were in no immediate danger of the dread disease, but in the neighbourhood of the towns there was nothing more to be done in the way of devastation, and the only fresh food they got was what they took from the enemy. As an instance of the thoroughness of the system of destruction, Naudé related how he and his corps of hungry men had one day come upon a *kraal* containing the bodies of over 500 sheep in an advanced stage of decomposition, with their throats cut or their heads cleft in two by swords. Too far away from towns or camps to be driven to some place where they could have been kept for the use of starving and suffering humanity, they had been slaughtered and left to rot—anything to prevent their falling into the hands of the Boer commandos.

No provisions of any sort were left within their reach and they lived entirely on what they took by main force from the enemy.

A precarious existence indeed!

Not to know from day to day where the next meal would come from and with appetites sharpened by the healthy, roving, outdoor life they led, no wonder these men uttered imprecations on the heads of those responsible for the systematic devastation of the country and wholesale destruction of food.

The privilege too of stripping their prisoners of their clothes had its disadvantages, for in many cases they swarmed with vermin and had to be boiled before they could be used, while a camp deserted by the English had to be approached warily and with the utmost caution on account of the vermin with which it frequently was infested.

English prisoners were set free (what could the Boers do with them otherwise?), but the traitors caught with them red-handed were shot without mercy—and it was Naudé's duty, as captain of the Secret Service, to see that these executions were carried out. This was to him the hardest task of all.

"His fallen brothers" he called them, and voice and eye when he spoke of them betrayed compassionate horror and wrath unspeakable.

Armed natives met the same fate, and in a few words he described to his shuddering listeners how it was done, how he informed the doomed man of his fate, how the prisoner pleaded for mercy and offered to join the Boer ranks, how he prayed in despair when he found no mercy, no relenting, how he covered his face or folded his arms, how the shots rang out and he fell down dead.

Scenes such as these were witnessed without number, but the execution of a "fallen brother," when the details were arranged, took place some distance apart, beyond the vision of the burghers who had captured him.

But it was when the subject of the concentration camps was broached that the darkest gloom settled over Harmony.

Captain Naudé had a young wife and two children in one of the camps in Natal, and Mrs. Malan had procured, as a surprise for him, snapshots of his dear ones taken in the camp. When they were placed in his hands he gazed on them for a long time in silence, finally muttering under his breath, "For this the English must die!" and from that moment he was moody and silent.

His thirst for information on the condition of the Irene Camp, as Hansie had found it, was insatiable, and hours were spent in discussing the subject and its probable effect on the duration of the war.

"What do the men think of the concentration camps?" Hansie asked. "Will they give in for the sake of the women and children?"

"No," was the emphatic answer—"never. We all feel that our first duty is to fight until our independence is assured. *We* are not responsible for the fate of our women and children, and they let no opportunity pass of urging us to be brave and steadfast in the fulfilment of our duty to our country. Our spies come from the camps continually with messages of encouragement and hope; but that the mortality among them is more bitter to bear than anything else, you can understand—"

There was a long pause, and then, the captain continued gloomily:

"I did not recognise my wife on that photo—she has become an old, old woman.... Sometimes on commando we actually enjoy ourselves. You must not think that it is all hardship and trouble! I gave a concert, quite a good one, on the president's birthday, and occasionally, when we come to a farm where there are still some girls left, we take them out riding and driving."

Chapter 36

A Silent Departure. "Fare Thee Well"

As the afternoon wore on, an extreme nervousness came over all at Harmony, a feeling of tense anxiety which no words can describe, and was betrayed in a restless flitting through the house, arranging something here, peering through the blinds at the camp of the Military Mounted Police.

Unconsciously voices were lowered and final instructions given in hushed tones.

Only a few hours remained of the captain's visit to Harmony and much had still to be arranged.

The tension was broken by the arrival of Mrs. Malan, with large parcels containing the articles of clothing, etc., ordered by Naudé—hats, boots, riding-suits, soap, matches, salt, and a number of the small necessities of life. This gave the women something to do, for everything had to be sorted and made up into smaller parcels as compactly as possible, while Naudé donned a surprising quantity of clothing and disposed of various articles about his person.

In the excitement of the moment Captain Naudé, while he was dressing, must have forgotten to take off a waistcoat lent to him by Mrs. van Warmelo and clearly marked D.S. van Warmelo.

This caused her a great deal of anxiety for some days after the departure of the spies.

Had Naudé reached the commandos in safety or had he fallen into the hands of the enemy with the tell-tale waistcoat on?

They wondered and speculated, but as the days went by and no startling reports convulsed the town, they once again settled down—not to the same old sense of security as far as they were personally concerned, but to the comforting conviction that all was well with their friends.

Their own fate—but this is coming presently.

Mrs. Malan did not stay long, and there were fortunately no unexpected visitors that afternoon—except, strange to say, the English colonel who had all but ceased his visits and was on this occasion entertained by Hansie and her mother in turn.

His presence gave a great sense of security!

Hansie walked with Mrs. Malan to the gate, where her carriage was waiting for her, and the sergeant-major, slowly sauntering past and saluting to the girl as she gave the coachman her directions, little knew that the words spoken in Dutch were:

"You must be here at 7 tonight, and bring your residential pass without fail."

Van der Westhuizen, with the bandaged arm, was going to help to carry their parcels through the bush and escort the three men through the most dangerous parts of the town.

When all the preparations were complete there was an hour or two to spare before the other men, under cover of darkness, should join Naudé near the six willow trees at the foot of the orchard. That time was spent in making plans for the future.

"Promise me that you will never take in strange men," Naudé said earnestly. "Do not even harbour any one who professes to come from me unless he gives a watchword. What shall our watchword be?"

They thought for a few moments, and then Mrs. van Warmelo said:

"'*Appelkoos*' (apricots), because you came to us in the apricot season!"

"So be it." This was agreed upon.

"And if anything should happen to us before you come again?" Hansie inquired. "By what sign will you know that we have been taken and that Harmony is a pitfall instead of a refuge?"

Again they pondered. This was indeed a serious problem, for in the event of an arrest they would not be allowed to see or communicate with any of their friends, and there would be no possible chance of sending out a warning.

After a great deal of discussion it was decided that they should use one of the posts of the enclosure dividing the upper part of Harmony, where the orchard was, from the lower, on which the vegetable gardens of the Italians were.

On one of the posts they would, if they had time to do so, fasten a small piece of plank, and this would serve as a warning to the men not to approach the house.

In case the enemy was not considerate enough to give them time to put up signs and signals, it was agreed to have this done at dead of night by one of the few remaining men in town, van der Westhuizen for instance, at the first news of their arrest.

This arrangement eased their minds of some anxiety, and the rest of the time was spent in quietly chatting about other matters.

"I suppose you cannot let my wife know that I have been here and am well?" Naudé asked.

"I am afraid not," Mrs. van Warmelo answered thoughtfully. "We know no one in the camp in which she is, and her correspondence will no doubt be closely watched, but we could write an ordinary, cheerful letter, urging her to be hopeful and strong."

"Thank you very much," he answered gratefully, "but do not use your own names on any account. Get other people to write, people less implicated than yourselves."

Towards 7 o'clock Hansie walked slowly down to the willows, the faithful Carlo by her side, wistfully looking into her face. Did he feel the suppressed agitation, the unrest in the air?

I do believe Carlo knew and felt every changing emotion in his young mistress, and sympathised or rejoiced accordingly.

There was no one in the garden.

Hansie waited ten minutes, twenty, half an hour, then she went back to the house.

There the form of the tall young man in his English officer's uniform, from which the traces of blood had been removed as well as possible, was to be seen walking to and fro in restless nervousness.

"Have the others not come yet?" he exclaimed impatiently. "Where can they be so late?"

"I think it is too light still for them to be abroad," Hansie answered; "you should have made the appointment for 8 o'clock."

"But then the moon will be up," he objected. "I hope they will be here soon."

Hansie once more walked to the six willows, and the next half-hour was spent in a restless pacing up and down between the orange trees of the avenue.

"Will they never come? Have they fallen into some unforeseen pitfall?

"At this, the most critical moment of our whole adventure, when all arrangements seem to have come to a smooth and successful termination, must our plans be frustrated, and a bloody encounter be the climax?"

Hansie walked boldly towards the Military Camp, whistling to Carlo and admonishing him thus audibly:

"Why can't you leave the kittens alone, Carlo?" Then more softly: "A peaceful serenity pervades the camp. Evidently nothing brewing here!"

With a lighter heart she went back to the house, but one glance at the face of the captain was enough, and once more she sped down the garden-path to the ill-fated trysting-place.

As she neared the spot she heard no sound of life and her heart once more sank, but only for a moment. Suddenly she started violently. "What is this?"

The place seemed in a moment alive with silent figures. From the depths of the overhanging willow branches they emerged, one by one, and approached the tense form of the girl as she stood immovable, with straining eyes trying to distinguish the moving, silent figures in the darkness.

The white dress of a woman fluttering among the leaves reassured her.

"What is this?" she whispered. "Who are you? Why are you here?"

One of the men came forward.

"Venter and Brenckmann," he said softly, "come for the captain."

"Yes, yes," Hansie said hurriedly. "I know. We have waited for you more than an hour. But these people? Who are they?"

"Our friends and relatives come to see us off," came the unexpected reply.

Hansie was silent, trying to hide her indignation, her rising resentment, as another and yet another form cautiously emerged from behind the foliage.

"Do you know," she said at last, "that you are not only exposing us to great danger by coming here at a time like this, but that you are making it a thousand times more difficult for the captain to depart unobserved? How could you be so indiscreet?"

"These people are all trustworthy," one of the men volunteered.

"I have no doubt of it." Hansie extended her hands cordially to them. "But you must all go now as quietly as you came. Say goodbye and go, please, before I go to call the captain."

She turned away with a lump in her throat, for no sounds broke the stillness of the night save those of stifled sobs and murmured caresses.

"Fare thee well. God be with you!"

There was Brenckmann with his three sisters, there was Venter with one sister and a sweetheart, and there was the sweetheart of one of Brenckmann's sisters, to say nothing of the other relatives and friends whom I have been unable to place.

Some distance from the scene, and unobserved by all save one, was the figure of the ever-cautious and discreet van der Westhuizen, guarding the parcels which had previously been conveyed there, lurking among the trees.

Swiftly and silently Hansie sped up to the house to meet the captain, just as he, unable to bear the suspense any longer, had made up his mind to set out on his perilous expedition alone and was cautiously emerging from the bath-room door, concealing himself under the vineyard as he went.

"They are there, captain," she said in a quick and lowered voice, "waiting for you under the willows. Lower down near the bush van der Westhuizen is also waiting. He will distribute the parcels when you come. I think everything is in order and the coast clear. The military camp is quiet, the sergeant-major is in his 'tin villa.' Goodbye, captain. God bless you."

The man removed his helmet and stood before her in the pale light of the rising moon. His face was very white.

"I shall never be able to thank you. God keep you. Goodbye, goodbye." He clasped her hand and was gone, as silent as the shadows into which he disappeared.

When Hansie rejoined her mother a few minutes later no word was said on either side. The extreme tension was over, the reaction had set in, and they could not trust themselves to speak, but set to work at once, firmly and decently removing every trace in the house of confusion and disorder.

In the room vacated by Captain Naudé they found the snapshots of his wife and children taken in the concentration camp.

Mrs. van Warmelo held them up to her daughter's view with a significant look.

"I am not surprised that he would not take them with him," she said.

Chapter 37

Betrayed

Hansie was one of those unfortunate women who cannot cry, but I believe she cried that night when the awful strain was over, the house quiet and deserted, and the feeling of "nothing to do but wait" creeping over her.

She and her mother lay for hours listening for sounds of commotion in the suburb, following in spirit the brave men on their route to the free *veld*, so perilous and insecure, watching and praying for their safety.

At last Hansie fell into a heavy, unrefreshing sleep, from which she was roused in the early dawn by her mother's voice, hurried and extremely agitated.

"Hansie, Hansie, come here quick!"

"Where, mother? Where are you?"

"In the dining-room! Come at once, come and look!"

Hansie sprang out of bed, alarmed and now thoroughly roused, and ran into the dining-room, where she found her mother concealing herself behind the lace curtains and cautiously looking out of the window to the Military Camp.

She half turned as her daughter approached and said in a whisper: "Don't show yourself. Look, Hansie, we have been betrayed. Our house is suspected. See how it is being watched."

Hansie looked and looked again. There was no doubt of it.

The sergeant was in excited conversation with a man on horseback, well known to Hansie by sight as a detective in plain clothes. Here and there the soldiers were grouped around other private detectives, on horseback and on foot, talking and gesticulating and pointing to the house in wild excitement. What struck Hansie as almost ludicrous, even at that moment, was the *unbounded astonishment* betrayed by them.

Their looks and gestures spoke as plainly as the plainest words: "Can it be possible? Has that been going on under our noses? And pray, how long?"

"There is no doubt about it. We and our house have been betrayed. But cheer up, mother; forewarned is forearmed. Oh, silly fools, to give away their game like that!"

"They have not seen us yet, Hansie. They think we are asleep."

"Even so, the servants are about. Oh, mother!"

"Go and get dressed, Hansie, and let us behave exactly the same as usual. All we can do now is to see that we do not betray that we *know* we have been betrayed. How do you think this has come about?"

"The crowd under the willows last night?"

"Gentleman Jim?"

"Flippie?"

They looked at one another inquiringly and slowly shook their heads.

Good reader, after more than ten years, when they talk about this period of their lives, they still look inquiringly at one another and slowly shake their heads.

Who could it have been? How did it come about?

✶✶✶✶✶✶

When Hansie went out into the garden an hour or so later to gather roses for the table, Harmony was flooded with the exquisite morning sun, the birds were twittering and bickering among themselves, and Carlo sprang up to meet her, barking an affectionate "good morning," as he playfully capered round his mistress.

As she stooped down to pat him she glanced through her hair to the camp, where some of the men were bending over their camp-fires and others were rubbing down and feeding their horses.

Will you believe it? At the first sight of the girl every man dropped his work, stood up straight and stared at her in open-mouthed astonishment as if he had never seen her before. They even got together again in little groups of twos and threes and began talking rapidly to one another. Their amazement, their consternation was so obvious that Hansie found it difficult to pretend that she saw nothing unusual in their behaviour, and when she joined her mother at the breakfast-table and told her what a commotion her appearance had created, Mrs. van Warmelo said: "It is the same with me. Wherever I show myself under the verandahs or in the garden, I am met with stares that can only be described as thunderstruck."

"And that, after all the months they have spent within earshot of all that went on at Harmony! Why, mother, those men have never lifted their heads when we have passed them for a year and more, they had got so used to us, but now——!"

She went on more seriously:

"We can never be thankful enough that you found this out in time. The members of the committee must be warned not to come to Harmony, but we must invite lots of other people. Let us give a few fruit parties and musical evenings for the young people, and above all, let us invite the consuls and their families." Hansie was feeling hopeful, buoyed up by the unlooked-for privilege of having been put on her guard, but Mrs. van Warmelo was silent and depressed.

"I am thinking about the spies," she said at last. "How can we ever harbour them here again? How can we let them know that Harmony is being watched? How shall we get through the anxiety and suspense when we begin to expect them again? Naudé's last words to me were, 'We shall be with you four weeks from now, when the moon is young again.'"

Hansie looked thoughtful, but brightened up again immediately.

"We have always the sign on the gatepost to fall back on, you know, mother dear, but I hope it won't be necessary to put that up. In the meantime let us watch developments. We have nothing to be anxious about *yet*, and when the time comes we shall know what to do. Just think how terrible it would have been if this had happened yesterday while Naudé was in the house!"

But poor Mrs. van Warmelo could not shake off her gloom, and Hansie, who, strange to say, was usually most hopeful and strong in the presence of depressed folk, but pessimistic and downhearted when others were most bright, sighed for once and allowed herself to be cast down by her mother's forebodings.

They realised that an anxious time was before them, their worst fear being that Naudé and his companions had been captured the previous night and that some time would probably elapse before they knew with any certainty what his fate had been.

That they were safe in his hands they never doubted for a moment, but there were too many others, practically unknown to them, concerned in this enterprise, and every conspirator more added to the list made their own position less secure.

"I think I must go to Mrs. Joubert this afternoon, mother, to see if

I can get hold of van der Westhuizen. Perhaps he can throw some light on the subject. At any rate he will be able to tell us whether he parted from Naudé under favourable conditions last night."

"Do that," Mrs. van Warmelo answered, "if you can make sure beforehand of not being watched. Don't go to that house if you have any reason to think you are being followed. We are on the black list now, but that makes it all the more necessary for us to protect our friends."

"Yes, mother; but the Jouberts have been under suspicion so long and have so successfully escaped detection that I am sure their names have long since been removed from the black list."

"Don't be too sure. Jannie's transportation was not a sign of the cessation of hostilities. The enemy is not asleep, but merely slumbering, as far as they are concerned—that is, if this thing" (waving her hand over Harmony) "has not roused him completely."

All day long, and in fact for many days after, an unusual commotion was apparent in the Military Camp.

Detectives could be seen coming and going, little groups of soldiers clustered together, and even "Judas-Boers" made their appearance on the lower portion of Harmony, examining the ground and following the tracks made by the spies in their escape from the town.

Beyond that the van Warmelos could not follow their investigations, and whether they found conclusive evidence in the marks made by the men at the closely barbed and netted drift, under the railway bridge, will never be known, but there was reason to believe that the last remaining route of the spies had been discovered. Brave hearts sank at the thought of their probable fate when they tried that route again.

But, thank God! the birds had flown—for the time at least.

That afternoon, when Hansie cycled to Mrs. Joubert's house, the streets were quiet and practically deserted. She was quite sure that no one followed her, for she dropped her handkerchief once and had suddenly to turn and pick it up.

Carlo was some way ahead of her and did not notice the interruption until she was on her bicycle again, when he came tearing back to find out what had happened, furious with himself for having missed the smallest piece of excitement. After that he did not leave her side again, but trotted quietly along, watching her every moment from the corner of his eye.

When Hansie entered the house in Visagie Street, Carlo stretched himself as usual beside her bicycle, ostensibly to sleep, but in reality on guard and alert with every nerve in his quick body. Hansie was thankful to find van der Westhuizen in; in fact, he was expecting her and wished to see her, but did not think it advisable to go to Harmony.

"Tell me all about last night," she said. "Tell me everything, and then I have something to tell you too."

"Well," he said, and the inscrutable face was for once turned to her in frank confidence, "after we left Harmony last night things did not go as smoothly as we expected. It was all right as long as we were in the bush, and we were able to get our heavy parcels through safely, but when we came to the drift we found it strongly guarded. We retreated at once without a sound and lay down in the thick shrubs to wait. The men were nervous and impatient, and after a little while Brenckmann borrowed my residential pass from me and walked on ahead to see if the coast were clear.

"He soon came back and said it was impossible to get through.

"After a short consultation, Naudé advised me to come home. They would stay in the bush and wait until the moon went down, he said. I hated leaving them in such a plight, but Naudé insisted, and I only came away when he said he thought there would be more chance for them to get through unobserved if they were fewer in number. How they managed without residential passes and handicapped by those parcels, I do not know."

"God only knows how they *do* manage," Hansie answered sombrely. "Well, I have nothing good to relate either."

She told him in a few words what had happened at Harmony, and the steadfast face opposite her, so calm and strong, grew more grave as she proceeded.

"This is very serious," he said at last; "then the fact of their being in town, and the route they had taken, must have been known to the enemy yesterday. That is why we found the drift guarded. But do not be downcast. I am sure they got through unharmed, for there has been no commotion of any sort in town. I always know when prisoners have been taken. We must be thankful they were not discovered in your house."

Hansie nodded, and the quiet voice went on:

"You are in no danger now———"

But the girl broke in impetuously:

"Oh, that does not trouble me at all, but I would give my life to know that those men were with General Botha now. I am only anxious about them."

"I am not," he answered. "The captain is a man of vast experience. This was not his first visit to Pretoria. Venter has been five times in Pretoria and nine times in Johannesburg under the same conditions. Brenckmann, too, can speak of unique experiences—but I can bet you anything that *he* will never come in again."

"Why not?"

"Oh, he had an awful time here. There are khakis and handsuppers living all round his house, to some of whom he is well known by sight. It was found necessary to conceal him, and for three days and two nights the poor boy was stowed away in a tiny attic, just under the corrugated-iron roof and hardly large enough to hold a man. There he lay in the suffocating heat of those endless days, only coming out at night for a few hours like the bats and owls. No, he won't trouble us again!"

Before she left she told him what had been arranged about a sign on the gatepost and asked van der Westhuizen to warn her friends of the "inner circle" that Harmony was no longer a safe place to visit, begging them to keep this information to themselves, "because," she added, "the enemy must not know that we know." Later on she hoped to see him again when the time approached for Naudé to come again, but she advised him not to visit Harmony unnecessarily, as much would depend on him in the event of a raid on Harmony and the transportation of its inhabitants to other regions.

I can only say in conclusion of this chapter that the friends of the "inner circle," Mrs. Malan, Mrs. Joubert, Mrs. Armstrong, Mrs. Honey, and a few others, bravely scorned the idea of avoiding Harmony.

"Why should we not come?" Mrs. Armstrong asked, with her cheerful, ever-ready laugh; "don't other people come here still?"

"Oh yes, but——"

"Then why not we? The more the better, say I! Surely we cannot *all* be arrested and sent away!"

CHAPTER 38

The Raid on Harmony

It was the peacefullest, decentest raid I ever heard of, and it would be difficult to think of anything with a termination more tame and commonplace.

But we have not got there yet.

The events which led up to it must be got over first as briefly as possible, and then we go on to what was called a formal declaration of war between the inmates of the Military Camp and the two principal actors at Harmony.

After the van Warmelos had discovered on December 20th, through the enemy's rank stupidity, that they had been found out, a regular game of hide-and-seek began to be played in and around their beautiful garden.

The curious thing about this game was that it was only carried on under cover of darkness and intense silence, a silence which could almost be felt, and which became so uncanny as time went on that the women found it quite insupportable and had no peace by night or by day until the day on which, a month later, the enemy took the initiative and made what may be called an attack in front. There was only one noisy actor in the game, which was played for four solid weeks before the crash came, and as many after, and that was Carlo, but, although his feelings found relief in constant growlings and furious barkings, I do believe even his nerves suffered under the constant strain, for he became more and more irritable and restless as time went on.

That dog gave a lot of trouble in those days and was a source of great anxiety, as my reader will see presently.

The fruit season was at its height. The garden, heavily laden with the burden of luscious fruits and blooming flowers, was a scene of beauty and riotous luxury impossible to describe; and as the different fruit trees bloomed and bore their rich harvest in rapid succession, each after its kind—apricots, figs, pears, plums, apples, peaches, and, last but not least, the noble vine with its great bunches of purple and white—Hansie and her mother revelled in the wealth of Nature's extravagance from morn till eve.

Mrs. van Warmelo, an energetic and tireless gardener, spent all her time amongst the fruit, while indoors the task of putting up in jars for winter use fell mainly on Hansie's shoulders.

Nothing was allowed to run to waste, and that year was always remembered as an exceptionally fine fruit season.

It was nothing for Mrs. van Warmelo to have 100 lb. of grapes cut before breakfast and have them conveyed to the early market, and even then the vines bore no trace of having been robbed or tampered with.

The soldiers, too, got their share, and the sergeant-major's small basket was often filled—for were they not on the best of terms with one another?

But when the shades of night fell over the land, and silence settled on the birds and beasts and flowers, the sense of careless freedom and security deserted our heroines entirely.

Unseen eyes watched them from behind the leaves, and they knew that the very trees under which they sat had ears, straining to catch up their every conversation.

The Military Police—unknown to the women, as they thought—were guarding them and their property from intruders, and this was known by Carlo's incessant growlings and his furious, sudden fits of barking whenever he came upon some midnight prowler hidden under the trees.

I am sure the good dog never understood Hansie's apathy on this point.

After all he did to warn her of foul play, to have his efforts rewarded with a scolding or a careless "Do be quiet, Carlo. The kitty is only catching moths," seemed unjust and quite unlike his mistress's usual ready sympathy.

In time he got used to finding strangers in the privacy of his domain and only showed his dissatisfaction with an occasional low growl or a vicious snarl.

Perhaps "Gentleman Jim" was not so bad after all, or perhaps he was only stupid, because a few days after the flight of our friends he came to Mrs. van Warmelo with the information, given with an amused smile and more drawl than usual, that "the officer had promised him plenty money" if he ever caught a Boer on the premises or in the garden, and that in future a strict watch would be held over the property and an extra vigilance preserved whenever the dog barked.

What more proof could be wanted after that? Now they knew exactly how the land lay, and in their hearts they thanked their simple servant and still more simple foe, for the confirmation of their suspicions.

As the weeks went by and the time for the captain's next visit drew near, Mrs. van Warmelo again and again urged the necessity of putting up the danger-signal (a small block of wood, which was kept ready with a nail through it, lying hidden behind the post), only to be met with an obstinate refusal from her daughter.

"How can you be so reckless and foolhardy, Hansie?" her mother would exclaim. "We know that the men may come in any night, and we know that the house and grounds are being watched, and yet you want me to let our friends run right into the trap, without lifting a finger to save them! It would be an unpardonable thing, and I do believe you are only longing to have the excitement of harbouring spies again!"

Hansie laughed.

"Perhaps that is it! But think of the disappointment of the men to be turned back at our very doors after having come so far through untold dangers! Depend upon it they will not come in again for nothing. They went through too much last time, and there will be work of some importance for us all to do if they come in again, you may be sure of that. No, dear mother, let us risk it, I beg of you. We are still in the house, and Naudé is no chicken. He will reach us in spite of guards and fences, and———"

"Be followed right up to the house and be taken here like a rat in a trap," Mrs. van Warmelo continued gloomily.

"I am not so sure," Hansie exclaimed, as cheerfully as her sinking heart allowed, when this horrible picture rose before her.

"You know what our experience has been of English vigilance and English sagacity; now, if they had some of Carlo's intelligence we would have some reason to be anxious."

The danger-signal was not put up, but that things would have ended exactly as Mrs. van Warmelo predicted I now have not a shadow of doubt.

The spies would have glided into the house in the false security occasioned by the absence of the danger-signal, they would have been watched and followed to the very doors by the hidden foe, the house would have been surrounded and stormed by armed men, and a fierce, an unspeakably horrible encounter would have ended in death and destruction—*if they had come*. But they were prevented on commando from keeping their appointment that month—and at the very time when they expected to be safely housed under Harmony's hospitable roof, the place was surrounded, an entry forced and every corner of the house searched for spies.

It happened "like so," and we must now turn our attention for a moment to a matter of small importance in order to understand why Hansie was from home at a critical time, and how she missed the keen enjoyment of being present at the "raid."

For some weeks the advisability of leaving home on a pleasure trip had been discussed. While the moon was on the wane their friends from commando would not be likely to pay them a visit, but Mrs. van Warmelo, who never had much inclination to leave her little paradise, persuaded Hansie to go to Johannesburg for a few days alone to a dear young friend, newly wed, who had repeatedly begged her to come.

They hoped that such an attitude of innocent pleasure-making on their part would avert some of the suspicion which rested on their heads and cause a part, at least, of the surveillance to be withdrawn from Harmony.

Hansie hoped to be back home before the appearance of the new moon, the time appointed for Naudé's next visit, and it was red-tape, nothing but red-tape, through which she was undone.

So many difficulties were placed in the way of her obtaining the necessary permits that by the time she got away she should have been on her return journey.

Let us see what her diary says.

January 10th, Friday.
My poor old diary! I begin to foresee that it is going to die a natural death, simply because I am tired of recording lies and rumours (this was the black-and-white diary, kept on purpose to mislead the enemy, should it fall into their hands).
I am now busy preparing for a little trip to Johannesburg, but oh dear! the difficulty one has in getting permits!
The English have never been so strict before!

Major Hoskins (who could have helped me without further reference had he wished) sent me to the Commissioner of Police, who asked me to produce a note of recommendation from my 'ward officer' in B. Ward.

My 'ward officer' refused to give me a permit without a medical certificate that I required a change of air.

I told him shortly that I was going for pleasure and that I would appeal to General Maxwell if he could not assist me. He said 'that made all the difference!' (what did he mean?) and asked me for the name and address of the people with whom I would be staying in Johannesburg, so I gave him Pauline's box number.

No, that was not sufficient, he must have the name of the street and the number of the house.

'I do not remember the number, but I shall go home to look it up and come back at once.'

'It will—er—be more convenient if you bring it tomorrow,' he said.

And Hansie understood that he was gaining time.

After all the fuss that had been made, she was not surprised next day when the Commissioner of Police asked her, very politely, while closely inspecting the "note of recommendation," to call for her permits on Monday (this was Thursday), as there would be some delay in having them "approved" by the other officials.

This was again done to gain time while the authorities were putting their heads together, trying to find out "what the dickens" she could want in Johannesburg.

Hansie knew this well enough, although she filled her diary with lamentations and wonderings.

"Will you be all right alone, mother, at a time like this?" Hansie asked, as, with her permits at last in her possession, she hugged her mother in affectionate farewell.

"Oh yes, I am well guarded, as you know," Mrs. van Warmelo answered, laughing; "there is plenty of time, and you will be back before anything can happen."

Hansie looked doubtful. Was her mother play-acting? Did she mind being left, and was she only eager to have her daughter out of danger's way? Or did she intend putting up the danger-signal, after all?

You see, Hansie was getting so used to plotting and scheming that she could not help turning her newly acquired detective propensities on her nearest and dearest when occasion offered, and she even misdoubted the behaviour of her mother, tried as she had been, and never found wanting, in many a crisis in the past.

"You will wire for me, won't you?" she asked suspiciously.

"Of course, of course—but there will be nothing to wire about, I am quite sure."

With a sigh and many anxious forebodings, Hansie drove to the station on her way to her "pleasure trip."

She was met in the Golden City, now more like a Dead City, by loving friends and a magnificent St. Bernard dog, Nero, who soon made her feel at home, although they could not altogether banish the cares, dimly guessed at by them, with which she was oppressed.

The most reassuring news from home continued to reach her until one morning, on the sixth day after her arrival, a brief postcard from her mother informed her in a few bald words that Harmony had been searched on "Sunday morning the 19th inst."

A few hours later Hansie was in the train, speeding, with remorse tugging at her heart, to her mother's side.

It was something of a disappointment to her, on arriving at Harmony, to find everything exactly as she had left it.

Carlo greeted her with his old extravagant demonstrations of affection and delight, and when she looked searchingly into her mother's face she was met with a beaming smile. There was no trace of the ordeal she had faced alone, and Hansie's anxious heart gave a throb of relief.

She was soon in full possession of the details of the adventure, and it appeared that the "raid" had been made in the early hours of the 19th (Jan.), Sunday morning.

It had been raining heavily all night, and the torrents were still coming down drenchingly when Mrs. van Warmelo was aroused by a knock at her bedroom window and "Gentleman Jim's" voice, with all the drawl gone, calling out anxiously, "Missis, come, the police want you!"

Mrs. van Warmelo dressed hurriedly, and on opening the front door was met by an officer, who informed her that he had been ordered by the Commissioner of Police to search her house.

Armed soldiers were standing about, guarding the different entrances.

Mrs. van Warmelo led the way, and the officer went through the house with her alone, glancing under beds, opening wardrobes and moving screens in his search "for men," as he said in reply to her questions.

"I am surprised that you should have been sent to search my house for *men*," she said, with righteous indignation.

"I was surprised to see *your* name on the black list, Mrs. van Warmelo," he answered.

She watched him in puzzled silence.

Evidently he knew her, or her name. Quite evidently he was no Englishman—only a South African could pronounce her name like that.

When they reached the passage leading to the kitchen the officer suddenly started at the sight of Flippie's form lying curled up in deep sleep. He bent over him, pulled his blanket down cautiously, and said below his breath, "Oh, a boy!"

The house having been thoroughly searched, he turned to Mrs. van Warmelo and, courteously thanking her for having allowed him to do so, asked permission to go through the out-buildings, which was instantly granted. There was no one, of course, and the military, if they had expected to make any sensational discoveries that morning, were grievously disappointed.

******

"Well, I am glad it is over, mamma," Hansie said when the story came to an end.

"It is better to have the house searched *in vain*, than not to have it searched at all, when one is on the black list. Perhaps the surveillance on Harmony will now be removed, at least to some extent, and the danger to Captain Naudé, when he comes in again, considerably lessened."

That this was the case we shall see in our next chapter.

Chapter 3

The Watchword

Three weeks went uneventfully by.

Visitors at Harmony were few and far between, for the story of the "raid" went quickly through the town, and many people who had been in the habit of visiting the van Warmelos, all unsuspecting of the cloud under which they rested, took alarm at this first open hint of danger and discreetly withdrew from the scene.

When Hansie thought of them it was with some contempt and bitterness, but her mind was, at the time, occupied with more important matters, and her fair-weather friends soon passed from her life, never to return again.

Only about a dozen remained, mostly women, friends staunch and true, upon whom one could depend through days of the most crushing adversity.

How close we came to one another in those days only those who have been through similar experiences can ever realise.

Those three uneventful weeks were by no means the least trying of the long war. Sorely tested nervous systems were giving way, fine constitutions were being broken down, and powers of resistance had reached their limit. It needed but the acute nxiety and intense strain of the last adventure which I am about to relate, to reduce our heroines to a state bordering on the hysterical.

The phases of the moon were watched in suspense, and when the time drew near for the next visit from the spies, Mrs. van Warmelo took the precaution of locking Carlo up in the kitchen before retiring for the night. Although she let him out very early every morning in order not to arouse the suspicions of the servants, "Gentleman Jim," ever on the alert, soon found out that something unusual was taking place.

"Why you lock up the dog every night, missis?" he inquired one morning.

Mrs. van Warmelo was completely taken by surprise, but answered with great presence of mind:

"Oh, because he barks so much that we cannot sleep. But I think I will have to let him out again, because thieves will help themselves to the fruit if there is no watch-dog about."

The ruse had been found out and Carlo had to be released, although his vigilance added greatly to the dangers of the situation.

The grapes were ripe, great luxurious bunches of purple and golden fruit were weighing down the sturdy old vines.

"I wish Captain Naudé would come," Hansie sighed. "Harmony is at its very best."

"He won't come again, I am convinced of that," her mother answered mournfully. "No more news from the field for us. The dangers are too great, and nothing could be gained by coming into town now that our friends have nearly all been sent away."

"We shall see," Hansie said cheerfully. "I have a strong presentiment that the men are coming in this very night. I am going to put everything in readiness for them, and we must go to bed early, dear mother. Perhaps we shall have very little rest tonight."

This was Sunday night, February 9th.

Hansie packed away various little articles lying about the bedrooms and bathroom, and generally prepared herself for the midnight adventure which she felt more than ever convinced would take place within a few hours, while Mrs. van Warmelo went about with a feather and an oil-can, oiling the hinges and locks.

She was soon sound asleep in her mother's bedroom, for the two women were not as brave as they had been during the first part of the war and had got into the habit of sleeping together "for company."

Suddenly at about 2 a.m. they both started up violently, at the sound of Carlo's furious barking near their window, where he usually kept guard.

Mrs. van Warmelo sat up and panted "Here they are," but Hansie's heart was beating so loudly in her throat that she was unable to reply.

Mrs. van Warmelo went quickly to the window, and on cautiously raising the blind saw the forms of two men close to the window, undistinguishable in the darkness but quite evidently the cause of Carlo's startled and furious barkings. She ran through the bathroom and, opening the door leading to the garden, asked softly, "Who is there?"

"*Appelkoos*," the welcome answer came clearly and cautiously, and Mrs. van Warmelo drew the men unceremoniously into the room, noiselessly locking the door.

"Not a word, not a sound," she commanded, "remove your boots—you have never been in greater peril."

"Hush! What was that? A man's voice outside! The sergeant-major? The police? My God! then we are lost indeed!"

But no! Only one moment of agonising suspense and the familiar voice of "Gentleman Jim" could be heard, reprimanding the growling watchdog.

"What for you make so much noise, Carlo? Go to sleep, bad dog—you frighten everybody when you kick up so much row."

Muttering discontentedly, he retired to his room, evidently reassured by the dead silence which pervaded the house.

For some time the four people inside stood close together without a word. No lights were lit, no sound whatever made until Carlo's restless growlings ceased and he had settled himself to sleep again.

Then only were a few whispered words of welcome and greeting exchanged and a breathless account given of the dangers with which Harmony was surrounded.

"How did you come in?" Mrs. van Warmelo asked.

"Through the *drift*," Naudé replied. "There were no guards—in fact, we did not see a soul from first to last, and the dog was the only one to object to our midnight wanderings. We were nearly on top of him before he woke."

Nearly on top of the sensitive and alert watchdog before he became aware of their proximity! No wonder, then, that the Boer spies frequently glided up so close to the English outposts that they were able to knock them down with a wooden stick or the butt end of a gun before they could give the alarm or utter a sound!

The men were tired and exhausted, and gladly stretched themselves on the beds to get what sleep they could before morning, having first divested themselves of their outward trappings, helmets, etc., which they buried under the floor. As before, the captain came in a khaki uniform, while his orderly, Venter, was dressed like a soldier.

As it was necessary for them to remain in Mrs. van Warmelo's bedroom in order to be near their place of refuge under the floor, mother and daughter retired to the dining-room, there to watch and wait for the dawn of day.

Would the long night *never* end?

Every time Carlo barked the two women started up from their couches and listened with straining ears for sounds of commotion outside—but in vain. Nothing disturbed the serenity of the night, and when the rosy glow of dawn broke in the eastern sky and gradually spread its glory over the hushed and expectant earth, Hansie fell into a fitful slumber.

Not so her mother. Mrs. van Warmelo had been quietly pondering over "Gentleman Jim's" unexpected appearance at the first sign of commotion in the night and had come to the conclusion that something should be done to disarm his suspicions.

That the guard of Military Police had been withdrawn from Harmony was very evident, but it was quite possible that the task of maintaining a vigilant watch had been transferred to Jim, with promises of a liberal payment if he succeeded in getting information which might lead to the arrest of Boer spies.

Mrs. van Warmelo therefore cautiously rose, while the rest of the household lay in sleep, plucked clusters of grapes from the vines and strewed them about the garden paths. The ruse answered excellently.

"Gentleman Jim" himself discovered the grapes lying about the garden and was loud in his expressions of indignation.

"Them thieves have been at the grapes again," he called out.

"Look here, missis, here is a bunch—and another, and here is some more." He shook his head in despair.

The sergeant-major too was sent for and informed of the plundering that had been carried on in the small hours of the morning.

"What is to be done?" he asked. "Shall I put a guard here again?"

Mrs. van Warmelo thanked him for his kind offer, but thought that very little damage had been done, and was of opinion that Carlo's vigilance would be sufficient to prevent the thieves, whoever they might be, from returning on a second pilfering expedition.

When Hansie woke it was past six o'clock, and the captain was sitting near her, drinking coffee and chatting with her mother in a matter-of-fact way, evidently quite at home and glad to find himself in such comfortable quarters again.

The whole of that eventful February 10th was spent in writing dispatches and procuring articles of clothing and small necessaries for the men to take out with them; three pairs of riding-breeches, shirts, brown felt hats, leggings, boots, soap, salt, cotton, etc., etc.

Fortunately, among the few remaining men in town who could be trusted to carry out these commissions was the young man behind the counter in *the* store in Church Street.

To him Hansie went with a small list, which she laid before him without a word.

He glanced over it and whistled softly.

"Leggings? Riding-breeches? When must you have them?"

"If possible this evening," she replied.

"I'll do my best," he said, and she departed joyfully.

"Now, I could never have got those things myself without rousing great suspicion," she thought as she cycled rapidly to the next person whom she had been instructed to see—van der Westhuizen with the bandaged arm.

"The captain came last night with Venter," she whispered hurriedly. "They are at Harmony, and Naudé wishes to see you as soon as possible on a matter of great importance. No one must know of his presence in town this time, not even our best friends, for he has a dangerous mission to fulfil and you must help him."

"I shall be there some time today," he said.

Hansie thanked him and departed.

Much writing work waited her at Harmony, and the rest of the day was spent in drawing up dispatches at the captain's dictation and making notes of the condition of the various commandos.

In the course of a long conversation with him he told her the object of his visit and why he required van der Westhuizen's services.

"My flying column of scouts is over sixty strong, picked men and wonderfully brave," he said. "They are all in khaki and scour the country, doing the enemy incalculable harm, but they would be of more service to the commandos if they had better horses. Our horses are worn-out and underfed, their life is very hard, and it is imperative that we should have them reinforced. Now, we have heard that there are many magnificent horses kept at Skinner's Court, remounts kept in good condition for the special use of officers. Those horses we must have, and we have come to get all the information we can about the strength of the guards at Skinner's Court. For this I require van der Westhuizen's assistance."

Hansie felt a thrill of excitement.

The adventure was very much to her taste, and she remembered with delight that first successful raid on British stables. She wished she could supply the desired information. To steal the enemy's best horses seemed to her an enterprise worth toiling for, for there would probably be little or no bloodshed connected with it and, if successful, the reward would be very great.

But she felt assured that the adventure could not be in more capable, more trustworthy hands than in those of the silent van der Westhuizen.

When van der Westhuizen arrived, he and the captain were closeted together in the bedroom for nearly an hour, and then he departed as silently as he had come, but Hansie had observed the look of steadfast determination on his face, and was satisfied.

Very unlike the previous visit was this, the last sojourn of the Secret Service men at Harmony.

There was no entertaining of shoals of trusted friends, no lying about under the trees, no sociable gathering of strawberries.

The men were not allowed to leave their bedroom during the day, but remained in safe proximity to the place of refuge under the floor, where their belongings lay buried.

Of the many plans devised by Mrs. van Warmelo for the safety of her guests, the following was decided upon as being the most ingenious:

A large bath was brought into her bedroom and half-filled with soapy water, bath-towels, sponges, and other toilet requisites being placed near by in readiness for use. In the event of a raid, Mrs. van Warmelo (if she had time to do so) would rush into the room, locking the door on the inside, while her daughter (if she had the presence of mind and kept cool enough) informed the police that her mother was having a bath. Thus time would be gained to enable the men to creep into their hiding-place.

The bath of soapy water, standing in readiness night and day, was a constant source of amusement during that time of suspense.

The men begged to be allowed to smoke, but Mrs. van Warmelo protested strongly. In case of an unexpected search, how was she going to account for the smell of smoke in her bedroom?

Seeing, however, that this restriction was becoming a source of great discomfort to them in the monotony of their imprisonment, she gave them permission to smoke in the dining-room while she and Hansie kept watch outside.

Even with these precautions Mrs. van Warmelo seemed to feel very uneasy, and Hansie coming into the kitchen unexpectedly one afternoon, found the captain standing beside the stove and blowing vigorous puffs of smoke up the chimney!

Volcanoes and earthquakes would have been a welcome change to everyone after those never-to-be-forgotten days of strain and tension; and much as Hansie had longed to see some one from commando again, her longing to see these men depart became a hundred times more intense. There was no pleasure for any one during that visit of two days, for the very air was charged with treachery, and not even the servants could be trusted with the dread secret.

The men were waited on stealthily, food was brought in unobserved and the plates and dishes washed surreptitiously by the two watchful women, who took turns in guarding the place and enjoyed what conversation they could get in fragments from their guests.

That night was spent in anxiety and unrest, and again the glorious day was hailed with joy and relief.

Van der Westhuizen was an early visitor that morning, and the report of his investigations of the past night must have been highly satisfactory to the men, to judge by their faces. The women were not taken into their confidence, but Hansie watched and wondered, and dared not even ask whether the attack on Skinner's Court was to be made or not.

It was better not to know.

The long summer's day went slowly by, broken only once when Hansie rushed into the bedroom with a breathless, "Danger, danger—hide yourselves!"

It was not at all funny at the time, but afterwards, when Hansie thought it over, she laughed and laughed again at the recollection of those two men, diving for the hole in the floor, and of their resentful looks when they emerged, on hearing that the alarm had been caused by the unexpected appearance of "Um-Ah."

The departure that night was in dead silence. There was no hearty "send-off" under the six willows, no escort through the bush, van der Westhuizen alone going on ahead to see if the coast were clear.

The events of that night are blurred and vague in the memory of the two solitary women, and Hansie's diary contains but meagre information on the subject—in fact, her war-diary practically ends here.

Frail womanhood had reached the breaking-point.

A period of dull suffering, of deadly indifference followed, broken one day by the news, with which the whole town rang, that Skinner's Court had been stormed by the Boers and that every horse had been taken, fourteen in all, valuable remounts of the officers.

Hansie just glanced at her mother and then asked hoarsely, "Was anyone hurt? Was anyone taken?"

"No," the answer came, with a curious look at her strained face; "the attack was so wholly unexpected, and the Boers so evidently informed of every detail of the place, that they were gone with all the horses almost before a shot could be fired."

This meant not only that the captain had reached his men in safety, but that the enterprising object of his visit had been successfully carried out, beyond his most sanguine expectations.

******

And now we take our leave of the brave captain whose name appears so often and so honourably in this book, and in leaving him, we quote, at his request, the tribute with which he closed his little book *In Doodsgevaar* (*In Danger of Death*)—published in August 1903—a tribute to the women who assisted him.

> I feel it my duty, before closing this story of our personal experiences of the war, to direct a word of thanks and appreciation to those faithful South African mothers and sisters who personally supported us during those difficult days and did what they could in Pretoria to further our cause in the field. But how can this be done? I have no adequate words at my command, and I feel that the work of these women is above all expression of appreciation.
>
> When I look back on those days, there floats across my mind not only the names, but also the personality of each of these worthy women, and I remember to the minutest detail their self-sacrifice and the zeal with which they stood by us during our visits to Pretoria, while exposed to the danger of themselves being plunged into the greatest difficulties. But for this they had no thought, no care, as long as the sacred cause could be advanced. I feel, however, that it would be out of place to mention the names of a few where so *many* risked their all, willingly offering even the sacrifice of their lives, if necessary, to further the interests of our cause.
>
> How fervently I should have wished to see their great work crowned with a well-deserved reward!
>
> He who rules the destinies of nations decreed it otherwise, however, and we must bow in resignation to His will, but, faithful women and girls of South Africa, rest assured that your noble work and self-sacrifice have not been in vain. For myself

I find in that which was performed by you this great abiding comfort, that so long as South Africa possesses women and girls of your stamp, so long can we go forward to meet the future hopefully and cheerfully; so long as the spirit, nourished by you, still lives and thrives in our midst, so long may we pursue our way fearlessly.

The struggle is over, brought to an end more than a year ago, and some of us have already learnt to adapt ourselves to our altered circumstances. We have been taught by those whose position, as leaders of the people, gives them the fullest right thereto, how to conduct ourselves, and we require no further encouragement to follow that advice.

But we feel that we cannot lay sufficient emphasis on the injunction to be true to one another as a nation, to be true to our traditions of the past, true to the lessons we have learnt in the recent conflict.

We have seen to what a pass one can be brought by infidelity.

Let us in future live in such a way that nothing may be lost of the honour which is our inheritance from the battlefields of South Africa.

   Farewell.

CHAPTER 40

Peace, Peace—and There is No Peace!

If I may dare to hope that there are, among my readers who have followed me with so much patience through this book, some sufficiently interested in the heroine to desire information on what befell her in her future lot, I should wish to give to them just a glimpse or two into scenes as totally different from the events recorded in this volume as night is from day. And to do this freely, unreservedly, I must endeavour to forget my close connection with the heroine, a connection the thought of which has hampered and restricted me, from first to last, in choosing and rewriting the material from her diary.

Her diary, as I have said before, had ended soon after her last adventure with the spies, never to be resumed again.

I do not, however, write from memory in this brief chapter on her subsequent experiences, for I have before me for reference a pile of letters from her to her mother.

Almost her last word when she left her native land was an injunction to her mother to preserve her letters for the future,—"for when I am married, mother dear, *you* will be my diary."

Hansie's health gave way.

Not in a week or a month, not in any way perceptible to those around her, but stealthily, treacherously, and relentlessly the fine constitution was undermined, the highly strung nervous system was shattered. This had taken place chiefly during the desolate and dark hours of the night, when, helpless in the grip of the fiend Insomnia, the wretched girl abandoned herself to hopelessness and despair.

And the time was soon to come when she feared those dreadful waking hours even less than the brief moments of fitful slumber which overcame her worn-out, shattered frame, for no sooner did she lose her consciousness in sleep than she was overpowered by some hideous nightmare, and found herself, shrieking, drowning in the black waters of some raging torrent, or pursued by some infuriated lunatic or murderer, or enveloped in the deadly coils of some hideous reptile.

Shuddering from head to foot after each of these most awful realities of the night, she was soothed and comforted by the tender hands of her distressed and anxious mother.

Something had to be done, of that there was no doubt. Not even the strongest mind could have endured such a strain for any length of time, and that Hansie's reason was preserved at all I put down to the fact that she had never once throughout the war entertained the idea, the possibility, of the loss of her country's independence.

The blow, when it came, found her so far from the scenes of her recent sufferings, as we shall see presently, that she was able to endure it, as one, far removed from the death-bed of her best beloved, is spared the crushing details, the cruel realities of that last parting scene.

The thought of the strong heart across the seas, waiting to receive her, would have been of more support to her in those days had she known by experience what it *could* mean to a woman, tried as she had been, to place herself and all her grief in the protecting, understanding love of a good and noble man.

But even this comfort was denied to her; in fact, the thought of her uncertain future, and her fear that the step she was about to take might prove to be a great mistake in her abnormal condition, were an added burden to our sorely tried and now completely broken-down patriot.

Plans were made to send her out of the country.

Her sister, Mrs. Cloete, who had for some months been trying to procure a permit to visit the Transvaal, was, after great trouble and inconvenience, successful in her endeavours and arrived at Harmony on Saturday, March 29th, 1902.

What words from my poor pen can describe the emotions of *that* meeting?

Even Hansie's diary has nothing to say except "let us draw the veil," but memory is strong and the bands of love and kinship are unbreakable, even under the adversities of long and bitter years—nay, rather are they strengthened by the threads of common woe, woven into their very fibre at such a time of bitter trial.

The mother spent hours with her elder daughter, happy beyond power to express, relating her experiences and adventures, comparing notes and making plans for their future.

All that month of April was filled with rumours of an early peace, and hopes were buoyed up with the certainty that "peace with honour" would and could be the only termination to the peace conferences. Incredible as it may seem to some of my readers, the Boer opinion was that England was about to end hostilities and that, under certain terms, the independence of the two Republics would be assured.

No reliable information reached our friends at Harmony, for the activities of the Secret Service had ceased entirely—at least, as far as the town was concerned.

Uncertainty, excitement, expectation filled the air, reaching their height on April 12th, when the news of the Boer leaders' arrival at the capital spread like wild-fire through the town.

Steyn, Botha, de Wet, de la Rey, Reitz, and a host of others were amongst "their own" again, under circumstances of unique importance. They were not allowed to mix freely with the crowd, but kept in a state of highly honoured captivity in the beautiful double-storied house known as "Parkzicht," opposite Burghers Park, well guarded night and day by armed patrols, who kept the crowd at bay with a friendly "Move on, please," when they touched the limit of their beat.

Mrs. van Warmelo and her two daughters, like so many other citizenesses, lost no opportunity of walking in the neighbourhood of "Parkzicht," and they were fortunate beyond their wildest hopes in being greeted by the generals on more than one occasion.

One day as they were passing they observed the familiar figure of General Botha on the balcony.

They waved their handkerchiefs and there was no doubt about his recognition, for he took off his hat and waved it, kissing both his hands to them.

(General Botha it was who, after the war, said to Mrs. van Warmelo, clasping her hand and looking earnestly into her eyes:

"You have done and risked what even I would not have dared.")

After six or seven days in Pretoria the Boer leaders left for their commandos, to deliberate, with what result Hansie did not know until nearly two months later in mid-ocean, where at a distant isle the news of the declaration of peace was made known to her.

The three women at Harmony now turned their thoughts into

another channel.

The mother being far from well herself, arrangements had to be made to leave her in the companionship of some suitable and congenial woman, until her "boys" came home—one from the front, if he were still alive, the other from captivity. A girl friend offered to take Hansie's place at Harmony and promised not to leave Mrs. van Warmelo until the country was in a settled state again.

This was Hansie's only crumb of consolation during those last days at home.

Many difficulties were made about her permits when she applied for leave to go to Holland, and many were the questions asked, her interview with General Maxwell being the least unsatisfactory when she told him of her approaching marriage.

"You may go with pleasure," he had said; but a few days afterwards Hansie received a letter from the provost-marshal, saying that "the present regulations do not allow *burghers* or their families to leave South Africa."

Hansie wrote to Lord Kitchener, but received no reply, and it was nearly the middle of May, after some weeks of uncertainty, harder far to bear than trouble of a more decided character, when she and Mrs. Cloete left the capital for Cape Colony.

Hansie's last words in her diary are:

"There is quite a history connected with the procuring of my permits, which I shall relate another time. *I am too tired now.*"

Words significant of what the girl had endured in parting from her mother and leaving her beloved country at a time so critical!

★★★★★★

On an ocean-steamer she found herself at last—alone, for in that crowd there was no face familiar to her to be seen.

She mixed freely with the crowd; she sought, in the games with which these voyages usually are passed, to forget—to forget; but the nights of sleeplessness remained—her waking terror, with which she was consumed.

Two men there were who proved sympathetic, one a Scotchman, the other an Englishman—both anti-Boer and sadly misinformed when first she met them, both "converts" by the time they reached their native shores.

Sitting at table she listened intently to the conversations on the war—the war, the never-ending war. On no occasion did she breathe a word of what *she* knew, of what *she* felt, until one day at dinner a young English lieutenant, "covered with glory" and returning home a hero of the war, enlarged on the services rendered by one brave officer, well known by name to Hansie.

"It is not only what he achieved with so much success in the field," he continued. "I am thinking now of those two years he spent in the Pretoria Forts *before* the war, as a common labourer, doing menial work with other men, and secretly making plans and drawing charts of the Pretoria fortifications. Every detail was made known to our military before we went to war."

Exclamations of surprise, a murmur of admiration, ran along the table.

Hansie waited until there was a lull, and then she asked:

"The work carried out by him, was it done under oath of allegiance to the Transvaal Government?"

There was one moment's painful silence before the young lieutenant answered, with a laugh:

"Of course; it could not possibly have been done otherwise—but *all is fair in love and war.*"

"War?" Hansie exclaimed—"I thought you said that this was done some years *before* the war."

"Yes, but we all knew what things were leading to!"

This incident was the first hint among the passengers that she was not one of them.

At first they looked at her askance, but as the days went on and the girl steadfastly avoided every allusion to the war, refusing to express her opinions to any one, except the two men mentioned above, the feeling of discomfort passed, and she was once again included in the pastimes of the ship's company.

As they were nearing Teneriffe the longing for news, for the latest cables from England and South Africa, possessed every soul on board—and now I find that, search as I will, within the recesses of my mind, for words with which to describe adequately such scenes, brain and hand are powerless.

※※※※※※

There was peace in South Africa—peace "with honour" for England, peace *and defeat* for the Boers!

※※※※※※

In a moment the ship's crew went mad, as the wild cheering rolled over the waves.

Hansie stood stupefied until (and strange it is that at a time like this an insignificant detail should stand out in sharp relief against the background of her dulled sensibilities) an hysterical woman ran up to her with outstretched hands, crying:

"Oh, my dear, my dear, let me congratulate you! Let us shake hands!"

The girl, thus taken by surprise in all that crowd, recoiled in shuddering distress, while, with hands clasped convulsively behind, she murmured:

"Oh, I *could not*—I *could not!*"

A wave of deep resentment passed over the ship's passengers, and hostile eyes looked on her frowningly.

******

That night, as the good ship was ploughing the waters on her way once more, a solitary figure stood on the deserted decks.

In the saloons great bumpers of champagne were passing round, while the strains of "God save the King" and "Rule Britannia" floated over the ocean waves.

A man in search of her, fearing perhaps, I know not what, approached the drooping figure of the girl, and pressed her hand in silent sympathy.

"There is no peace!" she said. "Do you think I believe these lying cables? The Boers will *never* yield. If you knew what I know, you would take these reports for what they are worth. I have been trying to think what it all can mean, and this is the conclusion I have come to. If it be true that peace has been proclaimed, then the Boers have preserved their independence, and this last fact has been excluded from the cables in view of the approaching Coronation. But my own conviction is that there is no peace at all, but that these cables have been sent to reassure the English public, and to make it possible to celebrate the crowning of the king in a splendour unclouded by the horrors of the South African war. Believe me, when the Coronation is over you will hear of a mysterious renewal of hostilities."

The man was silent, troubled. He had not the heart to argue with the girl, perhaps he thought, and rightly thought, that this strange illusion of the brain, this confident belief in her own convictions, would help to tide her over the first days to follow.

"I cannot understand," he said, "how Mrs. —— could have asked you to shake hands with her."

"Oh, I was wrong," Hansie said. "She meant it kindly. How could *she* understand? I will apologise—tomorrow."

★★★★★★

It had been arranged that Hansie should spend a few days in London to see some friends before proceeding to Holland.

She found the mighty metropolis in the throes of preparation for an event of unparalleled magnificence.

Every sign of splendour and rejoicing was a fresh sword through the heart of our sorely tried young patriot.

The people with whom she stayed, old Pretoria friends, had not an inkling of what was passing in her mind.

Their warm and loving greetings, their loud expressions of delight that the war had come to an end at last, were so many pangs added to her grief.

"You will come with us to the Coronation?" her hostess said; "we have splendid reserved seats, and this event will be unparalleled in the history of England."

Again the unfortunate girl found herself recoiling, taken by surprise; again she said:

"Oh, I *could not*! Not to save my life!"

"Not go to see the Coronation! I am surprised at you. Very few South African girls are lucky enough to benefit by such an opportunity. I must say I think it very narrow-minded of you. You disappoint me. The war is over now, and while we are all trying to promote a feeling of good-fellowship you nourish such an unworthy and narrow-minded spirit."

Narrow-minded, unworthy!

The iron entered deep into her soul; and when she looks back now and takes a brief survey of what she suffered throughout those years, that moment stands out as one into which all the fears, the hopes, the agonies of one short lifetime had been crowded.

Sometimes the human heart, when tried beyond endurance, will reach a point where but a trifling incident, an unkind word, is needed to break down life's stronghold.

This point our heroine had reached.

Something passed out of her soul, an undefinable something of which the zest for life is made, and as she felt the black waters of despair closing over her she almost gasped for breath.

She turned away.

"You will never understand. I think it very kind of you to make such plans for my enjoyment, but—to the Coronation of the English king I *will not go*. Leave me here—I have some writing to do—no need to be distressed on my account. My one regret is that my presence here, at such a time, should be a source of so much painfulness to us both."

With cold courtesy the subject of the approaching Coronation was dropped, until the next day, when the appalling, the stupefying news of the postponement of the Coronation spread through the hushed streets of the great metropolis.

The king was dying, was perhaps already dead. The king had undergone a critical operation and his life still hung in the balance.

The king could not be crowned.

Already the black wings of Death seemed to be stretched over the mighty city, with its millions and millions of inhabitants. The multitude was waiting in hushed expectancy, in breathless suspense.

Hansie, walking through the streets with one of the men whose sympathy on board had been of such unspeakable comfort to her, never felt more unreal in her life. Her mind was in a maze, she groped about for words with which to clothe her thoughts, but groped in vain, for even the power of thought had been suspended for a time.

Her companion, glancing at her face, asked suddenly, curiously:

"Would you be glad if King Edward were to die?"

There was a long pause, while the girl strove to analyse her feelings.

At last she answered slowly, simply, truthfully:

"No; I would be sorry."

And in these words, good reader, when I think of them, I find a certain solution to the problem of her behaviour on many occasions when brought into close contact with her country's enemies.

There was never anything personal in the most bitter feelings of resentment and hatred of her country's foes, and never at any time did she belong to the ranks of those among her fellow-patriots who deemed it an unpardonable crime to recognise and appreciate the good qualities possessed by them.

A love of fair-play characterised her, even as a child, and it is certain that the cruel circumstances of the war developed this sense of justice to an abnormal extent, often bringing upon her, in later years, misunderstanding and distrust from those who should have been her friends.

******

It is June 28th, a glorious, cloudless summer's morn.

Speeding swiftly, almost silently, cutting its way through the calm, blue waters of the English Channel, a passenger-boat is fast approaching Holland's shores.

The hour is early, and of the few figures moving on the pier, one stands apart, watching intently, as the ship draws near.

He waves his hat, he has recognised the figure of the girl who stands on deck and waves her handkerchief in response to his greeting.

His strong hand clasps hers; and now the discreet reader need not avert his eyes—no need here to "draw the veil"—for Hansie had written from London to this tall, broad-shouldered man:

"What is left of me is coming to you now, but we must meet as *friendly acquaintances*, until we are both certain of ourselves."

How long this "friendly acquaintance" lasted it is difficult to say, for there is a difference of opinion on the point.

She says, not less than sixty minutes.

He asserts, not more than thirty-five!

******

The exquisite serenity of her father's native land, especially on such a perfect day in midsummer, had never seemed to her so sweet.

Here, indeed, she felt that peace *could* come to her at last.

******

But not yet—not yet.

Strong emotions of a different kind awaited her, the meeting of beloved friends and relatives, after seemingly endless years of pain, proving no less trying than the introduction to a large circle of *future* relatives and friends.

Hansie had to be "lionised" as heroine of the war, and this was done in a whole-hearted, generous way which was a constant source of wonder to her.

She was "carried on the hands," as the Dutch saying goes, by all who had the remotest claim on her.

Functions were arranged for her, receptions held, to which white-haired women and stately venerable men came from far to shake her hand, because she was a daughter of the Transvaal, nothing more—not because of what she had done and endured, for this was known to only one or two.

Old friends from South Africa there were in scores, and for the time the State of Holland was transformed into a colony of Boers, which seemed complete when the Boer leaders, Botha, de Wet, and de la Rey, arrived with their staffs. Then it seemed as if the people of Holland lost their heads entirely, and scenes such as those which took place daily in the streets are never to be forgotten by those who witnessed them.

All this, though wonderful, was not the best thing for our heroine, who was "living on her nerves," though in a different way, as surely as she did during those cruel years of war.

Added to this she was frequently tried beyond endurance by the questions:

"Why did the Boers give in? How *could* the Boers give in and lose their independence?"

One conversation in particular was burnt into her brain.

"Was it the concentration camps?"

"No," the answer came slowly, "no, it was not the concentration camps. The high mortality was past, the weakest had been taken, and there was no cause for anxiety for those remaining in the camps. Their rations had been increased and improved—there was no more of that first awful suffering."

"What was it, then? The arming of the natives?"

The answer came more slowly:

"No, it was not the arming of the natives. Their forces were more scattered, for they were chiefly employed in guarding the railway lines, in protecting stock and guarding block-houses. Though their addition to the British ranks undoubtedly weakened our strength to some extent, their inborn respect for the Boer would have prevented them from ever rendering valuable services to the English. How we laughed, my sister and I, when, on the railway journey from Pretoria to Cape Town, we saw the line patrolled by hundreds of these natives, with gun in hand, stark naked except for a loin-cloth and a bandolier! So much waste of ammunition! No, the arming of the natives would have been the last thing to induce the Boers to surrender."

"Then it seems to me incomprehensible! surely death were preferable to defeat!"

"Yes, a thousand times; but you forget the National Scouts—the Judas-Boers. *They* broke our strength. Not by their skill in the use of arms, not by their knowledge of our country and our methods—no!"

"They broke our strength by breaking our ideals, by crushing our enthusiasm, by robbing us of our inspiration, our faith, our hope——"

With averted eyes, and seemingly groping for one last ray of light, the man continued:

"But where were your heroes—your heroes of Magersfontein, Spion Kop, and Colenso?"

"Where were our heroes?" the girl echoed bitterly. "In their graves—in our hospitals—in captivity! Ever foremost in the field—one—by one—they fell—— '*But the remnant that is escaped of the house of Israel shall again take root downward and bear fruit upward.*'

"Although, under the shadow of this great national calamity, we cannot see it now, there is hope for our sad South Africa. It is too soon to speak of a united race, but the time will surely come when, in the inter-marriage of our children and our children's children, will be formed a nation great and strong and purified."

Through all those weeks our heroine never slept. It seems incredible that the frail form of a girl should be endowed with so great a power of endurance, and that the human mind can stand the strain of smiling self-control by day, abandonment of grief by night.

Those nearest to her, divining something of what she was passing through, lavished countless proofs of tender sympathy on her, innumerable acts of loving care for her personal comfort, and well-thought-out plans for drawing her away from herself into the charmed circle of the B—— Labouchere house.

And when her marriage-day drew near she turned away with a superficial glance at the array of costly presents, to devour once again the cables from South Africa, the telegrams from her generals, the letter and the photograph of her beloved President, inscribed in his illegible hand, "For services rendered during the late war."

Last, but not least, there came to her official-looking documents from Het Loo, the personal congratulations of the queen, the prince consort, and the queen-mother—and the ancient blood of Holland coursed more swiftly through her veins as she thought of Wilhelmina, the dauntless young Queen of the Netherlands, now *her* queen.

In all the ranks of the "Petticoat Commando" there was not one woman who had dared more, risked more, than the brave Queen of Holland when she dispatched her good man-of-war to bear away from the shores of Africa the hunted President of the South African Republic, to the refuge of her hospitable land.

★★★★★★

Flowers, flowers everywhere, first in baskets, then in cartloads, then in waggon-loads, they were deposited at the doors until they overflowed from the reception-rooms into the halls and staircases, and even the verandahs—chrysanthemums and roses in riotous profusion, nestling violets, rarest orchids, bright carnations, heavy with the richest perfume.

Each flower had a separate message for the bride. They understood, and they enveloped her with their unspoken sympathy.

Some there were adorned with her beloved, her most tragic "*Vierkleur*," and over them she lingered long, breathing a prayer to merciful Heaven to still her beating heart for ever.

Not in the wild beauty of the Swiss scenery did she find rest, not by the calm lakes of sapphire blue in which she saw reflected the rugged mountains, soul-satisfying in their majestic grandeur, not in the soundless, the mysterious regions of the eternal snows—but in the north of Holland, where she found herself when autumn fell, Hansie slept.

Languid and more languid she became; drooping visibly, she sank into oblivion in that northern village home, conscious only in her waking hours of the cold, the driving sleet, the howling wind, the ceaseless drip, drip of the swaying trees.

As the long winter months crept by, her sleep became more and more profound, less haunted by the hideous nightmares of the past, and though she at first rebelled, ashamed of her growing weakness, she was soon forced to yield to the resistless demands of outraged nature.

In this she was supported by her husband, who, unknown to her, was acting on the advice of the famous nerve-specialist who had watched her unobserved.

"Let her sleep, if need be for a year, and in the end you will find her normal and restored, of that I am convinced," he had said; and in these words her husband found his greatest comfort, as he tucked his little dormouse in and tip-toed from the darkened room.

Hansie lost count of time, but there were two days in the week of which she was quite sure—the day on which the South African mail reached her and the day on which it was dispatched. In between she slept, as we have seen, but when she woke she always knew that her enfranchised spirit had been to her native land.

★★★★★★

A full year had gone by, fifteen months, and when the first breath of winter once more touched the land she gradually became aware of voices calling to her, insistent, imperative voices from across the seas.

"I must go," she said. "What am I doing here? South Africa is calling. My people want me there. You and I must go. There is a great work for us both." And he, no less ardent and enthusiastic, yielded to her prayers, bade farewell to home and fatherland, sailed away with her to the unknown.

"In all the world," she said, "there is no pain to be compared with the pain of being born a patriot; but a patriot in *exile*—may Heaven protect me from the tragedy of such a fate!"

Conclusion

The veil is lifted for one last brief glimpse.

Ten years have gone by since the declaration of peace, (as at time of first publication), ten years each more wonderful than the last, full to overflowing of life's rich experience of joy and grief.

By some strange turn in the hand of Destiny, our heroine finds herself, after many vicissitudes, an inhabitant of the Golden City—that Golden City which had wrecked her youth and very nearly wrecked her life.

For years it has seemed incredible to her that she should have been destined for the position she now holds, a position of so much trust, so difficult, so critical.

A plaything in the hand of Fate, she thought at first, when looking from her balcony she saw the Golden City, with its extensive suburbs stretched out at her feet, and heard the distant, never-ceasing roar of the innumerable mine-batteries of the Rand. But the resistless hand of Fate was drawing her into the sphere of work for which she longed most ardently—woman's work, at home, abroad—and the glamour of Johannesburg stole over her in time.

✶✶✶✶✶✶

The terms of peace have been fulfilled, responsible government for the Transvaal and Free State, and Hansie thinks with an intolerable pain of that day at Teneriffe. Had she but known—had she but known—but the cables (she had called them "lying cables" then, and she was not far wrong) had spoken only of a glorious victory for the English and unconditional surrender on the part of the Boers. No word about the terms, the *only* terms on which the Boers would ever have yielded their independence.

Responsible government has been followed by the Union of the South African provinces.

South Africa is united *in name*, if not yet in reality, but the time will surely come, as we have said before, when, under the softening influence of time, a great united race will be born.

★★★★★★

Closely pressing around Hansie as she writes are eager little faces, reverent little fingers touching the scattered pages before her, brave eyes of blue and brown, looking wonderingly into hers.

"Writing a book, mother? About the spies? And the lemon-juice? Oh, mother, what will the English say?"

And the accents falling on her ear are in the expressive sweetness of the South African Dutch, in its most cultured form.

★★★★★★

Hansie ought to be a happy woman. None of the joys of life have been withheld from her, and yet—and yet——

On Commando

Dietlof Van Warmelo

Contents

Preface	291
Foreword	293
At the Boundary	295
Siege of Ladysmith	300
The Eight-Day Battle of the Tugela	305
Return to, and Flight from, Pretoria	310
Battle of Selikatsnek	314
Narrow Escape of President Steyn and General de Wet	321
With President Steyn to President Kruger	326
Lost	330
Adventure on the Sabie	335
From Roossenekal to Pietersburg	340
Battle of Nooitgedacht	344
Paardekraal Day	349
Commando Sufferings	355
Battle of Boesmanskop	359
Battle of Chrissiesmeer	364
Camped Near Tafelkop	369
In the Hands of the Enemy	373

Preface

This book was written in 1901, while its author was a prisoner at Ahmednagar. It was written in Dutch, and has been put into English by a young lady from what was the Orange Free State.

The author is a friend and relation of mine, son of a clergyman in the Transvaal, and of old Afrikander stock on both sides. His book is the more valuable because of the absence of all literary pretensions, and it may be taken as truly representative of the Afrikander spirit, which has been so much misconceived in England.

Frederik van Eeden

Walden, N. Holland,
July, 1902

My Life on Commando

Foreword

Could I have known that the war would last so long, I might from the beginning have taken notes. They would have brought back memories in a way pleasant to me now, and perhaps also to those who have asked me to write down my adventures.

Often it occurred to me to keep a diary, but I was obliged to give up the idea because my clothes were sometimes so thoroughly drenched that the letters in my pocket were not readable. Later on, when clothes were scarce and pockets past mending, I often made the unpleasant discovery that caused the fool, on his journey from the land of Kokanje, to cry to the king: 'We have ridden at such a breakneck pace, see, everything has slipped through this little hole!' Now I am obliged to write down my adventures without any notes, so dates, numbers, and names of places will occasionally be missing. It stands to reason that I— being an exile in a strange country, in the fort of —— in ——, cut off from the world outside and without any official reports—should simply limit myself to my own personal experience. And, lastly, I must apologise to my readers for so often speaking of myself and my friends; but that is inevitable in this tale.

I shall pass rapidly over the first part of my life on commando. If my memory plays me false—which is not very probable, as I still have a lively recollection of the events—I shall be grateful for correction.

July, 1901.

CHAPTER 1

At the Boundary

When that part of the Pretoria town commando to which my brother Frits and I belonged left for the Natal boundary on September 30, 1899, we were all very enthusiastic, as could be seen from the nice new suits, the new shining guns, and the sleek horses. Many ladies had come to the station to see us off, and we were proud of having the opportunity to fight for our country. Our departure seemed then to us a great occasion, as we were inexperienced in war. We had not yet learnt that one could pass unscathed through many a fierce battle. We knew nothing of 'retreating' and we knew all about the enemy with whom we were to come in contact. We imagined that several sharp engagements would take place—that these would be decisive battles in which many of our men would be killed, and therefore the parting with relatives and friends was sad indeed.

Our field-cornet, Melt Marais, had told us that we had nothing to see to except provisions for a day or two, as government would supply us with all necessaries at Zandspruit, where the commandos were to concentrate; so many of us took neither pots, pans, nor mugs.

What a disillusion it was to find on our arrival at Zandspruit that there were no tents, and as yet no provisions of any kind! So we were initiated by having to pass the first nights of our commando life on the open *veld* with insufficient food. And in the daytime our work was cut out for us, as every other minute our horses disappeared—lost among the thousands of horses that all looked exactly alike in the eyes of an inexperienced townsman. Then it meant a running and seeking, an examining of marks and tokens, until the stupid among us were obliged to tie ribbons to our horses as a means of recognising them. And one, the story goes, even tied a nosebag, with a bundle of forage, to his mount so that it should not run away.

At length the provisions began to arrive, but the pots and pans were still scarce, and we could not even drink a cup of coffee till a tin of jam or meat had been emptied.

We were just beginning to feel comfortable, when the time stated in the ultimatum expired, and we had to cross the boundary of Natal. General Erasmus was at the head of our commando. We spent the night near Volksrust in a cold hail storm and rain. Those first days we are not likely to forget. They were wet, cold days, and we were still unaccustomed to preparing our own food and looking after ourselves. Fortunately, we had the opportunity, a few days later, of supplying ourselves with all necessaries at Newcastle.

Before we crossed the boundary General Erasmus had addressed us and told us the news of our first victory—the taking of an armoured train at Kraaipan; at that time we still made a fuss about such a trifle. Also, in those days, we still looked up with respect to our leaders.

Ds. Postma, who accompanied us everywhere, led us in prayer. Not one of the *burghers* seems to have known where the enemy were. We advanced slowly and carefully, as we expected *to meet with the enemy at any moment*; but we saw no signs of them until we came to Dundee. After a rest of a few days we undertook the momentous expedition to the mountains of Dundee, to the north of the town.

Towards evening we got the order to 'prepare for three days.' For three days! And we had not even provisions enough for one. But we understood that there could not yet be a proper commissariat, and we fought for our country willingly, convinced of the justice of our cause; so we 'prepared' cheerfully.

Before the commando started, a terrible thunderstorm came on that slowly passed over and was followed by a gentle rain. We rode hard in the dark, through *dongas*, past farms and houses, zigzagging in a half-circle, to the mountains of Dundee. No sound was to be heard except the dull thud of the hoofs of the galloping horses. Now and again we whispered to each other how delightfully we were going to surprise the enemy. When the horses came to a sudden pause, and an inexperienced rider, owing to a presentiment of evil, involuntarily uttered his wish to 'halt,' we turned upon him angrily and called him 'traitor.' We did not then know that we were far beyond earshot of the enemy. It stopped raining, and towards morning we reached the mountains; and after we had with great difficulty got our horses on to the mountains, we had to await the dawn in the cold, drenched to the skin. A mackintosh is of small service in such a rain. When the day dawned we led our horses higher up. A thick fog had come on. General Lucas Meyer was to begin the attack on the west, and we were to surprise the enemy from the heights.

When the roar of cannon announced the battle, we were full of enthusiasm, but General Erasmus forbade anyone to move on before the fog lifted. It was quite possible that the fog might be only on the mountain-tops, because of their great height, and that we would have clear weather as soon as we began to descend, therefore several of our men begged General Erasmus to be allowed to go on ahead as scouts. But he was very much against it, and said that the enemy might cut off our retreat, and 'if the enemy surround us it is all up with us,' said he. As soon as the roar of the cannon ceased, we withdrew some distance into the mountains to let our horses graze. But we had only just off-saddled, when from all sides came the cry of 'Saddle! saddle!' and from our left, in the valley, came the sound of firing. A detachment of 250 khakis, probably knowing nothing of our whereabouts, and intending to pass round the mountains and attack Lucas Meyer in the rear, was compelled to surrender in a few moments, after first having sought cover in a kraal near a house.

We remained three days on the Dundee mountains, and during all that time there was a steady drizzle, with intervals of hail and wind. Once when it cleared up for a few hours we got the order to attack the town, but it began to rain again, and that night we had to keep our positions in the intense cold, without any covering. Fortunately, the enemy abandoned their camp that night, and when we looked down upon the town next morning the khakis had vanished. We had only the preceding day placed our cannon in a position to command the camp.

When we returned to our saddles, the horses had strayed so far that it took us almost all day to get them back. My uncle, Paul Maré, formerly Volksraad member for Zoutpansberg, treated us to *kaboe-mealies* (roasted maize), the first we had on commando, and we ate with great relish.

Meanwhile the commando had left. We followed, and entered Dundee, where we helped ourselves hungrily to the good things from the shops placed at the disposal of the commandos.

In an unorganised army looting is a necessary evil. There are always some of the lower classes who are the ringleaders, and when the commandos reach a house or farm that has already been looted, they join in the looting 'because the *burghers* are on commando, and they must be well supplied with all necessaries, so as to be able to fight well.' So we reasoned, and we joined in the looting. I can affirm, to the honour of our *burghers*, that it was not our intention to plunder, and in the beginning much was done to prevent it. The lower class *uitlander*, who joined us for the sake of booty, and not for love and sympathy towards us, was largely responsible for the bad name we got among right-minded people who did not know the facts of the case. It was the same as regards theft.

If anyone missed his horse, he had but to look for it among the 'Irish corps,' or some other *uitlander* corps, and unless he knew his beast well he would fail to recognise it, as both mane and tail would have been cut short by the thief. I do not wish to pretend that we were always free from blame. It has happened that the *uitlander* got a very poor horse in exchange for his thoroughbred because a Boer had tied the token of recognition to his own horse and made off with the better one. The truth is that very few men are proof against the demoralizing influence of war, and I will not deny that this war has shown up our many faults; but in my tale I shall be able to take up the cudgels for my people in cases where the rest of the world turned from us because they were disappointed in their expectations of us.

After our departure from Dundee the looting went on freely. Then we began to witness the devastation that is the irremediable consequence of war. Here and there a house had been completely plundered. At Glencoe Junction I entered the stationmaster's house, a well-furnished house with beautiful pictures, books, and mirrors. Some massive silver mugs and other articles of value were lying about. The family had only just dined, for the cloth was still laid. I ate of the food on the table, wrote a letter home with pen and ink, and left the house. Later on, when I returned, it had been thoroughly looted and some of the mirrors smashed. There were many of the riff-raff, *kaffirs* and *coolies* in the neighbourhood, and in all probability they had done the mischief.

When our commando left Dundee to move in the direction of Ladysmith, part of the Pretoria town commando was sent to reinforce Lucas Meyer, who was to follow the troops fleeing from Dundee with his commando. My brother and I went with it. A terrible thunderstorm came on just then, and during the whole march to Ladysmith it rained heavily. Every moment we expected to come up with the troops, but they had too great a start, and we did not overtake them at all. We were too late again. An English general has said that 'the Boers are brave, and make good plans, but are always twenty-four hours late.' That can be explained in this way. We were accustomed to fighting against *kaffirs*, who hid in woods and mountains, and against whom we had to advance with the utmost precaution, so as to lose as few lives as possible. So we were too cautious in the beginning of the war. We would not make a great sacrifice to win a battle.

On October 30 we were present, under Lucas Meyer, at the battle near Ladysmith, but we did not come into action, as we belonged to a part of the commando that had to hold a position to prevent attack in the rear. The enemy did not attack our position at all, except with a few bombs, because they suffered a great defeat near Modderspruit, and had to retreat hurriedly. From our positions we could see how every time the bombs burst among them the fleeing troops seemed to get 'mazed' for a moment, and then went forward again.

At that time we were often in want of food. One must have suffered hunger to know what it means. In a few linen bags I had some biscuits that had first been reduced to crumbs through the riding, and then to a kind of pap by the rain and perspiration of the horse. Often when I felt the pangs of famine I added some sugar to this mess and ate it with relish.

Some days later we left Lucas Meyer and returned to our commando, which had meanwhile gone to the north of Ladysmith. During our absence Zeederberg had taken the place of Melt Marais as *veld-cornet*.

Chapter 2

Siege of Ladysmith

When we surrounded the town and the siege began, all talk of the bananas that we were to eat in the south of Natal came to an end.

Ladysmith ought never to have been besieged. On October 30 we should have made use of our advantage. If we had at once followed the enemy when they fled in disorder, we should in all probability easily have taken those positions that would have involved the immediate surrender of Ladysmith. Many lives would have been sacrificed, but not so many as were sacrificed during the whole siege. And we might have used those men who were necessary to maintain the siege elsewhere as an attacking force. Instead of following up our advantage, we deliberately prepared for a siege. The enemy meanwhile made use of the opportunity to entrench themselves well. Most of our *burghers* were against our attempting to take the town by assault when once it was thoroughly entrenched.

The Pretoria town commando and that from Krokodil River in the Pretoria district occupied the position nearest to Ladysmith. This was a hill to the north of the town, flat at the top, and surrounded by a stone wall. In all probability the enclosed depression of about 500 paces in circuit had been used as a cattle *kraal*. Against that *kopje* (hill) we gradually put up our tents. From our camp we looked on to a large flat mountain that we called Little Amajuba, because on October 30 the first large capture of prisoners had been made there. In front of our kopje, near the foot, ran a *donga*, and at a distance of about 1,000 paces, parallel to us, lay another oblong *kopje* occupied by the enemy. This *kopje* we called Rooirandjes.

On November 8 we received the order from our general to attack the Rooirandjes the following day. We were about 250 strong, and very willing, as that position had not yet been entrenched. On a mountain to our right a cannon had been placed that was to begin firing on the enemy's position towards dawn. Distinct orders were given that our *veld-cornet* was to be at the foot of Rooirandjes with his men before daybreak. But something went wrong again, and it was already quite light when we reached the *donga*. We found ourselves at a distance of about 700 paces from the Rooirandjes, and we had to cross an open space if we still wished to storm the position. The enemy's watch already began shooting at us.

The corporals let their men advance in groups of four from the donga to the *kopje*, using the ant-hills as cover when they lay down. Our turn came last, but meanwhile the enemy had received reinforcements, and the nearest ant-hills were nearly all occupied, so that only three men could go at a time. Such a shower of bullets fell that it was a miracle that we came out of it alive. Fortunately I found a free ant-hill. My brother had to share one with a comrade.

At last the cannon from the mountain fired a few shots, but stopped again almost immediately—why, I do not yet know. So we were obliged to lie in our positions. It was terribly hot, and not a cloud in the sky. We suffered horribly from thirst, and scarcely dared move to get at our water-bags. One of our comrades lay groaning behind me. He was shot through both legs. The bullets kept flying over our heads to the *kopje* behind us, where some of our *burghers* lay firing at the enemy. Every now and again a bullet exploded in our neighbourhood with the noise of a pistol-shot. I fancy only dum-dums make that peculiar noise. We had already seen many such bullets taken from the enemy by our *burghers* in the Battle of Modderspruit. Another *burgher*, Mulder, ran past me with a smile on his lips, threw himself behind an ant-hill, immediately rose again with the intention of joining some of our *burghers* in the front ranks, who sat calmly smoking behind some rocks under a tree, but had not gone two paces when he was shot in the thigh. There he had to lie groaning until our brave Reineke, who was killed later on at Spion Kop, saw a chance of carrying him away.

Some of us fell asleep from fatigue. One of our men on waking heard the hiss of a bullet over his head at regular intervals, and thought that a khaki had got closer up to him, and was firing at him from the side. When he lifted his head he found that he had rolled away from all cover. One, two, three, back he was again behind his ant-hill, and the scoundrel stopped firing at him. It was lucky for us that the enemy were such bad shots, or not many of us would have lived to tell the tale.

When our cannon at last, towards evening, condescended to bombard the enemy, the firing almost wholly ceased, and we made use of that favourable opportunity to get back to the *donga*. We had lain nine hours behind those ant-hills, and, strange to say, there were only two wounded on our side. We decided not to run the same risk again. In this way we lost our confidence in men like the brothers Erasmus, general and commandant, who, in the first place, were incapable of organising a good plan of attack, and, secondly, never took part in a battle.

The months spent near Ladysmith were to most of us the most tedious of the whole war. We had so little to do, and the heat between the glowing rocks of the *kopjes* was awful. The little work we had was anything but pleasant; it consisted chiefly in keeping guard either by day or by night. In the beginning a very bad watch was kept. Later on we had to climb the *kopje* at least every alternate evening to pass the long nights in our positions, while not far behind us stood our empty tents.

When we got back in the morning with our bundles on our backs, dead tired, we simply 'flopped' on to a stone, and sat waiting for our cup of coffee, either gazing at the lovely landscape or at the dirty camp, according to the mood we were in, or exchanging loud jokes with our neighbours. Constantly being on guard and constantly being in danger wears one out. We much prefer active service on patrol or in a skirmish to lying in our positions. It is not in the nature of the Boer to lie inactive far from his home. He soon wants to go '*huis-toe*' (home), and very soon the 'leave-plague' broke out in our camp. That plague was one of the causes why the enemy succeeded in breaking through our lines.

Through unfairness on the part of the officers, some *burghers* often got leave, others never, and the consequence, of course, was a constant quarrelling. Many *burghers* got leave and never returned—either with or without the knowledge of the officers. No wonder we never had a proper fighting force in the field.

The difficulties we had to contend with through want of organisation prevented the generals from putting their plans into execution.

Fortunately, many *burghers* were very willing, and if there was to be a fight they always went voluntarily. It was noticeable that those under a capable general fought well, while those under a bad or incapable general were very weak indeed. Sometimes wonders were done at the initiative of some of the *burghers*. We had a few games in the camp to pass the time, but we were kept busy in a different way also. Sometimes, when we were all just comfortably lazy, the order would be given to 'mount.' That meant a hurried search for our horses and snatching up our guns and *bandoliers*. But after a while we had had enough of those false alarms, and they failed to make any impression on us. The call of 'The English are coming! saddle, saddle!' became proverbial.

When we did not keep such constant guard, we sat or lay listening of an evening to a most discordant noise caused by the singing of psalms and hymns at the same time at different farms. We sometimes joined in. As a people we are not very musical.

The day-watch we liked best. Then we often got a chance of firing a shot at a careless khaki on the Rooirandjes. To some of our young men there was something very exciting in the idea that they were in constant danger. Every now and again a bomb, too, would come flying over the camp, and the whole commando would make for the rocks amid shouts of laughter.

At that time we still felt rather down when there was a fight in prospect. When, some time after our attack on the Rooirandjes, we went to the west of Ladysmith to attack Platrand, we did not feel at all comfortable, although we went voluntarily. It was a lovely ride in the dark at a flying gallop, but when we found on our arrival at Platrand that the promised number of men was not there, we rode away again quite satisfied that we had not to attempt the attack. For had we not made up our minds not to risk a repetition of the attack on Rooirandjes?

The blowing-up of the cannon at Ladysmith is one of the episodes of the war that we look back upon with a feeling of shame. A few days after a Long Tom had been blown up on Umbulwana Kop, east of Ladysmith, I warned our field-cornet that the enemy were busy spying in our neighbourhood at night. While on guard, we could distinctly hear the flapping of the saddles and the neighing of the horses in front of us. I foretold a repetition of what had happened on Umbulwana Kop. The field-cornet promised that the guard would be doubled that night. Towards morning those of us who were not on guard were waked out of our sleep by a loud cry of 'Hurrah!' from the throats of a few hundred Englishmen who were blowing up two cannon on a mountain to our right, close to us.

We sprang towards our positions, stumbling and falling over stones, not knowing what was going on, and expecting the khakis at any moment. It was the first time that we had heard a fight at night, and it gave us a creepy feeling. We saw the flames of the guns and from the exploding bullets, and heard the rattling of the shots and the shouting, but we could not join in the fight, as we—eight of us—were not allowed to leave our positions. Now and again a bullet fell in our neighbourhood, and the Free State Artillery, who were on the mountains to the right, fired some bombs at the enemy, nearly hitting us in the dark.

When it got lighter we went to look at the dead and wounded, perhaps from a feeling of bravado, perhaps to accustom ourselves to the sight. The enemy had paid dearly for their brave deed. They know the number of their dead and wounded better than we do, for they had opportunity enough to carry them away. On our side only four were killed and a few wounded. Niemeyer, Van Zyl and Villiers were among the killed. Pott was severely wounded. Niemeyer had several bayonet wounds.

After that we were, of course, doubly careful. We have never been able to discover who failed in their duty on guard. Cooper and Tossel were suspected and accused. They were sent to Pretoria under arrest, but the investigation never led to any result. We have every reason to believe that our *burghers* were guilty of treachery more than once near Ladysmith, Government ought from the start to have taken strict measures against traitors and spies.

Some days after the blowing up of the cannon I sprained my left knee, which I had already hurt before the war began. General Erasmus gave me leave to go home for an unlimited time. On my way home I passed my brother Willem without being aware of it. He had come from Holland, where he was studying, to take part in the war.

What a meeting with relatives and friends! How much there was to tell! Even then we had not experienced very much, and how much more will our burghers have to tell their dear ones on returning from their exile in strange countries! There will, alas! be much sorrow, too; for many of our friends and relatives have been killed in this war, and many more will have yet to give their lives for their country!

Chapter 3

The Eight-Day Battle of the Tugela

Before my knee was quite cured I returned to Ladysmith. The first thing that caught my eye on my return to the camp was the balloon above Ladysmith. It looked just like a large crocodile-eye as it followed all my movements. When I went to look for my horse or to fetch water or wood, there it stood, high up in the sky, and I felt as if it kept its eye specially fixed on me, and as if I might expect a bomb at any moment.

We had never in all our lives seen so many flies as at Ladysmith. We had to hurry over our meals as they made eating almost an impossibility to us. Fortunately, I was only a short time there, as towards the end of January, 1900, part of our commando, including my brother and myself, was sent to the Tugela as reinforcement. We had a distance of four and a half hours to ride, and we had to ride hard, as the enemy were determined to force their way through. We arrived the same day, just two days after the enemy had tried to force their way through to the right of Spion Kop and had been defeated. On nearing the high Tugela mountains we heard more and more distinctly the constant rattling of bullets, interrupted by the roar of the cannon and the *bom-bom-bom* of our saucy bomb-Maxim, that made our hearts expand and those of the enemy shrink. As we raced on to the foot of the mountains, the bullets that the enemy were sending over the mountains to find the Boers raised the dust around us.

The following morning we went to lie in a trench that had been dug by our men on a rise to the right of Spion Kop. The previous day eight *burghers* had been wounded there. Red Danie Opperman was field-cornet. Not far from us, to our left, stood a few of our cannon, and facing us, to our left, on the long mountain slope, we could see fourteen guns of the enemy's. In front of us was a large wood, and close to that the English camp. We could see the enemy moving in great close square masses. It was a terribly hot day; we had to lie in the trenches, as all day long the enemy fired at us from the smaller positions facing us, at a distance of 15,000 paces; and constantly the bombs burst over our heads. At regular intervals a lyddite bomb—that gave us a shock through our whole body—came from the wood towards the cannon on our left. Once only part of our entrenchment, where, fortunately, no one happened to be, was blown to bits.

Whenever there was a moment's pause, we lifted our heads above the trenches to have a look at the lovely landscape and at the positions of our enemy. That day not one of us was wounded. Only the artillery suffered. If our few cannon ventured to make themselves heard, eight or more bombs followed in quick succession to silence them. Next to me lay a man whose servant, a restless, impatient Bushman, most amicably addressed him as Johnny. The Bushman went to and fro continually to a 'chum' of his who lay hidden behind a rock close to us. Once, on one of his visits to his 'chum,' a bullet struck the ground close to his heels; he stood still, looked slowly and defiantly from his heels to the enemy, and said in a most emphatic tone, 'You confounded Englishman!' and calmly proceeded on his way to his chum.

To the right of this position was an open space, almost level with the immediate surroundings, but ending in a steep decline some 900 paces further on. There we went towards evening with a reinforcement of the Pretoria town commando that had followed us. The field-cornet made us stand in rows, and told off forty men to dig a trench that night. The rest of the men would relieve us the following night. My brother and I were in the first shift. Towards morning, While we were still digging at the trenches, fire was opened across the whole line of battle. We imagined that we were being attacked, and jammed ourselves in the narrow trench. But as the attack did not come off, and the bullets flew high over our heads, we went on digging until daybreak. Then we noticed that the enemy were lying in a trench about 800 paces ahead of us. We fired a few shots at them, but saved our ammunition for an eventual storming.

The whole of that day and the two succeeding days there was a constant salvo over our heads. The bullets flew over our heads like finches, and did us no harm, but we had to be on our guard against the sharpshooters, who occasionally fired close to us. That day (January 24), the heroic Battle of Spion Kop took place, where our *burghers*, after having been surprised in the night by the enemy and driven off the *skop*, obliged them, after a stubborn fight, to abandon it again. The Pretoria men, who were to have relieved us in the trench, took a great part in that battle. Reineke, Yeppe, Malherbe, De Villiers, and Olivier were killed. Ihrige was severely wounded.

All day long we lay listening to the fighting, for we could not sleep. We had to stay in the trench three days and four nights before we were relieved. Water and food were brought to us, or fetched by our men at night, as we did not venture to leave the trench by day. We were safe enough, for the bombs had not much effect on the sand-walls of our trench, and there was always time to stoop to avoid them. The following morning news was brought to us that the enemy had abandoned the whole line of battle and were retreating in the direction of Chieveley.

The Battle of the Tugela had lasted eight days.

I had again hurt my knee, and had to leave Ladysmith for Pretoria, from whence I went to Warmbad at Waterberg to stay for a few weeks with Mrs. Klein-Frikkie Grobler, who received me most kindly. My brother Frits got leave for the first time then, too, and Willem remained at Ladysmith. During my absence the English broke through at Pieter's Heights, where Willem was made prisoner and Lüttig, Malherbe and Stuart de Villiers were killed. Meanwhile Frits had gone, with some other Pretoria men, to the Orange Free State, where the enemy had surrounded General Cronje.

Since the beginning of the siege our *burghers* always thought the town would fall soon. 'The khakis cannot hold out any longer! They have no provisions, and their ammunition must be coming to an end! Buller can never cross the Tugela, our positions are too good! What does it matter if *I* do go on leave? The khakis cannot get through!' That was the opinion of most of the *burghers*. And if anyone ventured to point out that the enemy *might* force their way through because we did not all do our duty, he was either not believed or looked upon as a traitor. Meanwhile enthusiasm was dying out. The *burghers* lay in their *laagers* or went home, trusting to the few willing ones, who ultimately proved not strong enough to withstand the overwhelming force that Buller brought to bear upon one point of our positions when he was obliged to force his way through at no matter what cost.

No leave should have been given during the war, and here I may as well mention—although this tale does not pretend to be a history of the war—that it has been carried on with far too great laxity, owing to the ignorance of our generals and the demoralizing influence of self-interest and nepotism. We should have sent our forces far into the Cape Colony to get help from our brothers in a war that had been forced upon us by England. The Colonial Afrikanders never had the opportunity of standing by us, because we did not supply them with the necessary ammunition or stretch out our hands towards them. Unless they had help from our invading forces, they dared not risk a rising, because of the confiscation of their property in case of failure.

We have had to suffer—to suffer cruelly for our sins. Our enemy forced his way through the dyke that surrounded us, and like a stormy sea he ruined our homes, devastated our fields, and caused us endless suffering. Besides this, the talk of intervention had an enervating effect on the commandos. In our commando, which was largely composed of ignorant men, the strangest stories went round. One was that the Russians had landed somewhere in South Africa with 100 cannon. There was always talk of a great European War having broken out; and the consequence was that the Boers counted on intervention or help from the powers, instead of depending on their own strength and perseverance. The most sensible among us recognised the improbability of intervention. It was not to the interest of any foreign power to intervene in South Africa where it had no firm footing, particularly as Chamberlain had, by most cunning artifices, forced us to be the aggressors.

War was inevitable. Sooner or later it had to come. After the Jameson Raid, which was really the beginning of the war, the Transvaal Government recognised the dangerous position in which it stood, as an isolated Republic, and was therefore obliged to arm itself with the most modern of military equipments. Before the Jameson Raid race hatred was dying out rapidly. The consequence of the raid was that the gap between Boer and Englishman widened, the sympathy of the *uitlanders* for us grew deeper, and the Afrikander Bond grew stronger. England's prestige in South Africa was threatened, and with it her rank as first Power in the world. She had to maintain her supremacy in South Africa; while for us it had become a question of all or nothing. England has evidently succeeded in keeping up such friendly relations with the other Powers that no intervention seems possible.

The relief of Ladysmith took place on February 28—a Majuba Day—a day that had been marked as a red-letter day in our calendars. For nineteen years the enemy have longed to wipe out the remembrance of that day, and they have done so brilliantly and malignantly. Since that time we have been humiliated and belittled. Our fall was great. For the first time there was a general panic. The two Republics, being forced to venture on war against a powerful kingdom, felt themselves staggering under the heavy blow.

Chapter 4

Return to, and Flight from, Pretoria

After the relief of Kimberley and Ladysmith we imagined that the decisive battles would soon follow. Although my knee was not yet cured, I went to Glencoe, whither our commandos had retreated. I was not five days there when I had to leave, being unfit for active service. Again I went to Warmbad for some weeks with Mr. Burgemeester Potgieter and his family, and on my return to Pretoria remained in my office until the beginning of May.

Meanwhile Frits had returned from the Free State, and my knee was cured. We each bought ourselves a sturdy pony, and left, with some other *burghers*, by train for Klerksdorp, from where we went on to Dewetsdrift, on the Vaal River. General Viljoen was guarding the drift there with some hundreds of *burghers*. We rode from there some four or five hours into the Free State to spy the movements of the enemy.

From Dewetsdrift we went, under Commandant Boshoff, to Schoemansdrift, Venterskroon, and Lindequidrift. Our division formed part of the escort for the guns. Our route lay through beautiful scenery. The Vaal twists and bends between two high mountains that curve on either side like the roads the khaki makes with his double row of waggons over the hills of the Hoogeveld. In every opening of the mountains lies a farm, a mean little house, but among well-cultivated fields. In nearly every farm the family was grieving for one of its members who had been taken prisoner along with Cronje, and of whose fate they were in ignorance. The people received us very kindly. Everywhere we got milk and biscuits, and we found afterwards that those people were the kindest who had suffered the most from the war.

As the enemy were already on their way to Johannesburg, we had to retreat as rapidly as possible, first to Bank Station, near Potchefstroom, and then by train to Langlaagte. To the north-west of Johannesburg we had a skirmish with the enemy, who attacked us as we were feeding our horses. It appeared that our guard was not on duty. I have never seen horses saddled so quickly. Most of the *burghers* rode off and left us behind with the guns. One ammunition waggon stuck in the mud, and was left behind, but was brought in safety to Pretoria by Frans Lottering, a comrade of mine, who rode back for it with some gunners when we had fled. Lottering was given a sword by General de la Rey for his brave conduct. Through negligence on the part of our officers we lost on that occasion one gun, several waggons, and some of our men.

Almost all night long we retreated with our guns to Pretoria. We had not lost courage. We all spoke of the thorough way in which our government would have fortified Pretoria, and of the great battle that would take place there. We had all made up our minds to a stubborn resistance at our capital. What a bitter disappointment it was to find that our government had decided not to defend the town! The causes that led to such a decision will be brought to light by historians. The consequences were that many of the *burghers* were discouraged, and rode '*huis-toe*,' and nothing came of the great battle that was to have been fought.

Frits and I decided to give our horses a few days' rest in their stables before going to meet the enemy.

On June 4, at about twelve o'clock, while we were at luncheon, a lyddite bomb fell close to the fort, raising a cloud of dust. My mother went outside, and came back quickly to tell us that it was not a shot *from* the fort, but from the enemy. The bombs followed in quick succession. They flew over Schanskop fort, and fell close to our house at Sunnyside. As the ground was rocky they exploded well. My mother and sister fled with our neighbours to the town, and my brother and I saddled our horses and rode off to Quaggaspoort.

From over the mountains, to the south of the town, the bombs came flying as a gentle warning from the khakis that it would be better to surrender in order to avoid a great calamity.

It was sad to see how few horses there were at the foot of the mountain. Here a group of four, there of ten—a sign that the number of *burghers* in the positions was very small indeed. When the enemy appeared at Quaggaspoort, we noticed that the *burghers* from the direction of Krokodil River were retreating, and a moment later they were all in full flight. One of my comrades, a brother of Lottering, was wounded in the arm by a shell as he fled, and had to remain behind in Pretoria. That night my brother and I spent in our own home, but we left the town the following morning in the direction of Silverton, just before the enemy entered.

It would be well to try and understand the condition of our country and the temper of our *burghers*.

As the capital was in the hands of the enemy, it was easy enough to convince our simpleminded men that our country was irretrievably lost to us. Therefore a period of discouragement and demoralization followed. Many *burghers*, also, who had all along fought bravely now remained behind in the towns or on their farms, not daring to leave their wives and daughters at the mercy of the soldiers. We may not judge those men, neither need we consider it to our credit that we, either from a sense of duty or from a spirit of adventure, acted differently. There were many also who argued that the government was corrupt, and that the war should have been prevented, or that the Boers did not want to fight. So they also became unfaithful to the cause, and to those along with whom they began the war.

And the name of 'hands-upper' was earned by those *burghers* who of their own free will surrendered to the enemy. The chaff was divided from the grain; cowards and traitors remained behind, and the willing ones went to the *veld*, even though it were in a retreating direction. We were still very hopeful. There were still the good positions in the Lydenberg district, and we had heard that De Wet had cut the line of communication behind the enemy. We also still had an intact line to Delagoa Bay.

My brother and I met our old comrade Frans Lottering, and the three of us went in search of General Grobler of Waterberg, who lay with his commando to the east of Pretoria at Franspoort, near Donkerhoek. There we joined his commando. Our camp was put up near a *kaffir* location, and as the *kaffirs* were clean, we often bought boiled sweet potatoes and crushed maize from them.

Nothing particular happened at Franspoort. To the right and left of us some desperate fighting went on for several days, and at Donkerhoek a fierce battle took place, but we were not attacked.

When the news came that the enemy had broken through our lines at Donkerhoek, and that we had to retreat, my brother and I left Grobler's commando. Thinking that the commandos would fall back upon the positions of Belfast, we went to Middelburg to an uncle of ours, the missionary Jan Maré, in order to give our horses a rest. We had lost sight of our comrade Frans. On our way we bought bread at the farms, or had it given us, cut a piece off an ox that had been slaughtered for the commando, and slept either in a manger or, as was more often the case, in the open air of the cold Hoogeveld. We arrived at Middelburg completely exhausted, and are not likely to forget our uncle's great hospitality.

We accidentally met our former Commandant, Boshoff, who told us that he was on his way with ten men to join General de la Rey, who had gone in the direction of Rustenburg to cut the enemy's line of communication between Mafeking and Pretoria, and we very willingly joined him, after a delightful rest of ten days.

The commando of Commandant Boshoff consisted of nine *burghers* with an ambulance waggon—that was used for the commissariat and for our bedding—a French doctor, two *kaffirs* and two tents. It seemed as if we were going for a picnic. But it was necessary that we should be well provided with all sorts of things, as our journey would be through the Boschland, where fever and horse-sickness play havoc with man and horse in summer. In winter it is endurable for a few months only, so the country is very scarcely populated and almost uncultivated, and in winter the Boers trek there with their cattle from the bare, chill Hoogeveld. I had always longed to see that part of the Transvaal.

CHAPTER 5

Battle of Selikatsnek

Come hours north of Middelburg one suddenly leaves the high plateau of the Boschveld for a difficult road that curves steadily downwards between two high mountains until it reaches a wide, thickly-wooded valley. In the *kloof* (mountain-pass) a swiftly-flowing river cuts the road that goes along its banks, in several places, before it loses itself in the Olifants River. There the song of many birds, not to be found on the Hoogeveld, can be heard, and there it was delightfully warm, in comparison with the chilly air of the Hoogeveld. Of an evening we made large fires, as there was plenty of dry wood. We sat round the fire, chatting or listening to the comic songs which one of our comrades sang. It was a happy time—away from khaki, far beyond reach of the roar of cannon—a time of rest in preparation for the evil days that awaited us.

Everywhere we saw flocks of sheep and herds of cattle grazing among the bushes—always a sign that we should find a waggon or two with tents close to them, under the nearest trees. Sometimes, near a *drift* or a good place to outspan, quite a small *laager* had been formed of the trek Boers, or, rather, of their wives, for the husbands and sons of many had gone to the war. The Boers who fled with their cattle in that way we called 'Bush-lancers.' We came up with De la Rey's *laager* near the Elands River, and later on made the acquaintance of Captain Kirsten's scouts, to whom we offered our services. In those days it was very pleasant to belong to the reconnoitring corps. When we went to reconnoitre our horses got plenty of forage on the farms, and as we were few in number and always ahead of the *laager*, there were always eggs, bread, and milk to be had.

We had enough to do, also, as we had to keep a sharp look-out, and we were in constant danger, but not at all afraid of the patrols of khakis, which, being small in number and without their guns, were pretty harmless. We advanced almost parallel to the Magalies Mountains, that stretch from Pretoria to Rustenburg, until we came to the neighbourhood of Selikatsnek. Unless one was well acquainted with the highways and byways of that part of the country, one was in constant danger of losing the way; it is a long stretch of bush, consisting of the well-known thorn-bushes of the Hoogeveld, for a distance of about ten miles deep. The principal passes of the Magalies Mountains were occupied by the enemy—Wonderboompoort, Hornsnek, Selikatsnek, Commandonek, Olifantsnek. General de la Rey had made up his mind to take Selikatsnek, and on July 11 he succeeded, by his strong will and military talent.

While we were reconnoitring with Captain Kirsten's party we got the news that De la Rey had attacked Selikatsnek—about an hour's ride from where we were—and that the battle was still going on. We all rode to the scene of action, but my brother and I, with a few other men, remained behind to wait for Captain Kirsten, who was absent at the time. As soon as he arrived we rode off, and arrived at Selikatsnek at about nine o'clock. Our *burghers* had already taken two of the enemy's guns.

Selikatsnek (or Moselikatsnek) is a narrow opening in the Magalies Mountains, with high shoulders on either side, that slope gradually to a white *kopje* in the centre. If an attacking party once occupies the shoulders, it can easily keep the enemy on the *kopje* or on the two slopes. When we arrived our *burghers* already occupied the principal positions—both shoulders and the smaller positions to the front of the *kopje*. The enemy had been obliged to draw in their clipped wings, and to concentrate on and in the neighbourhood of the white *kopje*.

But as the shoulders of the pass were very steep on the other side, our men could not surround the enemy or attack them in the rear; and as there was not sufficient cover for them to go down the slope without great loss, in order to drive the enemy by force from their positions, the *burghers* remained 'rock-fast' in their positions, and made no progress at all. Thus, the enemy would either get reinforcements from Pretoria or escape when it got dark. Both our flanks kept up a constant fire on the slopes, and on the white *kopje*, but the shoulders were too high for a proper aim, and the khakis lay fast behind the boulders and in the clefts of the rocks.

Captain Kirsten, with about ten men, was ordered by General Coetzee to hold a position to the right of the white *kopje*, and prevent the enemy from taking it. This position consisted of a small rise, from which we could fire at the *kopje* with a sight of 550 paces. To the right of this rise, at a distance of 80 paces, was a small *kloof* overgrown with bushes, and on the other side of the *kloof* ran a reef of rocks in the direction of the white *kopje*. Here some of the *burghers* had before our arrival forced eleven khakis to surrender, but they had not succeeded in occupying the position, as some khakis had remained in the *kloof*, and had shouted to them that they would not surrender. We were therefore warned against that *kloof*.

But while the others were shooting at the enemy on the white *kopje*, one of our men went by himself to see if there really were any khakis left there. He kept under cover wherever he could—behind the rocks and behind the walls of an old *kraal*—and came close up to the *kloof* without being fired at. On the other side, at a distance of fifty paces, he heard a wounded man groaning and begging for water; but, as he was alone, he did not venture to cross the *kloof*. He returned to his comrades, but they would pay no attention to his request to cross, as they thought the enemy were only waiting until more men came under fire before they began firing.

We continued shooting at the white *kopje*, from which the enemy were firing at us. The captain had a good telescope, through which he could distinctly see the faces of the enemy on the *kopje*. If a khaki showed himself from behind a rock, the captain pointed him out to one of our marksmen, Alec Boshoff, who studied the position through the telescope, and took such good aim that the captain declared he could see the blood on the wounded man's face.

The *burgher* who had gone to the *kloof* tried to persuade the rest to cross with him to the other side, as he was sure the enemy were not inclined to make any resistance there. At length, after twelve, he went with two others to the opposite side, but first told a few of the best marksmen to keep an eye on the reef. They crossed the *kloof* very cautiously. It was dangerous work, as a shot might come at any moment from behind one of the numerous shrubs or boulders. But they did not advance in an unbroken line. Every time they sought cover behind a rock, from which they watched to see whether the enemy would make their appearance. They did not all three advance at the same time, either, but first one and then the other. Whenever they had advanced a few steps, they stopped to ask the wounded man, who lay groaning there, whether he was alone. When they reached him they put some grass under his head, and gave him some brandy from a flask that they always carried with them. The poor man lay in a pool of blood on a rock under some shrubs. He had been shot through the leg. His name was Lieutenant Pilkington.

The wounded man took hold of the hands of one of the *burghers* and begged him to stay with him. He, however, considered it his duty to advance, but first assured the poor man that the *burghers* who were following could also speak English, and would look after him. Most of our men followed the three. The rocks and boulders on the reef that we were climbing afforded us splendid cover from the enemy on the white *kopje*.

To our left we found some more wounded. My brother took charge of one with a ghastly wound in his head. We made some prisoners there, who were too cowardly to defend themselves. A few of our comrades took them down. We could notice by the guns and rugs that were lying about that the enemy had fled in a panic, or else we should never have ventured to do what we did later on.

We could fire at the enemy from a much shorter distance now, but were not yet in their rear. It was necessary that we should occupy the next position—a reef running parallel to the reef we were climbing, at a distance of eighty paces. But it was impossible to take that position, as our guns were firing bomb after bomb from the valley at our back, somewhat to the left of us, so that the stones flew up in the air. We also ran the risk of being taken for khakis, as our men knew nothing of our venture. The captain sent down a message to tell them to stop shelling that position, as we wished to take it. Meanwhile, we kept on firing at the white *kopje*, and the khakis kept on firing at us.

I went back to the wounded officer, who was being looked after by the captain. While we were standing talking, he died from loss of blood. Oh the cruel brutality of war! The poor man was not dead five minutes when we sat smoking his cigarettes.

We moved slightly more to the left towards the boulders. Khaki was on the one side, we on the other. Some of our men had a most original and amusing way of getting at the khakis. 'Come out, you rabbits, come out of your holes, else well shoot down the lot of you!' Then the poor things answered: 'We're afraid to come out. You'll kill us!' They really thought we would shoot them down if they surrendered. The officers had lost all control over the soldiers. Later on, at Nooit Gedacht, where *we* had cover as well as the enemy, it was proved that as soon as the officers lose control over the men they remain lying behind the rocks without firing a shot, as they are too frightened to expose themselves. Most of them still had their *bandoliers* full of cartridges—there, too, when they surrendered.

Before the war the English used to say they would fight us in our own way, from behind rocks; but they forgot that as soon as an officer, having to seek cover himself, fails to keep his eye on his men, they are too cowardly to lift their heads from behind the rocks, as they are not fighting for their independence. On a field like Selikatsnek we are by far the better men.

To get the khakis from behind the rocks, one of our men ran as hard as he could to a rock in their neighbourhood, and aimed at them. Then some of them threw down their guns and put up their hands. Others surrendered more calmly. So he sometimes made five or six of them surrender without their having fired a single shot at him. A shower of bullets always came from the white *kopje*, but, as his movements were quick and unexpected, they could not take proper aim at him. One of the khakis said as he surrendered: 'It is better to surrender than to be a dead man.' Another: 'Just fancy, in the hands of the Boers! I wonder what poor mother'll say!'

Meanwhile the gunners had received the captain's report, and ceased bombarding the reef that we wanted to storm. As it was getting late and there was no other means, one of our men ran forward as hard as he could, making use of every small covering, while the rest kept firing at the white *kopje* to prevent the enemy from taking a proper aim at him. There were not many khakis behind that reef, neither did they fire at him. The rest of us followed at intervals, while those who arrived at the reef again fired at the white *kopje* to cover the others.

The few khakis who surrendered at the reef we first disarmed, and then we allowed them to seek cover behind the rocks from the bullets of their friends. From that position we could see the enemy from the rear. In the narrow road, at a distance of about 150 paces from us, stood an ammunition waggon with splendid horses harnessed in it; there was no room for them to turn to draw away the waggon. A few khakis showed themselves next to the waggon, but were immediately shot down. A little further on an ambulance waggon, also inspanned, stood against the *kopje*; one could distinctly see how the empty litter was carried up and brought down again with some of the wounded

Once a man walked next to the litter as it was carried down; I pointed him out to my brother, as I suspected his motive. I was right. Just by the ambulance waggon he disappeared in a donga leading to the valley. My brother, who was a little higher up the reef than I was, could not hit him, as he appeared again only for a moment. He was most likely a despatch-rider who went to warn the guard at Commandonek to retreat.

Further on there were some horses to be seen, and a little further still the small tents of which the camps consisted. We kept up a constant fire, but the enemy seemed to have sufficient cover on the *kopje*—and they were very obstinate. For some time the firing from the shoulders of the pass ceased, and in the dark shadow between the high mountains we for a moment had the feeling that we had been deserted by our men—only for a moment, for we knew it could not be! The game was in our hands.

The sun sank lower, and we felt if the enemy were not soon compelled to surrender they would escape in the dark. There was still one position which must be taken—the last reef, to which most of the enemy had retired from the position we now occupied. One of our men, therefore, let the other six fire a salvo at the *kopje*, and ran as hard as he could to a rock at a distance of twenty-five paces ahead, about halfway to the last reef. But now both the enemy and our own *burghers*, under Commandant Coetzee, fired at him so persistently that he was thankful to reach the rock. He lay there as still as possible, with his gaze fixed on the reef—as he lay without cover on that side. It was a most critical moment.

Fortunately he heard, almost at once, one of his comrades. Van Zulch, call out 'Oh, the white flag! Hullo, the white flag!' and he saw them climbing down. He lay still a moment longer to convince himself of the fact, and then calmly went to the last reef, where many khakis surrendered—and he descended with them. Now the rest of the *burghers* came running along from all directions to disarm the enemy in the dusk—and to take what booty there was to be had. In their eagerness to get as much booty as possible, they allowed an officer, Major Scobel, to escape.

As I arrived rather late on the battlefield, I cannot give any account of the order in which De la Rey placed his men, neither do I know the number of the enemy's dead and wounded, nor how many lives our victory cost us. I have never seen any official report concerning this battle. Field-Cornet Van Zulch, who with Commandant Boshoff, took the officers to Machadodorp, and who is at present a fellow-prisoner, tells me that three officers—Colonel Roberts, Lieutenants Davis and Lyall—and 210 soldiers of the Lincolnshire Regiment were taken prisoners, and that four companies of the Scots Greys had early that morning escaped with two guns. Our loss, both dead and wounded, was not more than thirteen or fourteen men. The enemy had made a stubborn resistance, judging from the number of dead and wounded that were lying on the field. Of the seven of us who forced the enemy to surrender by attacking them in the rear, not one was injured, although we were the attacking party. They say that the khaki prisoners whom we left on the reef remained there all night, and came down the following morning with little white flags made of the bandages that a soldier always carries with him, tied to twigs.

Chapter 6

Narrow Escape of President Steyn and General de Wet

Commandant Boshoff had been ordered to take the prisoners to Machadodorp. He left my brother and me with Captain Kirsten, who had to reconnoitre in the direction of Rustenburg along the Magalies Mountains. We first of all passed through Commandonek, and found that deserted by the enemy. We had no adventures on our way to Rustenburg.

The Rustenburgers, who had nearly all laid down their arms and taken the oath of neutrality, took courage when they saw De la Rey's big commando, and joined us one and all.

Then we recognised a great fault in the character of our people. Without the slightest compunction, they first fail in loyalty to their own country, and then break the oath of neutrality, although the enemy had in no single respect violated their part of the contract. Some of them we, in a way, forced to join us, as we took the guns and horses of the unwilling ones or of those who acted at all in a suspicious way. We also called them traitors. But most of the *burghers* joined us of their own free will. Many had not taken the oath of neutrality, as they had been beyond the reach of the enemy; others had, after Lord Roberts' threatening proclamations, ridden over to the enemy to give up their arms, but had given up their old rifles and kept the Mausers for 'eventualities,' to use the now historical word of Sir Alfred Milner.

A few of the oath-breakers tried to excuse themselves by the Jesuit plea that either they did not mean what they swore or else they had purposely changed the form of the oath. In judging those who broke the oath of neutrality later on, we must remember that the enemy did not keep to their part of the contract, and so our men were justified in considering it as null and void, and, according to William Stead, their forcing us to take the oath of neutrality was against the Geneva Convention. But it is too difficult a question for me to discuss.

When the enemy, a few days later, drove us from Olifantsnek, General de la Rey sent Captain Kirsten with twenty men to the neighbouring kopjes to prevent the enemy from going on a plundering expedition. Then I for the first time saw a farmhouse burnt down by the enemy. From a high *kopje*, by the aid of a telescope, we could distinctly see the movements of the khakis. The bitter feeling that was roused in us in our helplessness is not to be described.

General Baden-Powell was in Rustenburg, and Magatonek was also in possession of the enemy.

It was a most interesting and adventurous time that we spent near the Magalies Mountains. By day we went reconnoitring along the hills near the mountains in the direction of Olifantsnek, and towards evening we withdrew into the thick woods of the *kloofs*, where it was delightfully warm both for ourselves and for our horses. When a small number of the enemy came in our direction, we fired at them unexpectedly from the hills, and so protected the farmhouses on the mountain-sides. Occasionally the khakis ventured a little nearer, but always had to retreat in disorder.

I once nearly fell into the hands of the enemy. As we were reconnoitring on one of the *kopjes*, I suggested to a friend that we should go to the farm in front of us, where none of us had been since Olifantsnek was in possession of the enemy. We had to ford a *donga* closed in by barbed wire. When we got to the farm, we were told that the enemy had not been there, with the exception of a khaki who had lost his way. He had taken six eggs from a nest in a *kraal* and swallowed them greedily, and had then passed on to the garden without speaking a word to the harmless, inquisitive women of the farm.

For safety's sake I put the boys on guard and had the horses tied. The view was so enclosed on all sides that the enemy could appear most unexpectedly from Olifantsnek. We had been there only a short time, when we were told that the enemy were coming in large numbers from the direction of Rustenburg. We mounted at once and rode back, but could not get back to our comrades on the hills because of the barbed wire in the *donga*. We had gone only about 250 paces along the drift, when the enemy came riding along. Fortunately, they were intent on plunder and did not see us, as they kept their eyes fixed in the direction of the house. If we had been a few seconds later we should have fallen into their hands. The few *burghers* on the *kopjes* began to fire at them, and when I got to the top of one of the *kopjes* I saw the enemy—about 100 in number—fleeing in great disorder. This expedition cost them several dead and wounded, besides their plunder—meal, fowls, and other things—that they dropped in their flight.

When I went back to the farm later on, I was told that one of the girls had clapped her hands with delight when the enemy fled past them. That must have been the reason why she and her family were so cruelly insulted and plundered by the khakis afterwards. We met with great kindness during our stay in the Magalies Mountains. We always got something to eat, and towards evening we bought some loaves of bread to take back with us to our hiding-place. In those days we could always get forage for our horses, and they were in very good condition.

Meanwhile General de la Rey had gone with a commando to the west of Rustenburg, and had left two *commandants* in the Zwartkoppen, to the north-east of Rustenburg.

When we got the tidings that the enemy had taken possession of Selikatsnek, we went as rapidly as we could to the Zwartkoppen. We had many adventures on our way. My brother and I rode on ahead, thinking that the others would follow, but they went a roundabout way, and so did not catch us up. When we left the wide tract of wood that stretches along the Magalies Mountains, we noticed that the enemy from Rustenburg had come to meet the column from Selikatsnek. Fortunately, our horses were good, and we escaped the danger by riding back into the wood to a farm that I knew of. While we were giving our horses a rest there, a despatch-rider came along looking for a reconnoitring corps. We rode with him in the track of our comrades, who had taken a great circuit round Rustenburg. We arrived safely at Zwartkoppen, and immediately joined Commandant Boshoff, who had just returned from Machadodorp.

The *commandants* now followed General de la Rey. We came up with his commando to the west of Rustenburg, where he had surrounded a party of the enemy. Commandant Boshoff, however, was immediately sent to Olifantsnek, as the enemy had left Rustenburg and the pass was clear. Our men were most changeable in their moods. The slightest favourable tidings raised their spirits, but any unfavourable news made their courage sink into their shoes. There was much talk about the retreating movement of the enemy. Some spoke of intervention; others said the English soldiers had refused to fight any longer, or that the whole of the colony was in rebellion. This talk went the round even among the officers, probably because they did not understand the enemy's movements.

Now we know the meaning of it all. It was De Wet who was being followed. We were not two days at Olifantsnek, when, to our great surprise, De Wet arrived with a commando of 2,800 men, followed by 40,000 English. He had been by treason separated along with Steyn from the chief commando, and had been chased by the enemy a month already.

It was a great *laager* that advanced through Olifantsnek—the largest commando that we had seen yet, with numerous carts, waggons, beasts of burden, and other belongings. And it was then I made the acquaintance of President Steyn and De Wet. Our Commandant with his men accompanied President Steyn to Machadodorp to President Kruger. We put up our tents for the time being next to those of President Steyn, so that we had time and opportunity enough to learn to know him. When the enemy a few days later broke through at Magatonek, to the west of Rustenburg, General De Wet sent for me one evening and ordered me to take a report to Rustenburg, and gave me some instructions for the *commandants* there.

I had to take a message for President Steyn also, that the ambulance of the Orange Free State was to follow the *laager* in the direction of the Krokodil River.

Late at night I arrived at Rustenburg, only to find that the *laagers* had already taken flight. The enemy were expected at any moment. But the ambulance was there still, and all night long I led it in the direction the general had told me the *laagers* would take.

Late the following morning I arrived at De Wet's *laager*, which had moved a few hours further on to Sterkstroom. The commando left there that afternoon, and went along the Magalies Mountains to Commandonek. That day and that night we had a first experience of the long tiresome marches that enabled De Wet to mislead the enemy.

That night President Steyn made a most favourable impression on us with his talk. He did not try to encourage us with hopes of intervention, but merely pointed out that the war might last a long time still, and that we would have to enter the Colony.

At Commandonek we rested a few hours while De Wet himself went to reconnoitre. He sent a message to the English officer in charge of the pass that he must surrender. The officer replied that he did not quite understand who must surrender—he or De Wet. I think this was merely a dodge on De Wet's part to find out by the signature of the reply who was in charge of the army at the pass, and so to make a guess at the numbers of the enemy.

He decided not to attack the pass, and before daybreak next day we were on the move again. Some time afterwards at Warmbad I heard that an English general had related this dodge of De Wet's, but he thought De Wet had threatened him with a very small force, as his commando must still have been at Olifantsnek. It is an example of the way we misled the enemy by our mobility.

CHAPTER 7

With President Steyn to President Kruger

Near Krokodil River, on Carlyle's Farm, President Steyn and his attendants separated from De Wet's commando, and went in the direction of Zoutpan to Machadodorp. We were about seventy-five men in all. The little commando consisted of carts, a few trolleys, and horsemen on strong, well conditioned horses. The Free Staters nearly all had one or two spare horses. Our own commando still always consisted of twelve or thirteen men, and the small ambulance waggon which we used for provisions. The French doctor had remained behind with De la Rey. We moved very fast. At Zoutpan—a sunken *kopje* like the mouth of a crater, with a pan at the bottom, from which the salt is got—I met some old acquaintances, who pretended to have come there for salt.

During our talk my suspicions were roused by their curiosity, and by their knowledge of President Steyn's arrival. I also doubted their tale that their trolley stood behind a *kopje*, and not at Zoutpan, and I warned the *commandant* against them. He became very anxious, and made us move on as rapidly as possible, for once we had crossed the Pienaars River all danger from khaki would be past. It was a good thing that the *commandant* made us travel so fast, for we had only just outspanned at Pienaars River the following morning when the khakis' bomb Maxim began firing at the outposts of General Grobler's Waterberg commando, which was stationed there. We had only just time to inspan and ride off to the Boschveld, towards the Olifants River, where we would be safe, while General Grobler disappeared in the direction of Warmbad.

At Pienaars River I made the acquaintance of General Celliers, who was loudly proclaiming the way in which he would squash khaki if only the *burghers* would fight. He is the exception to the rule that all braggarts are cowards. Most of the braggarts have gradually disappeared from the scene, but the deeds of this hero were always in accordance with his words.

We heard afterwards that a detachment of the enemy had followed us, but we had had too great a start, and had besides taken a short-cut of which they knew nothing. It would not have been easy for the khakis to overtake a well-mounted commando like President Steyn's.

We were also told that the enemy knew of the arrival of President Steyn, which strengthened my belief that the two suspicious characters at Zoutpan were the informers. Whenever we, as the attacking party, made prisoners, they always declared that they had known all about our plan of attack—probably to discourage us with the thought that through the treachery of our own people the enemy always knew all about our movements.

For a long way we followed the same road that we had taken with Commandant Boshoff to Rustenburg. We arrived safely at Waterval-Boven (President Kruger having already retreated from Machadodorp), where we stayed a few days and heard the famous Battle of Dalmanutha (August 27)—the most awful roar of cannon that I have ever heard.

From Waterval-Boven we went to Nelspruit, to which President Kruger had moved in his railway-home. We gave our horses a week's rest and passed the time fishing and hunting. We were content there, as we got plenty to eat, and our horses, too, were well fed—an important matter to us just then. Circumstances were forcing us to attach much value to all sorts of trifles that we would formerly not even have noticed.

If once one has suffered the pangs of hunger, one learns to value the comfort and luxury of home; and if one has wandered about for weeks without seeing woman or child, one learns to appreciate their gentleness and charm and to understand Schiller's Züchtige *hausfrau* in *Das Lied von der Glocke*. How often in our wanderings we longed for good literature during our long, tiring, monotonous rides! And how terrible was the thought of the moral hurt we were suffering—voluntarily in a way, yet forced to it by a sense of honour and duty. For in this lay the grievousness of the war, that a powerful nation—influenced by a few unscrupulous leaders—was trying to annihilate a small nation that demanded the right of existence, and was therefore forced to defend that right. It was a happy time for us when we had the opportunity of turning our thoughts towards literature and other things than commando work.

The privations that we had already endured were small indeed in comparison to those which awaited us. It was well with the *uitlander* optimist who remained in our country while the Republics could give him the comforts he demanded as his right, but who, as soon as things went wrong, and he saw nothing but misery in the future, left for his own country—there to sit in judgment on our peasant-nation. How I long for the gift of being able to express myself, to give a true account of the self-denial of our *burghers* and of the misery that we endured! How my heart bleeds when I think of the great sorrow that has come upon my poor people!

When the enemy approached the Delagoa railway-line, President Steyn left with his escort for Hectorspruit. I had to follow with a trolley for which there was no room on the train. Because of the disorder that reigned everywhere I had to wait nearly three days before I could start. I was pretty nearly famished on my arrival at Hectorspruit, and ate greedily of the remains of the porridge left by some *burghers*, among whom were two sons of State Secretary Reitz. President Steyn's *laager* had in the meanwhile become 250 men strong, under Commandant Lategan, and was then at Krokodil River.

At Nelspruit I met a couple of old friends, Malherbe and Celliers, with whom I left for the *laager*. They were both Transvaalers who had been studying in Holland, but had returned before finishing their studies on account of the war. The commando was well supplied with weapons and ammunition, as the Delagoa Bay line brought plenty to our store. What became of the rest I do not know, as President Steyn was in a hurry and our commando left first for the North.

The ford at Krokodil River was about fifty paces wide—made for the occasion and difficult to cross. The trolleys and waggons that had to cross to the *laager* on the opposite side gave us much trouble, as they sank deep into the sand. We harnessed a double span of oxen to the waggons, undressed ourselves, and had to swim alongside the animals to get them through. Occasionally something dropped from one of the waggons and had to be fished up in a hurry to save it from the strong current. There was much shouting and laughter, and if any crocodile had been in the neighbourhood he would have suppressed his hunger until the storm was over.

On the banks of the river there was a constant shooting at fish and game, and even at crocodiles, who showed themselves occasionally. There was game in abundance. It seemed as if all the game of the Transvaal, that is becoming so scarce, had fled to this part.

We were on our way to Pietersburg through the Boschveld of South-East Lydenburg, which might be called a desert in winter. It was a journey difficult even for a trek Boer, and more than difficult for a large commando. A man called Hester was our guide. Some two years before he had made the same journey on a hunting expedition, and now he was able to follow the ruts which the wheels of his waggon had made then, and which would be in all probability deepened by the summer rains. Our means of transport were chiefly carts and trolleys, on which we also put our bedding to lighten the burden of our riding horses.

Chapter 8

Lost

On September 12 we left the Krokodil River early in the morning, after first watering our cattle and filling our water-bags. Our guide did not expect to come across any water before the Sabie—a river several days' journey further on. There were several springs on the way, but as that part of the country was so little known, because of its unhealthiness, no one could tell when the last rains had fallen.

The shrubs and bushes had grown high above the ruts made by the waggon two years ago, and were a great hindrance to us. The road we followed twisted and wound rather more than was agreeable, but it was certainly easy to follow for the *laagers* that came after us. The horsemen rode next to the *laagers* to shoot bucks. We had no 'slaughter-cattle' with us, so had to live on the game that we shot.

In the neighbourhood of the river we still came across birds and insects, but the further we went the more monotonous and *dead* Nature became. I could never have pictured such a lifeless wood to myself. No sound of insects was to be heard, no chirp or song of bird; and not even the trail of a serpent was to be seen.

There was a melancholy stillness. Traces of game were in abundance. It seemed as if only those animals lived there which, accustomed to the monotonous silence, withdrew noiselessly from the gaze of the interloper, or, in their ignorant curiosity, stood still until a hunter's bullet warned them or put an end to their lives. To them we must have been strange disturbers of the peace. Shots fell in all directions; sometimes a whole salvo was discharged when we came upon a herd of bucks. There were many thornless trees growing in their stately height far above the usual scrub of the Boschveld. Our horses often grazed on the sweet buffalo grass that always grows under trees. Looked at from a rise, the Boschveld appeared to be nothing but trees—trees as far as the eye could see. One shuddered at the thought of what would become of anyone who lost his way there, since for miles and miles there was no water to be seen and no trail to go by. It made one hurry back to the safety of the *laager*, trusting to the capability of the guide.

To our great joy, the first spring contained water. It was a large pool surrounded by rocks, where the game was accustomed to drink. We arrived there towards afternoon, rested a few hours, and continued our journey with fresh courage. As the waggons moved too slowly for our liking, we rode on ahead; but the consequence was that, when it got dark and we off-saddled, we had no bedding, for nearly all the waggons were obliged to outspan when darkness set in, as there was no road.

We knee-haltered our horses in case there were lions about, and collected a large quantity of wood to keep the fire going all night. That night our talk, of course, ran upon lion-hunting and shooting expeditions. Then we crept as close to the fire as possible, and were soon in a troubled, or untroubled, sleep, dreaming of lions and other wild animals. But I felt the cold very much, and could not sleep without my rug, and kept turning from side to side to get as much warmth from the fire as possible. If only I had made two fires! In a battle I have been between two fires, and did not find it at all agreeable, but in this case it would have been different.

I lay awake, waiting for the third fire, the red dawn, but not in a poetical mood. There is a time for everything; that I learnt during the war. Rain is lovely, and cold gives energy, but one must be warm to appreciate it. As I lay thus, four mules, tethered together, came closer and closer up to our fire, grazing all the while. I lay still, listening to the peculiar noise made by the biting off of each mouthful of grass. I seemed to expect a joke, and suddenly one of the mules fell on his back. In a moment all our heroes were up and ready to defend themselves against lions or khakis, according to their different dreams. I laughed, and laughed again, so that the hyenas could hear me a mile off, and the startled lion-hunters began to laugh also, so that we woke up the whole camp. This little episode made my blood circulate, so that I very soon also was in the land of dreams.

As the *burghers* chased all the game on ahead of the *laager*, the President and Commandant Boshoff agreed to go in advance, so as to have a chance of seeing the numerous kinds of wild buck and larger game. I went with them. Greatly to my distress I forgot to ask our guide what direction we would take that day with regard to the sun. An experienced hunter would not have forgotten it, as he knows from experience that in the excitement of the chase we often leave the beaten track. I had to pay dearly for my forgetfulness. I rode some distance to the left of the President, but took care to keep him in sight. But the Boer is wonderfully disobedient to any authority, and not long after two men made their appearance to my left, and I saw that if I did not look out they would be ahead of me in no time, and chase all the game away from me.

As the *donga* next to which we rode seemed to be a favourite resort for game, I took the same direction as they did, more to the left. The *dongas* ran into each other with numerous bends and curves, and were some times overgrown with high grass, then again quite bare. I paid no attention to the direction we took.

After a while one of the men wounded a buck, and they both rode into the *donga* after it. I rode on, to cross the *donga* a little further on, so as not to have to follow in the track of the other two, and saw a red buck on the other side, which I wounded so badly that it seemed unnecessary to fire again, and I rode leisurely towards it. But when I had crossed the *donga* the buck had disappeared, and I began to seek for the traces of blood, but I soon had to give up the search, not to lose sight of the other two men. They, however, seemed to be a great distance off, as I did not overtake them, and I did not succeed in tracing them in the direction that the wounded buck had led them, as the track in the grass was invisible to my inexperienced eye.

I rode back to the *donga*, and deliberated on the course to take. In all directions I heard shots, right and left, but I stood irresolute. I had no watch with me to find the four quarters of the wind, but the sun had only just risen, and I made a guess with an imaginary compass. It was lucky for me that I made such a good guess, and had paid great attention to the direction we had taken with regard to the sun. I was certain that I should come upon the traces of the *laager* if only I kept within the sides of a right angle, unless the *laager* had at the start taken a sharp turn to the right or left.

But it was possible that in our excitement we might have crossed the waggon track which the *laager* was to follow; then the *laager* would be far to the right. Standing thus like the ass between two bundles of hay, I was not in the mood to think lightly of my case, but had to act at once, so I chose the safest and more probable of the two sides of my right angle—namely, the left, as I would then in any case not be moving towards Portuguese territory, and could always turn to the

Krokodil River.

I felt pretty certain now, as it was more probable that we had not crossed the old waggon tract, and every moment I expected to hear the switching of the long whips. But when I had gone some distance I was obliged to return to the *donga*, and retrace my way to the place where we had slept. A clever Boer would have succeeded in finding the way back, but I soon lost my way altogether. I lost the traces of the horse's hoofs, and the *dongas* looked to me so different that in one place where a *donga* branched off I did not know which to follow. An intense feeling of desolation took possession of me. Lost in a wilderness without food or water! I thought of the twelve or thirteen men who got lost in this wood on a hunting expedition, and of whom only one was saved. A great fear came upon me. Gradually I became calmer, and tried to form some plan of action. I resolved to keep to the left, where I had already seen a solitary mountain. Perhaps water was to be found there.

My gun was loaded with dum-dum bullets, specially prepared for bucks. I had filed through the steel to the lead, so that the bullet would expand at once when it came into contact with bone. I found a buck tame in its very wildness, but I missed it, for the aim of my gun, a fine sporting Mauser, had been bent by the branches of the trees. It was a good thing that I did not come across a lion, or, rather, that a lion did not come across me.

I had to ride under trees, through shrubs and grass, and had to keep a sharp look-out, as the king of beasts sometimes takes the lords of creation unawares. And I had to look out for an opportunity to shoot a buck—the only food within my reach. The nearer I came to the mountain, the surer I was that I had lost my way completely, and the more I became reconciled to my fate. I planned how I should build a large fire in the night for myself and my horse, and how I should defend myself against a lion with a burning piece of wood.

Suddenly my horse went faster and pushed to the left. Greatly to my astonishment, I saw that the attraction was a little stream of water that he had scented in a *donga*. I off-saddled, and let my horse graze in the luxuriant grass.

Now I was strengthened in my belief that I had taken the wrong direction, for we were all under the impression that we should not soon reach water. I prepared some more dum-dum bullets with a small file that I carried in my pocket, and did not let my horse graze long, but hastened to the mountain to find a better shelter for the night. To my great joy, I came upon the wide road about a thousand paces further on. I followed the road along the mountain for half an hour, when I came upon the *laager*, camped near a stream—probably the same stream at which I and my horse had quenched our thirst.

As we sat round our fires that night we heard shots fired in the distance from the direction that we had come. Some men were sent out immediately, and returned after a while with a man quite exhausted from hunger and thirst, and paralysed with fear; he had been unable to overtake the *laager*.

Chapter 9

Adventure on the Sabie

Experience teaches us. The knowledge that we have gained in this war we must pass on to the coming generation. It may be of use in a war of the future, or on some other occasion. Therefore Oom Dietlof will take this opportunity to give his nephews in South Africa some practical hints that may be of use to a *burgher* in his travels or in a war. If anyone loses his way in the same way that I have just described, he must remember the following way of finding the four quarters of the wind:

The small hand of a watch describes a circle in twelve hours, while the apparent movement of the sun round the earth is in twenty-four hours. The movement of the small hand is therefore twice as fast as that of the sun. If one points the small hand of a horizontallying watch to the sun at twelve o'clock, then the hands and the figure XII. lie in the meridian as well as the sun.

In the northern half-circle the sun and the hands move in the same direction. In one hour's time the small hand goes a distance of 360° over 12 = 30°, and the sun goes a distance of 360° over 24° = 15°. If at one o'clock one points the small hand of a horizontal-lying watch to the sun, the line that divides the acute angle between the figures I. and XII. lies in the meridian. So one can always find the meridian.

In the southern half-circle the sun and hands move in opposite directions, therefore one must point the figure XII. to the sun, and then divide the acute angle between the figure XII. and the small hand to find the meridian.

In this way one can at any time find out the direction one has taken. But everyone has not always a good watch, and the sun sometimes hides behind the clouds. Then it is better to have a good compass—but better still not to lose one's way.

Besides such simple articles as a pocket-knife, a water-bag, etc., which are indispensable to a traveller in our country, everyone ought to carry with him a good plaster, a nosebag, and some snake poison; maize (mealies) for his horse, the cheapest and most strengthening food that we know of, can always be carried in the nosebag. Snake poison prepared by a good *kaffir* doctor is the only cure for snake-bites or the bite of any poisonous insect. The *kaffirs* prepare it from some (to us) unknown shrub, and from the poison of the most venomous snake, which they make into a powder. This powder is used as an antidote by swallowing a small dose—enough to cover the point of a pocket-knife—and also by applying some to the bite, after first having cut an opening into the bitten part with a pocket-knife.

Some people protect themselves against the poison of a snake-bite by regularly swallowing some of the poison and vaccinating themselves with it. One can even protect one's self in this way against the bite of the poisonous file-snake of the Boschveld—a snake the shape of a three-cornered file, sometimes from 3 to 4 feet long. It is a fact that the person whose body is proof against the poison of a snake-bite is never bitten, as he is feared by snakes. Formerly I doubted it, but I have myself seen people who have made themselves proof against a bite in this way, and I have also heard it from people in whom I have the utmost faith.

Alcohol is also a good antidote, provided one takes it immediately and in such quantities that it goes to the head. I would recommend everyone always to take a small quantity of brandy with him on commando, if experience had not taught me that some take even a mosquito-bite as an excuse to ' take a drop,' and I am against that on principle.

Often while loading my horse the thought struck me whether the poor brute ever had a wish to protest, 'Surely this is becoming too bad!' and that reminds me that one must be very careful not to overload. The knapsack must not be filled with *kaboe* mealies (roasted maize) for one's self, while the nosebag of the poor horse remains empty.

More than one prisoner of war has bitterly regretted that he did not take his horse's power of endurance into greater consideration. Now I must take up the thread of my tale.

The following morning the *laager* would start at three o'clock, and, as my horse was in good condition, the owner of the horse that had been left behind asked me to fetch it before the *laager* left. He explained to me where I would find it tied to a tree about half an hour's ride from the *laager*, so I started with a friend at about two o'clock at night. On the way we came across a mule that had wandered away while grazing, ignorant of all the danger he was exposing himself to in the uninhabited Boschveld. The creature gave us much trouble by refusing to be caught and constantly dodging behind a tree, so we lost a great deal of time. On our way back, close to the *laager*, we heard the whine of the wild-dog, the well-known feared wolf. We thought it very interesting to come across a wild animal of which we had no fear just then. But when we reached the camping-ground of the laager, where only the trolley stood to which the wandering mule belonged, we found to our surprise that both white men and *kaffirs* had given up the search for the mule for fear of the wild-dog. They had all congregated round large fires. The wild-dog, however, is harmless by himself; like the khakis, his strength lies in numbers. We had to leave the sick horse to join the bucks of the Boschveld on its recovery, until the horse-sickness came.

After a long, tiring, but very interesting ride we arrived at the Sabie, where the rest of the *laager* was already encamped. The Sabie is about the size of the Krokodil River, and its scenery of woods and valleys formed a sharp contrast to the deadly monotony of the Boschveld that lay behind us. We had crossed the bare desert and were now in a part of the country inhabited by *kaffirs*. The following day the *laager* was removed half an hour further on, and there we remained a few days.

At night four of us were persuaded to go eel-catching in a crocodile-pool that we had discovered a little further on. We made a large fire to entice the eels, and, as we were none of us great lovers of angling, we made a splendid bonfire, as there was plenty of dry wood to be had.

There was something particularly attractive in these large fires on those quiet, dark nights of the wilderness. The glow threw a sombre light on the water that gave one a creepy feeling, as if a crocodile were on the watch for us in the water, and lions at our back between the large trees. What must they have thought of us?

The bank of the river seemed to be about 6 feet high, and not very steep. We made the fire closer and closer to what seemed the bank. I saw someone lift up a huge branch, walk to the bank with it, and plant his left foot firmly on the ground. The reeds gave way beneath him. What seemed a firm bank, by the glow of the fire, proved to be a mass of reeds and grass, and the poor man fell down a height of 6 feet, his fall being hastened by the heavy branch he held. For a moment we stood irresolute. To jump after him into a crocodile-pool! But he called for help, and we had to act immediately. Fortunately, one acts almost instinctively in such cases. One of the others slid down the bank—the thought striking him: 'If only there are not two crocodiles!' Landing on a horizontal branch, he stretched out his hand to the drowning man, someone else took hold of his left hand, and so they were both saved. If a crocodile had been in the neighbourhood, he would probably have stood on the defensive. Such a queer, two-legged animal who led the attack in such a strange but decided way must have roused his respect.

This piece of fun put an end to our eel-fishing. We had caught only one eel—and a man.

The following morning there was parade for President Steyn. His speech to us was touching and to the point, and showed that he believed in a good ending to the war, if the burghers were capable of enduring such hardships as at present. Then he also told us in what a hurry he was to reach his burghers, as he was afraid that the enemy were doing all in their power to make them turn against him. We all liked President Steyn very much.

On our journey through the Selatie Goldfields, past the Marietje River to Pilgrim's Rest, we crossed the steepest mountain that I have ever seen. A double span of oxen was harnessed to each waggon. The oxen were lent us for the occasion by the Boers living on the plateau in front of us. After every few steps upwards we had to put stones under the wheels to prevent the waggons from slipping back. It took our little *laager* nearly all day to reach the plateau. Then we had a most magnificent view of the Boschveld that lay behind us. In the distance the Lobombo Mountains were visible on the boundary of the Portuguese and Transvaal territory. The first rains had fallen on the plateau, so the green grass was a refreshing change for our eyes. The horses would be able to graze well, and the good feeding would soon make them lose their old coats, and then they would be sleek and glossy again.

From the high plateau we descended, over a 'lumpy' *veld*, with an oasis here and there in a hole or valley, or on the top of a hill, to Pilgrim's Rest. Some miles before we reached this little town we passed beside the waterworks that supply a strong stream of water for the machinery of the gold-mines. We simply stormed the shops, that were still well supplied with provisions, and bought all sorts of luxuries and necessaries for our journey. From Pilgrim's Rest we once more crossed a steep mountain, along a road that for length and height has not its equal. In the neighbourhood of Ohrigstad, a little town that we left to our right, I asked a Boer woman whether the fever did not make one's life impossible there, and I got a very *naïf* reply: 'No; this year the fever was not so bad. We all got ill, but not one of us died.'

The rest of our journey to the north of Lydenburg, over Spekstroom River, along Watervalop, over Steenkampsberg to Roossenekal, was very tedious. The uninhabited Boschveld was very interesting, and we had sufficient provisions then, but the poor, uncivilized Boer inhabitants of the Lydenburg district were unable to supply us with necessaries, the want of which we were beginning to feel. We could not buy a loaf of bread anywhere. And it is anything but pleasant in a time of war to come across such lax and unenergetic people as they proved to be.

The men were nearly always at home, and appeared to be discouraged and unwilling to fight. We had all lost our sweet tooth. That one could tell by such expressions as: 'Even if you give me sugar—' But occasionally we got a more desirable substitute, when a beehive was discovered in a cleft of a rock. Some of our men are particularly clever at discovering a hive. I have often seen a man stand gazing up at the sky, walk on a short distance, and again stand gazing, and after awhile appear with a bucket of honey. By watching the flight of the bees they find out in what direction the hive is. A practised eye can see the rising and settling of the bees above the hive from a great distance.

Chapter 10

From Roossenekal to Pietersburg

We went in a very different direction from that of General Ben Viljoen's commando, which took the road to Pietersburg through Leydsdorp. President Steyn celebrated the anniversary of his birthday at Roossenekal, and addressed us in the same spirit as on the former occasion at the Sabie.

Roossenekal is famous for its caves, or grottos, in which the Mapochers hid themselves so well during the Mapoch War. We made use of the opportunity to visit the grottos, of whose formation I should like to know more. What appeared on the outside to be an ordinary hill proved a most wonderful natural building containing many rooms. The old *kraal* walls and the peach-trees and 'Turkish figs', (prickly-pears), overgrown by wild trees, and an occasional earthen vessel, were the remains of the *kaffir* city. Of course we cut our names into the rocks by way of becoming immortal. We could not help speaking with great admiration of the wild *kaffir* tribe who from such a hiding-place fought for months for a life of independence. We had no time to visit the grottos further away.

Although our horses were well fed during this time of rest, they profited little, on account of the constant cold rains that fell. We fortunately still had some tents, that we used only in case of rain. Our *commandant* was still always in doubt whether to proceed to Pietersburg, for we were quite ignorant of the enemy's movements during the last few weeks. Later on, when he got the information that the enemy were stationed at Pinaars River bridge, and that we could not with safety pass Warmbad and Pinaars River, we had to turn off at Kobaltmyn to the right to cross Olifants River lower down. We had already passed Kobaltmyn in the beginning of July on our journey after General de la Rey. The latter part of our journey, along Olifants

River, through Zebedelsland to Pietersburg, was exhausting for man and horse. Some of us often had nothing but a little rice and a small piece of meat for several days in succession. There was scarcely any grass for our horses, and yet we had to ride hard night and day.

After a tiring journey of fully a month. President Steyn's commando arrived at Pietersburg on October 11. Although we had always intended to follow President Steyn to De Wet, my brother and I, with Malherbe, now accepted an invitation from my uncle, Ignace Maré to stay awhile on his farm at Marabastad. President Steyn left with his commando for Nylstroom. Our horses were worn out, and could not follow the commando. Most of the men had a spare horse that was still in good condition, and although my brother and I had only one horse apiece, we often had to do the hardest work.

My aunt and uncle did their best to make our stay a pleasant one, and our horses were well fed. Soon General Ben Viljoen's commando arrived at Marabastad, and stayed there a few weeks, so that we also experienced the discomfort arising from a *laager* camped on one's farm. The Boer is deprived by it of all necessaries, and all sorts and conditions of men constantly visit his house. Some of them, the riff-raff of the commando, are very unwelcome guests, for they do much mischief intentionally, and thereby give the commando a very bad name. The poles to which the wire is attached for camping at a farm were yet left undamaged. The *burghers* were still accustomed to get plenty of dry wood in the Boschveld, and were not yet so demoralized as to work damage without scruple.

We stayed at my uncle's far longer than we at first intended. My saddle had chafed the horse's back so severely that I could not ride it for several months. My brother got an attack of malaria, and just as he was recovering had a relapse, so that President Steyn was so far. in advance of us that there was no question of overtaking him.

The commando had already left Marabastad when we started for Tweefontein, near Warmbad, on our now strong, sleek horses. There we joined Commandant Kemp, of the Krugersdrop commando, under Wyk III., who had parted from Ben Viljoen at Marabastad because the latter had on a Sunday afternoon during service fired off several cannon-shots for the edification of a few fast women.

Malherbe, my brother, and I formed a sort of comradeship under Corporal Botman—or, to put it simply, we were 'chums.' At Warmbad we heard many interesting things about the khakis, who had stayed there nineteen days on their hunt after De Wet. We could not understand why they destroyed the bathing-houses, unless it were to deprive our wounded of the chance of recovery.

The condition of the people in Zoutpansberg and in Waterberg, where the enemy had been, was not very cheerful. Everyone complained that there was no sugar to be had, that the meal was getting low, and that soon there would be no clothes. Pietersburg was exhausted by the commandos, and the courage of the inhabitants was nearly at an ebb. They would not yet make the sacrifice that would part them from their families. The enemy had not yet driven them to despair by the destruction of their fields and goods.

Every sensible person knew that the Republics would lose in the long-run in a guerilla war unless something unforeseen happened. At the time that we fled from Pretoria my mother said she would have hope as long as her 'gorillas' remained in the *veld*. Even if we clung to a straw, the possibility always remained that things might take a favourable turn as long as a fair number of *burghers* remained in the *veld*.

The *burghers* from the different districts now in Waterberg were earnest and full of courage. Noticeable changes for the better had been made. Beyers, a man in whom the men had the utmost faith, was made Assistant-Commandant-General, and was to lead a commando of 1,500 horsemen from Waterberg, Zoutpansberg, Krugersdorp, etc., to the Hoogeveld. The discipline was much stricter. Cooper and Fanie Grobler, who had been accused of high treason, promised to keep a sharper look-out for spies and traitors. And we still always hoped for an eventual rebellion in Cape Colony. That hope was our life-buoy on which we kept our eyes fixed.

We felt that there our safety lay, and the enthusiasm of the commando was heightened by the desire to celebrate Paardekraal Day in Krugersdorp on December 15, As a sailor longs for the sea, so we longed for a meeting with the khakis when we left for the Magalies Mountains in the beginning of December. Our commando was light and mobile, with provisions for a short time only. Such heavy cannon as the Long Toms were of no use to us now. Henceforward we were to live on the produce of the surrounding country, as there was no basis from which we were to operate. Besides this, the khakis very kindly made over some of their provisions, arms, and ammunition to us in a skirmish or battle, so that afterwards we had more Lee-Metfords than Mausers in our possession.

At Krokodil River I had the privilege of seeing how a honey-bird takes a human being to a bees' nest. As we were lying under a tree, a honey-bird settled close to us. Corporal Botman followed it as it flew chirping from tree to tree, and called to it that he was following, until the bird stopped at the hive. The grateful finder always rewards the bird with a piece of honeycomb that he puts aside for it. But I have never been able to discover whether the bird or the insects eat the honey. I know that the 'bug-birds,' that are always seen on or near cattle, do not feed on the bugs with which the cattle are covered, but on the locusts that fly about the herd. Last week, when our guards took us for a walk outside the fort, I noticed that a kind of sparrow in India has the same trick of catching the locusts that are driven on ahead by the cattle.

I shall not try to give a description of the works of the machinery that moved mechanically to the Magalies Mountains, for I should have to guess at the particulars in this historical little tale. Mechanical I call the journey, for. there were days and nights in which we were numbed, body and soul, exhausted by hunger and thirst and want of sleep.

When we were at Bethany, a convoy of the enemy was seen moving in the direction of Commandonek. When it noticed our guard, it dragged its curved body with great zeal through the pass. I think the khakis also must have been bored to death on those long, fruitless journeys. We left Bethany towards evening, and reached the Magalies Mountains the following morning after a tiring journey in the night past Sterkstroom, through the Kromriverskloof to the foot of Onuapadnek, or Boschfonteinnek. (I learnt the names from the inhabitants.) In the *kloof* we passed the burnt remains of the convoy that was taken by Commandant Boshoff—who joined De la Rey after having taken Steyn to his destination—and his brave little troop of *burghers*. They were obliged to abandon the convoy, however, on the arrival of reinforcements for the enemy. A sickening stench came from the corpses that they had left unburied in their flight.

We rested a few hours at the top of the steep *nek*. On descending on the other side we came, to our mutual surprise, upon De la Key's laager at the foot of the mountain on Barnard's farm.

CHAPTER 11

Battle of Nooitgedacht

We were busy all evening baking *vet-koek* (a kind of scone fried in lard), as we had received the order to be ready to leave the following morning at one o clock, and to take provisions sufficient for two days. Although our officers were beginning to see the advisability of keeping their plans secret, we were able to guess that we were going to attack General Clements' camp, an hour's ride further east at Nooitgedacht—particularly as the chances of success, in case of an eventual attack, were being discussed by some of the officers. The general opinion was that Clements' force was 5,000 strong.

We left quite three-quarters of an hour later than the fixed time in the early morning of December 13, 1900, and recrossed the steep, narrow neck, took a way to our right in the Kromriverskloof, making a sharp turn to Elandskrans, where a strong outpost had been placed by the enemy on the Magalies Mountains.

That was the crust through which we had to bite to get at the dainties of the booty. It cannot be denied that victory and booty, in our impoverished circumstances, were very close together in our thoughts. The enemy's camp lay at the foot of the long, high cliff that forms a precipice on that side of the mountain, while the slope of the mountain on our side was not steep, and there were a great many footholds and boulders. The artillery had been left in the neck of the pass to protect the laagers. Beyers, with some Zoutpansbergers, turned away from us to the right to reach Elandskrans along the mountain ridge. It appeared, therefore, that Beyers and Kemp were going to make the attack from the north, with 1,000 men, and that Kemp had the centre and the left wing. We were again too late. The sun had risen when we began the attack. Corporal Botman was ordered by Kemp to surround the extreme right of the enemy's right wing, with thirty men.

We had to storm the left to enclose the enemy in the half-circle. We were exposed to a rain of bullets, and had to storm through ravines and reefs, sometimes racing our horses, then leading them, and making use of every cover. General Beyers, with his splendid sharpshooters, was already in hot action with the right wing, and Commandant Kemp in the centre had forced his way close to the enemy. We tied our horses together behind a reef, left them in charge of a few men, and advanced, spreading ourselves in groups of three, four and five. A moment of extreme anxiety followed.

Not to expose ourselves unnecessarily, we had to peep from behind the rocks, shoot the course clear, and run to the next cover. Malherbe and I stayed as close as possible to our cool, collected, brave corporal, and we had to gasp for breath sometimes in trying to keep up to him. The others forced their way upwards more to the left, and so formed the furthest left point of the half-moon.

While the three of us were pushing our way from position to position into the neighbourhood of the few khakis who already dared not raise their heads from behind the rocks, I noticed, some 500 paces to our front, a number of khakis moving in our direction. I warned Malherbe to keep up his courage, as the enemy were getting reinforcements. A moment later, while our corporal had again moved onwards, I noticed several khakis on a stone ridge some 150 paces in front of us. It appeared that they were driven on by part of the centre and right wing, for just then two men made their appearance, whom I at once recognised as Boers from the colour of their clothes and the quick way in which they aimed at me. I stooped quick as a hare, and immediately rose again. The enemy now surrendered, I believe to the number of two or three hundred of the Northumberland Fusiliers, called the 'Fighting Fifth' on account of their courage and bravery. We also took on the mountain a heliograph that the enemy had broken.

The khakis acknowledged that we had taken the position with the greatest possible speed. We were in the majority. But it must not be forgotten that we were the attacking party and had to expose ourselves, and also that, although the battle on the mountain extended over a long line, our right wing had still to reckon with the reinforcements that were sent up through a narrow *kloof* from the camp. It was a repetition of Selikatsnek. The khakis had the good positions, and we had good cover behind the rocks on the mountain slope. In such a case he is no match for us.

We went on a few hundred paces over pretty level ground, and then looked down upon the camp at the foot of the mountain, which consisted of several hundreds of tents and many waggons. Some of these waggons were inspanned, some were already retreating, but most of them were not yet inspanned. The camp lay on the grounds and by the fields of a deserted farm.

Afterwards I heard that Commandant Badenhorst, of Pretoria (who had attacked the enemy before our arrival, at the foot of the mountain, and so suffered the greatest loss), was already retreating, but, hearing the fighting on the mountain, had renewed his attack.

The enemy could not stand the fire that we opened upon them, and had to retreat from the camp in the direction of Commandonek. The inevitable consequence was that the troops on the west, opposite De la Rey, had to retreat hurriedly so as not to be cut off by the wedge that was forcing its way along the mountains into the camp. They were far beyond reach of our bullets. Where De la Key's cannon were, and why they did not make themselves heard, I do not know. Neither do I know why General Smuts did not cut off the retreat of the enemy to the south-east. They had placed a few cannon to our left in the valley, and bombarded us fiercely on the mountain without much result. The balls of a small Maxim flew past us with a hissing sound and hindered us in our aim.

The waggons that were inspanned fled in the direction of Commandonek, and halted in the valley at a respectful distance from us. Although, the camp appeared to be almost deserted, a continual firing was heard below us. I could not make out from where it came until I suddenly discovered several small troops of horsemen who galloped at intervals from behind a wall in the shade of some trees. They were in all probability left there as cover for the waggons. The few shots we fired at them missed their aim. We saw De la Rey's *burghers* capture a large herd of cattle.

While Malherbe and I were peering from behind our hurriedly erected entrenchment, and occasionally firing a few shots, I discovered four or five brave khakis busy dragging along an ammunition waggon, or a gun; from such a distance we could not distinguish which. We fired at them with a sight of 800 paces, but did not hit them, as the horizontal distance to the camp was not more than 400 paces, and we should have used a sight of 600 paces, but the height of the mountain was very misleading. Immediately afterwards a span of mules came in the direction of the supposed gun, so Malherbe and I retreated as fast as we could, to find a better cover more to the left. It is strange how in a battle one always has an idea that all the threatened danger is aimed specially at one's self.

We had to be on the look-out not to fire at our own people, some of whom were already in the camp. My brother, Malherbe, and I went to the narrow *kloof* that I have already mentioned, after a fruitless search for our horses, which had meanwhile been taken to the entrance of the *kloof*, and I heard from my brother that our brave general had been wounded in the leg by a shell. During the search for our horses we had noticed a long dust-cloud at the end of Kromriverskloof, near Buffelspoort, moving from Rustenburg in the direction of Commandonek—in all probability reinforcements for the enemy, arriving too late.

The Waterbergers and Zoutpansbergers, who were most undisciplined, had descended through the *kloof* in quest of booty. But the Krugersdorpers, formerly notorious for their rough behaviour, were now the most orderly, and did not descend before all the men were collected. The *kloof* was strewn with bodies of khakis, who were sent up as reinforcement and pitilessly shot down by the *burghers*. The little stream of water was red with blood, so that we could not even quench our thirst. Some of the khakis had fallen from the high cliffs, where they had to lie unburied—like the soldiers on Amajuba in 1881.

We led our horses to the opening of the *kloof*, and then galloped into camp under the thundering noise of the shells that the enemy were firing at us from the distance. There was no control possible among the burghers. Each one loaded his horse with whatever he could lay his hands on, and there was no thought of following up the retreating enemy. They did not leave us undisturbed in our glory, but aimed lyddite at us, which had the desired effect, that we in our disorder did not storm the front positions, but retreated in the direction of our camp, a quarter of a mile in among the trees. There Veld-Kornet Klaassen ordered his men to off-saddle and give the horses a rest. Meanwhile the camp was burnt, flames arose in all directions, and thousands of cartridges exploded.

After we had watered our horses in a neighbouring *spruit* we lay down to rest. But ere long General De la Rey came galloping into our midst with a lash in his hand, calling to us whether we were not ashamed to lie there doing nothing, instead of following up our advantage now that we had the chance, when otherwise the enemy would ill-treat our women and children and burn down our homes. One of our corporals rather impertinently informed De la Rey that he served under another general, and would obey no orders but his. De la Rey thereupon rode up to him and gave him a heavy cut with his lash. I went up to the general, and told him that we were quite willing to fight, and had only off-saddled for a rest by order of our field-cornet. In his rage he lifted his lash, but, recognising me, lowered it again. If I had aimed at getting a cut from him, I might have called out like the Dutch farmers, who got a box on the ear from Peter the Great for pressing too closely upon him while he was building ships at Zaandam: 'I have had one too! I have had one too!' We then rode with the general to the burnt camp. The enemy had not found the game worth the candle, and had saved their shell for a more favourable occasion.

One can imagine De la Rey's indignation when he saw that waggons, provisions, and ammunition were nearly all burnt. He pointed out to us how ammunition and guns were required on every side. General Beyers, whom we met there, excused himself by explaining that he had ordered only those things to be burnt that we did not require. We then rode to the other positions on the opposite side of the camp, but the enemy were in full flight, followed by an occasional *burgher*.

I do not consider myself able to criticise the manner in which our officers organised this battle. But it was easy to see that a great mistake had been made. We had much to be thankful for, but the result might have been more advantageous to us. The whole camp with all its cannon should have been taken with a smaller loss than eighty men killed and wounded.

I do not know the number of the enemy's killed and wounded. If our first attack had been made unanimously and unexpectedly, we could easily have crushed the enemy. The prisoners, as usual, pretended that they knew all about our plans, but why, then, were their reinforcements too late, or, rather, why did they never arrive? When General De la Rey organises an attack, and his instructions are well carried out, the *burghers* have so much confidence in him, and like him so well, in spite of, or perhaps because of his violent temper, that they never have any doubt as to his ultimate success.

The prisoners were released. In my presence they were always well treated, and I have seen many khaki prisoners who have never on any occasion been ill-treated.

CHAPTER 12

Paardekraal Day

From Onuapadnek our *laagers* went to the farm Rietfontein, near Witwatersrandjes, where we celebrated Paardekraal Day on December 16—under sad circumstances, alas!

Ds. Kriel, who constantly accompanied us in the most self-denying manner, in all our battles and on all our long journeys, led us in prayer that day. Halfway up the *kopje*, which we climbed in most solemn earnest, he offered up a prayer to God, and then impressed upon us the importance of the occasion. On the top of the *kopje* he held a short service. It reminded me of that which my own father held for the assembled *burghers* at Paardekraal in 1880. How true and faithful he was in his position as preacher to the fighting men, and how well he served his adopted country!

After General De la Rey, Smuts, Kemp, and Mr. Naudé had all addressed us, Ds. Kriel read out a document in which was expressed, in a few words, the purpose each one of us should attach to his contribution of a stone towards the monument to be erected there. He exhorted the *burghers* not to add a stone to the pile unless they fully understood and were in earnest about its meaning. So the old covenant was renewed in a different place under different circumstances and in a different manner from the Paardekraal Day of former years, and when the *burghers* descended from the *kopje* they were strengthened by the renewing of an ancient pledge in their resolution to fight to the last for their country and their people.

The place where the monument was erected was called Ebenhaëzer.

Between the Magalies Mountains and the Witwatersranden stretches a long valley called the Moat. In the centre runs a gray ridge or rand, parallel to the mountains, and rising into *kopjes* to the east, near

Hekpoort. Thither our commando moved a few days later to meet the enemy, who were approaching from Commandonek, most probably with revengeful intentions. The Moat was well provided with corn, and asked for our protection. We stayed over a day on the gray ridge. When the enemy advanced towards us on the day following, General De la Rey had taken up his position near Nooitgedacht, and so formed the left wing.

Commandant Kemp, with his men, was at the south on the foot of the ridge, and Veld-Kornet van Tonder, with a small troop of Zoutpansbergers, was on the first *kopje*, while General Beyers, with the Waterbergers and Zoutpansbergers held the right wing to the west of Hekpoort, in Witwatersrand. The whole of that forenoon the enemy were ready to attack us, and we waited calmly. Towards afternoon their left wing moved towards the first *kopje*, beyond the reach of the Zoutpansbergers, who were on the Witwatersranden near Hekpoort They began firing at the position of Veld-Kornet Van Tonder, and when he fell mortally wounded his Zoutpansbergers were obliged to retire from the *kopje*.

Our Veld-Kornet, Kruger, a fine, brave fellow, then led twenty-five of our men towards Hekpoort, to try and stop the enemy in their forward movement. As Malherbe, my brother, and I were among the twenty-five, I cannot tell what happened to De la Rey on the other side of the gray ridge. We pressed too far forward, and soon had to retreat some distance. Our *veld-kornet* stayed behind with a few of us, on a small rise, while our horses were taken some 300 paces further back, and the rest of our little troop rode in the direction of Hekpoort. The enemy already occupied the first *kopje*, and were firing at us from a distance. We quickly made an entrenchment of stones and lay waiting. But our people were retreating from the other *kopjes*, and we had to get to our horses as quickly as possible. A few cowardly *burghers* on the ridge took us for khakis and fired at us. Then I experienced the difference between the aim of Boer and khaki. The latter's bullets always flew far above our heads, but the former's fell terribly close to us.

As yet we had retired in good order, but soon we fled in a panic. The enemy had come from Krugersdorp in very large numbers, and already occupied the high Witwatersranden behind us.

Whoever has an incapable horse had better hide in a ditch or behind a wall along with the poor, frightened women. More than once I have seen poor frightened women holding their crying children by the hand, and seeking a hiding-place near their houses during a battle.

It is indeed a tragic sight!—we men, with our weapons in our hands, not able to defend them at such a time. And then a great feeling of shame came upon us. These same women had only the day before called down God's blessing upon us, and now they cried to us to hurry, or we would be surrounded.

We rode at a flying gallop for fully half an hour—along the Magalies Mountains, between the Witwatersranden and the many smaller banks, while to the left the enemy were descending and firing at us. The Waterbergers and Zoutpansbergers, who learnt later than we did that the enemy were surrounding us, would all have been taken prisoners had they not forced their way bravely through thick and thin. As far as we can tell, our loss was, fortunately, only one killed.

At the Manharen, a peculiar kind of *kopje*, we halted, but had to retreat further towards evening.

Beyers' commando moved in the direction of Gatsrand, but had to turn to Zwartruggens, near Rustenburg, when it reached the farm Modderfontein, where we celebrated Christmas. The enemy was constantly at our heels, and made things hot for us; we often had to hurry most inconveniently not to be surrounded or cut off. We got a few days' rest on the farm Vlakhoek. We were camped near a small stream, and went from there to the different farms in search of the first fruit of the season.

On New Year's Eve General Beyers' commando moved on the wide hard Krugersdorp road. The bullock waggon *laager* had been left behind, as it prevented us from moving as quickly as was sometimes necessary. The *burghers* still longed to attack Krugersdorp, and on New Year's Eve, as we moved fast in the direction of the town, our hearts were cheered by the thought of Jameson's failure, when five years ago he passed along the same road in his notorious raid. We all hoped to add an immortal page to the annals of our history on the following New Year's Day. But we were sadly disappointed in our expectations. The Jameson Raid was not avenged, and we celebrated New Year's Day calmly and peacefully at Cyferbult, on Pretorius' farm, with *miliepap* (maize meal porridge) and beef and—green fruit!

Whenever we came to a farm we ate as much green fruit as possible by way of a change in our diet. On other occasions it would have been very bad for us, but now it seemed to have a very wholesome effect. As we moved on past Zwartkop over the Krokodil River in the direction of the railway, we realised that there was no chance of attacking Krugersdorp for the present, for General Beyers had apparently changed his plans. We were quite sure that it had originally been his intention, and some of our officers talked of the attack on the town as if it were an open secret.

Our capable Veld-Kornet, Kruger, had remained behind at Zwartkop to get the *burghers* of Wyk III. Krugersdorp from out of their hiding-places, as the generals wanted to concentrate all the small bands for some great undertaking. We joined Wyk I. Krugersdorp under Veld-Kornet Klaassen.

Near Hekpoort, as we were camped at Dwarsvlie, we attacked a convoy of the enemy in the valley, and very nearly captured it before it was reinforced. I was not present, so cannot give any account of the battle. After a sharp trek of more than one night, we crossed the rails between Kaalfontein and Zuurfontein Stations, just before sunrise one morning towards the middle of January. We captured a few guards who seemed to know nothing of our movements. Why General Beyers did not surprise one or both stations that morning early is still a mystery to us, as our movements were remarkably quick. It could not have been because he thought us too tired, for some twenty minutes further on, while we were resting on a farm, he ordered part of our *laager* to turn to the left and attack Kaalfontein Station.

Our corporal was unwilling to work us and our horses to death, so he first got breakfast ready. But when our cannon began to roar and Corporal Botman, who still limped from a wound, rode off without a word in his own peculiar way, our conscience began to trouble us, and several of our men followed him. My brother, whose horse's back was chafed, remained in the *laager* with the rest of the *burghers*.

When we reached our guns, we immediately saw that the station could be taken only at the cost of many lives—more than the success would be worth. Our guns had not the desired effect, and we should have had to charge across an open space without any cover. The enemy had no guns. They say our left wing very nearly succeeded in taking a small fort near the station, but I cannot give any particulars, for our *veld-kornet* rode with a small troop of *burghers* to the right of the station, and took another small fort which the enemy had abandoned because it was too far away from the station. What might have been expected happened.

Towards afternoon an armoured train came from Pretoria, and reinforcements arrived from Johannesburg and scattered our left wing over the valley. I happened to be with a few others on the outmost point of the right wing of attack—or, rather, since the scene was changed, of the left wing of flight. And as we were retreating at our ease an old man galloped towards us and pointed out that we were retreating in the wrong direction, as the enemy had captured our whole *laager*. He had never in his life seen so many khakis. They seemed to be on all sides of us. The only outlet for us was in the direction of Heidelberg. I asked him, 'Uncle, are you sure that our *laager* is in the hands of the khakis?' to which he answered, 'Nephew, I saw with my own eyes how they rode up to the waggons and made all our people " hands up!"' and he continued to give us a minute description of the occurrence.

If we had been greenhorns, we would have blindly followed the startled old man right through the stream of retreating *burghers* and exploding 15-pounders. But, fortunately, the war had taught us, and we moved on *with* the stream, but a little more to the left, and, I cannot deny it, with a feeling of great anxiety as to what was to become of us if the old man had indeed told the truth.

Fortunately, it appeared that fright had made the old man believe his own imagination, and the *laager* was quite safe. My brother told me that the slight attack made upon them by the enemy was easily beaten off.

The opinion of the majority was that we should have left Kaalfontein Station alone. We were thoroughly exhausted by our rapid journeys, particularly by the journey of the preceding night, and besides that the *burghers* were unwilling to make an attack of which they did not see the advantage. We had several killed and wounded.

The consequence was that we had to trek that night in a way that none of us will ever forget, to get beyond the reach of the enemy. One cannot imagine how terrible it is to sit for hours on horseback, dead tired and overcome by sleep. We did not even guide our horses; they simply jogged along mechanically, too tired even to object to ill-treatment. Our hands rested on the bows of the saddles, and as we sat leaning forwards, apparently lost in thought, but in reality suffering tortures from the effort to keep awake, we forced ourselves to look up and about us, but our eyes half closed in the effort, and everything about us took a strange shape, and the sky became chaos; with a nod we half awoke, only to dream again a second later that we were falling from our horses.

Not a word was spoken, for everyone was dozing. Whenever we had to wait for our guns or waggons, we simply flung ourselves on the grass with one arm through our bridles, and soon we were unconscious of the pulling and tugging of the horse, and if the order to mount woke us up, the tugging had ceased, and our horses were calmly grazing some distance from us. Then we lifted our bodies, loaded with cartridges and guns, into the saddle at the risk of toppling over on the other side, like a lizard sliding down a bank, and rode on in silence, drowsily and top-heavy.

CHAPTER 13

Commando Sufferings

The horsemen rode generally two by two, partly in front of the waggons as advance-guard, and behind as rear-guard, each corporal with his men in his place by his *veld-kornet*. The Krugersdorpers were no longer allowed to leave their places before they had permission from their corporal. Even those *burghers* who were most disorderly in the beginning now saw the necessity of discipline, and were obedient to the commands of their officers.

It was a mixed crew of old and young. But the majority were still in the prime of life, and proof against the privations of guerilla life. The old men among us were all men whose powerful constitutions were yet unbroken. It was praiseworthy of them that in their old age they were willing to suffer the difficulties and dangers of a wandering life for their country's sake, for although their constitutions were strong, they were susceptible to cold and damp, the effects of which they could not shake off. There were also many brave little boys, who were thus early initiated into the privations of commando life; but they shared all bravely, in a careless spirit of adventure.

Here and there were some *uitlanders* who had remained faithful to us. All the others had gradually disappeared, either because they were taken prisoners, or killed through their somewhat foolhardy courage, or because they had left the country in disappointment. The townspeople were by no means superior to the farmers. There were traitors and 'handsuppers' among them as well. We have been bitterly disappointed in people of all classes, but particularly in the so-called 'gentlemen.'

Our condition and appearance were indeed striking. During the heat of the day, when the dust lay thickly about us, we sat in our ragged clothes, with shaggy, uncombed beards, on our poor, hardly treated ponies, meekly staring in front of us, seemingly indifferent to the moral hurt that we were suffering and the after a long, tiring ride. At the start of one of our journeys an animated conversation sometimes helped to pass the time, but it soon flagged, leaving us staring in front of us in the usual dispirited, dull way. Our talk became daily more prosaic and superficial. We had not the energy to express our deepest sentiments, and things which were formerly pleasant were strange to us now. We had no spur to enliven our thoughts in our monotonous life. To the careless there was nothing startling in this moral numbness, but the more sensitive among us grieved over it, and were humiliated by the shallowness that had come into our lives.

The small necessaries of our material existence had become essential to our happiness. If we lost a knife, or if a pot or kettle broke, or a mug was stolen from us, we were depressed for days, as if a heavy blow had fallen upon us. It was not easy to fight against that bitter feeling of depression. Our only safety lay in the fact that we were conscious of the demoralizing effect of these small disappointments of commando life, for to know one's self is always the first step towards conversion.

Some qualities of our highest nature were systematically, suppressed. We prided ourselves on our fierce hatred of the enemy, and considered it a mark of patriotism, and we rejoiced when he fell beneath our bullets or when the plague broke out. We even wished that a great European war might begin, if only we might keep our country, and as a consequence of our righteous patriotism an inclination to cruelty became one of the predominant traits in the character of the *burghers*.

The commando life tended to make many of us melancholy. Wherever we came the thought was forced upon us that our beloved country was deeply injured, morally and materially. We ourselves saw everywhere homes and fields destroyed, women and children taken away by force, and cattle stolen; and rumours told of the most terrible outrages committed upon helpless women and children. If it were not that one becomes hardened to all outward impressions, our commando life would have been pitiful indeed. So we became hardened to almost all these things, but the thought of the ill-treatment of those dear to us, on whose happiness our own happiness depends, was constantly with us, and to that we did not become hardened.

It is impossible to enter into the sufferings of the married men. Much was suffered in silence. Some men got messages from their wives imprisoned in refugee camps, bidding them surrender for the sake of their wives, since fighting was of no avail and the country was already lost. Who shall blame the man who rides away with an anxious heart to his wife and children, no matter what the consequences may be to himself? Another woman, with a different disposition and a different heart, sends word secretly to her husband that life in the prison camp is endurable, and that he must fight to the end. Then he stays, and proves himself worthy of the courage of his wife.

Some men gave the impression that they were indifferent to the suffering of wife and child. These were the scum of our people, who in time of peace were not of much importance, but were necessary for our fight. But the majority, by far the greater majority, were men who, even in the most troubled times, were faithful to the comrades with whom they began this struggle, the struggle for our independence.

Whenever we came to a *'uitspanplek'* (a place where there is water to be found for the horses), some of us had to seek hurriedly for wood to make the fire, others to fetch water, and others to help in various ways. It was a regular struggle for existence. Those who came first got the least disagreeable work. Wood was scarce on the Hoogeveld where we happened to be, and the water was muddied by the first water-carriers. When the sun was very warm we made a shelter with our guns and our blankets.

Our meals were simple. They consisted of meat and *'mealie-pap'* morning, noon, and night, often for weeks without salt. We made coffee of burnt grain ground in a coffee-mill. During the war we learnt to drink all sorts of coffee—of wheat, oats, barley, sweet potatoes, maize, and even of peaches. We became so accustomed to a simple mode of life that our wants were few indeed. Even sugar we no longer missed. And we remained healthy and strong.

We lay in small groups round the fires, leaning against our saddles. Our moods were brighter after our tired bodies had had the needful refreshment and rest. The groups were often picturesque, some of us lying at our ease with soiled books in hands, others grouped round the fire, every now and again adding wood to the flames, and others, again, picking mites out of the biltong with a pocketknife.

A shower had not much effect upon us. We were accustomed to letting our clothes dry on our bodies. Nature is very kind to people who are day and night in the open air. If the sun did not shine soon after a shower, we made a very deplorable appearance in our dripping clothes. But we never grumbled. We were generally cheerful, unless we were exhausted from fatigue.

We suffered most on those long nights when, for some reason or other, we could not sleep, for many of the *burghers* were troubled with fears for their dear ones. Often, after a long ride, we were too tired to prepare a meal, but simply flung ourselves against our saddles and slept before we had time to let our thoughts wander. But if the enemy were not at our heels, we often passed the long nights in sleeplessness, gazing up at the stars with the most bitter feelings in our hearts. No wonder that many a *burgher* grew gray. We were often kept awake by the tethered horses stumbling among the groups. Sometimes a man would jump up and strike at them till all the others awoke, too, and then there was great hilarity in the quiet of the night.

Sometimes a constant rain cast a shadow over the sunny Hoogeveld and made our lives sombre and almost unbearable. Then our tattered garments could not dry on our bodies, and everything about us was wet and dirty. Even in dry weather fuel was almost unattainable, for the treeless Hoogeveld had been almost exhausted by the many large commandos which had visited the '*uitspan*' places. In wet weather it was almost an impossibility to make a fire.

Whoever had an ailment passed unpleasant nights then; each night meant a nail in his coffin. Even the constant rain the *burghers* bore cheerfully, and many a joke was passed along during an interval in the downpour. But in the morning, as we dragged our weary limbs out of our mud-baths, shivering from cold, we did not venture to put the conventional question, 'Did you sleep well?' to each other.

The spirit among the *burghers* was very different from what it had been. No swearing was heard, and quarrelling was exceptional. Thefts, too, were seldom committed. We called ourselves 'sifted'; traitors and thieves had gone over to the stronger party. I do not believe that any European army would have kept its moral tone so high under such demoralizing circumstances as did that small army of Boers with the help of their religion. Whereas in time of peace there was much difference in churches, especially in the Transvaal (although no difference in belief), now, during the war, the unity of belief in one Bible had become the means of raising the moral tone of the *burghers*.

During the last few months a plague had come amongst us that we had heard much about, and now caused us much trouble—a plague of lice. It is not an edifying subject, but anyone can understand how the itching caused many a sleepless night. We were not to blame. When we no longer were able to change our clothes, we could not guard against the vermin that had become a plague among the huge wandering armies of the enemy. Although we boiled our clothes, to our horror the nits appeared again.

Chapter 14

Battle of Boesmanskop

Fortunately, the enemy gave us a week's rest on the farm of Landdrost Schotte. During that time Veld-Kornet Meyer, with his small troop of Germans, blew up the electric factory at Brakpan.

Then we stayed a few days on Mr. Brown's farm, where a great many little commandos congregated that were camped on the banks of the river. Our horses became quite sleek again from the abundance of mealies they got there. On that farm we first used for fuel the poles that fenced in the farm. I distinctly remember how, after we had received the order from Commandant Kemp, we waited until after dark before pulling up the poles, and how grieved we were at the necessity for doing it. Since that time we have got over such scruples. Even if there were wood to be had on an outspan place, there was always a race to procure the best poles. Of course, when there was abundance of wood, the pulling up of poles was strictly prohibited.

At that time I made the acquaintance of a nephew of mine, Paul Maré, a boy of fourteen, with a noble countenance, who, like so many others of the same age, rode about with gun and bandolier, and was full of courage. When the enemy approached his mother's house he prepared for flight, but she took it for a joke. When she noticed that he was in earnest, she forbade him to go, as his father had been killed already, and he would in all probability be killed too. He merely answered, 'Because they have shot my father, I mean to shoot them now,' and rode away.

We did not like remaining long in one place doing nothing. We always became impatient, and wished to know when we could move on. But the *commandant* always answered that he could not tell. And the more sensible of us thought, 'It depends on khaki.' This was really the case now. On the evening of January 28 we got the order to be in readiness. While General Beyers, with 400 or 500 men, passed to the rear of the enemy to destroy the Boksburg mines, our commando of horsemen moved rapidly in the direction of Boesmanskop in the Heidelberg district, to cut off the enemy who were pushing on to our part of the Hoogeveld. We arrived at Boesmanskop the following morning.

The parts of the country that we now passed through had not yet been destroyed by the enemy, but everywhere else the houses and farms were burnt and ruined in the most barbarous way. We were very anxious, therefore, to cut off the enemy's advance. They were camped to the north-west of Boesmanskop. A strong Boer guard occupied this *kopje*—the only one in the neighbourhood; for the rest, the surroundings were the ordinary Hoogeveld with its mounds. We pushed up in a long line over a '*bult*' that ran north-west of Boesmanskop. Our guns—only a few, as most had been sent away to be repaired—stood on top of this mound without any cover. Lieutenant Odendaal, a very brave gunner, did not like *kopjes*, but always placed his cannon on a mound, as the enemy's guns always fired too short or too long on account of the misleading distances.

They did so in this instance, and the bombs flew far beyond us. Corporal Botman ordered me to stay with the horses at the foot of the '*bult*,' while the *burghers* crept on to the top a few hundred paces further, expecting eventually to charge the enemy. Suddenly I heard, twice over, a noise like that of a train in the distance. My brother told me afterwards how he had seen a detachment of the enemy storming Boesmanskop, and how the *burghers* waited until they were close by, and then beat them back completely with a twice-repeated salvo.

For some time the guns of the enemy ceased firing, because, as I heard later on. Lieutenant Odendaal had shot down the gunners. When they made themselves heard again, they were more accurate in their aim; I most narrowly escaped the bombs. Four or five thundered around me in quick succession, as I fell and stooped and grasped the bridles of the rearing horses. Some of the horses pulled the bridles out of my hands and raced down the valley.

But the left wing of the enemy was surrounding us, and, like a swarm of birds that rise on the wing, the burghers fled back in among the tethered and the straying horses, and retreated as fast as they could. The enemy now bombarded Boesmanskop, so that the retreating burghers in the valley had a bad time of it with the bombs flying over their heads.

Many waggons of Boer families, fleeing for their lives, were pushing along the sides of the long mounds, and the enemy's bombs burst in their midst more than once—perhaps accidentally, perhaps because they knew that the Boer nation must be swept off the face of the earth.'

The women seemed to be in a panic. From all sides families came in carts and waggons—long rows of vehicles filled with poor, terror-stricken women and children; large herds of cattle were driven along by the *kaffir* servants, but many of them fell into the enemy's hands. The *burghers* did their best to make a stand in order to give the waggons a good start, but retreated in good order when they saw no chance of checking the enemy's forward movement. Fortunately, a heavy shower fell in the afternoon and hindered the enemy in their advance, else many a waggon would have fallen into their hands.

It was no longer necessary for the *burghers* to resist for the sake of the waggons. The enemy had camped and left us, with the exception of the guard, to plod our way shamefacedly through the mud. Our ponies, with their quick, peculiar gait, soon caught up the heavily-laden waggons, and we supplied ourselves with mealies, flour, fowls, etc., that had been thrown overboard or left behind on a broken-down waggon. Such is the fortune of war, and the things were better in our hands than in those of the khakis.

When we rode up alongside the waggons, many a meeting took place between relatives and friends who had been parted for months. The women and girls drove the horses, and many of them walked with the *kaffirs* in the mud next to the oxen. They did the work of the men in time of peace. Many of them had been delicately nurtured, in spite of the simplicity of their lives, and were not accustomed to the hard work. They were all Transvaal women, and wives and daughters of the *burghers* who had to look on helplessly at their sad flight. And, oh! the dear little heads of the children that peeped at us from out of the waggons! It was a cruel sight, and it moved us strangely.

Although most of the women were drenched, they were all cheerful, and seemed proud of taking an active part in the great struggle. And if a young man asked a girl whether he should ride next to her to help her, the answer was: 'No, thank you, we can manage; the men must fight now.' There were many old men and boys who preferred the society of the women to the danger of the bombs. Some of the women were not kind, and reproached us for being the cause of all this misery, as our appearance in the Hoogeveld had brought the enemy in its train.

The waggons were heavily laden with furniture and grain, some even with stoves, and they sank deep into the mud, as the roads were one mass of mud after the numerous waggons and thousands of cattle that had already passed along them. Long rows of vehicles were continually approaching from all sides, all going in the same direction, and when we came to Waterval River a sad but grand sight met our eyes. The river was full. Hundreds of waggons had been outspanned on the banks on either side. The women and children were doing their best to light the fires with the wet wood, and to cook some food. It was just before sunset, but there was no sun to cheer them on their way.

Against the sides of the mounds (*bulten*) the cattle were moving in black dense masses, making an almost deafening noise with their bleating and lowing. As we rode through the full river, we saw in midstream a cart that had stuck fast. A woman was standing in the water pushing at the back, while a girl held the reins. A few of our men jumped down from their horses and soon succeeded in getting the cart to the other side. But we could not stay to help the poor women and children. We rode on, inquiring everywhere after the trolleys and the commissariat. These were higher up on the other side of the river, so we had to cross once more, this time in the dark, at the risk of our lives.

Two little girls were drowned that evening, and the wheel of a waggon had passed over a girl's body. It had been better if the women had stayed at home and depended on the mercy of the enemy. They should not have undertaken this terrible journey. A woman cannot flee from place to place like a man, and life in a 'refugee' (?) camp would have been better; she should bear her sorrow bravely at home. And this was only the beginning of the misery. If they had remained at home, they might have saved their homes, but now the enemy was sure to destroy and burn the deserted farms.

During the day, when the flight was still a novelty, the women and girls were cheerful enough, but who can describe their heartache and misery during their enforced journey on the rainy nights? I do not know how all those waggons and cattle got through the swollen river that night. Twenty paces from where I lay a waggon was being inspanned; I heard the voices of men and women. An old man was talking. He threatened to off-load all the women on the first available place, as he had never in his life had so much trouble. A small boy and a *kaffir* had their turn also; the boy was on horseback and led, or rather dragged, another horse that refused to move. He had to collect the cattle, which seemed to me almost an impossible task in the dark, among the many horses of the *burghers*. When he had found Kindermeid, Witlies had disappeared, and when Witlies was found, then Vaalpens was missing again. Kindermeid, a gray ox, was the most troublesome. Repeatedly it passed by me, followed by the boy dragging the unwilling horse. Then the boy exclaimed in sad, shrill tones, 'See how the mare jibs!'

When his father angrily asked, 'Have you found Kindermeid now?' he answered, 'Yes, father, but now Vaalpens is missing; the mare jibs so, I can't get the cattle together!' When he had found them all and the rumbling of their waggon was dying away in the distance, I still heard him complain of the unwilling mare, in his sad, shrill little voice. It was a small episode in my life that I shall not easily forget. This was the last I saw of the flight of the women, for we had to stay behind to fight as we were retreating. Later on I heard many sad tales about it, which I cannot repeat in this little book of mine.

The poor women and children were indeed to be pitied, but we had no sympathy with the men who fled in the winter with their cattle to the Boschveld, and now sought our protection, though they had never fought themselves. The flight with the cattle was necessary, as the enemy would otherwise have exterminated them, but many of the men took advantage of the necessity, and sometimes three or four strong, sturdy men went with one waggon, where one man would have been ample.

Chapter 15

Battle of Chrissiesmeer

I will not describe our retreat, as nothing of importance occurred. We were constantly on the alert to move before the cunning French entrapped us within the circle that he was trying to draw around us.

At Trichardsfontein Malherbe and I had to go in search of our horses, which had strayed, so we were separated from our commando for some days. When we found our horses we went to Ermelo, and stayed there until the enemy were so close upon us that General Louis Botha, who happened to be at Ermelo, and knew of our arrival, sent to say that we must leave the town. We then joined his force and rode to Spion Kop.

In the land of the blind the one-eyed is king!' Even so it was with Spion Kop of the Hoogeveld Ermelo. During the three years of my University life in that distant little country that stands by us now so well in our need, I often climbed a hill about the size of Spion Kop. That hill is famed for its height throughout the whole country, and bears the formidable name of 'the Amersfoort Mountain/

While the officers were holding a council of war, Malherbe and I rode off to our commando. At Klipstapel we were allowed a few days' breathing time, and there we prepared for the night attack on Smith-Dorrien's camp, to the north of us. But our guide lost his way in the dark, and we had to return. It was decided, nevertheless, to attempt the attack the following night at Chrissiesmeer, where the camp was then. We had everything in our favour. We were a strong force of many commandos, and the enemy's force was not much larger.

That evening we were placed in quite a different order from the usual one. The men of each corporal's division rode next to each other. The *commandant* or *veld-kornet* at the head, followed by the corporal with his ten or fifteen men riding abreast, was followed by the next corporal riding abreast with his men, etc. On looking back from the top of the hill in the moonlight, one saw a broad dark mass of fierce, determined men. Nearly every *burgher* had one or two extra horses, mostly mares with foals, that we had commandeered and trained during our retreat on the Hoogeveld. At that time every horse, trained or untrained, was put to use. It was a pity that the mares with their foals were not left behind, as they made a terrible noise with their whinnying. We walked our horses; we were not allowed to utter a word or to light our pipes—that was reasonable; but the neighing of the horses was not exactly in accordance with our silence.

Every now and again, when the whinnying of the mares was at its worst, some *burgher* or other would give vent to an exclamation of impatience. Every now and again someone or other would light his pipe, taking care that neither the *veld-kornet* nor the enemy should see it. A dead silence reigned everywhere, broken only by the mares and their foals. These beasts caused us great uneasiness, but so did the order we received that we had to shoot sharp at the beginning of the attack, but then slowly, until it became light, so as to save some of our ammunition in case of need. We had to attack in the dark then. But what if the enemy, prepared for our arrival, were to pepper at us unexpectedly from a different direction, or to point their Maxims at us?

The greatest mistake of all was that we took our horses right up to the hill on the other side of which the khakis were. The horses were tired and had ceased neighing, but we should have left them some miles behind and walked on to make the attack as soon as it was light. An uncle of mine told me that he saw some men on horseback riding over the *bult*, whom he took to be our spies, but they were of course the enemy's guard.

When we had tethered our horses at the foot of the *bult*, we climbed up slowly, but before we could fall into position the enemy opened a sharp fire at us. We charged shouting 'Hurrah!' in wild enthusiasm, and fired as fast as we could straight ahead. The sparks flew up some twenty paces in front of us, and even after the fight we could not tell whether they came from our own guns or from those of the enemy. At intervals we heard the *tick-tick-tick* of a small Maxim, but owing to the dark we were not mown down. Some of the *burghers* threw themselves down behind us, and involuntarily one thought of the proverb, '*to hide in another's blood*.' Whenever the firing slackened a few of our brave men charged, shouting out encouraging words, and again raised our enthusiasm.

Both *burghers* on my right and on my left were wounded. The latter had a most demoralizing influence on the rest of the men, as he lay groaning and moaning in a heartrending way. He was only slightly wounded, and eventually escaped on horseback. Our brave Commandant Botman went forward ten paces beyond the rest in his enthusiasm, and served as a target for the enemy. He was severely wounded, but walked back without a moan and fell down close behind me. I did not even know that he was wounded. I turned round to see if the *burghers* behind me would not take the initiative in the inevitable flight, as I was ashamed to take it upon myself. I did not take it at all amiss, therefore, when I saw several men looking round to see if the way were clear, and darting like an arrow back to their horses, for all round us our men were being shot down, and we did not know where the enemy's camp was, nor could we tell the effect of our shooting in the dark.

A slight fog had arisen, through which the moon occasionally succeeded in dimly appearing. The day had dawned; we reached our horses in the greatest disorder, and heightened the confusion by shouting inquiries to each other after friends and relatives. Some did not wait to find their horses, but fled on foot; others jumped on strange horses. Some even escaped on khaki horses that had strayed from the camp.

As my brother and I galloped off, a man fell wounded close behind us, and the bullet struck the ground between us. The *burghers* rallied at a farm in the neighbourhood of the enemy's camp. Some of our men fled on, but most of them retreated with the guns to the commissariat trolleys, many without saddle, mackintosh or blanket, more hopelessly impoverished than ever, but not discouraged, for although the attack had been repulsed we were not defeated.

In this lay our strength, that we were not disheartened by our defeats, but were able constantly to rally and to renew the attack. We kept on exhausting the enemy by slight skirmishes that are not worth relating, but their effect on the whole weakened him and strengthened us.

On our side that day there were forty wounded, but only a few killed. It grieved us all that Commandant Botman had remained behind on the battlefield. He was universally liked for his bravery and for his simple Christianity. To our great joy, we heard later on that he had recovered, and had somehow succeeded in reaching Krugersdorp. Fortunately, the fog prevented the enemy from doing us much harm, and towards afternoon our cannon put a stop to their advance.

The attack on Smith-Dorrien's camp was worthy of a better result. In this, as well as in the Hekpoort and Boesmanskop battles, where also we had no position, the *burghers* showed great courage and goodwill. In my opinion, the officers should have given up the plan of attack after we had missed our way the night before and been obliged to return. The *kaffirs* and traitors must have warned the enemy of our intention to attack, so that they could be in readiness for us.

The enemy were now all round us. We heard the firing of cannon on all sides, but that same night we undertook a cunning backward movement, and when the enemy closed their cordon an hour later the bird had flown. We were careful to avoid a repetition of Cronje's experience.

The *burghers* were very anxious about our laager. We had left it on Brown's farm on the Wilgeriver, when our commando advanced towards Boesmanskop. How the *laager* escaped I do not know, for we heard that the enemy were advancing from all sides—Standerton, Middelburg, etc. But we reached it in safety the very night that we slipped through the enemy's cordon.

We were now safely on our way back to Rustenburg, and had to leave General French with his 30,000 or 40,000 men to drive along helpless women and children, and all the cattle he could lay hands on. Commandant-General Louis Botha had strictly forbidden the women to leave their farms after the Battle of Boesmanskop, so that the enormous woman *laager* received no new additions.

Many of the farms were burned down, but some families had been left unmolested, because they said the enemy were ill at ease, owing to a rumour that General Beyers was going to attack them in the rear. The partly-burned granaries bore evidence to the great hurry the enemy were in. On some farms the very rooms that contained grain were set on fire.

Our constant retreat had a most demoralizing influence. This was felt even in our conversation and our expressions. We called this retreating '*kamping*,' (trappers), and it became one of our most common expressions in our daily life. For 'Let us go!' we said 'Let us *kamp!*' or for 'This evening we start!' we said 'This evening we go on the *kamp!*' A typical expression was '*kamping*' for our independence, when we could no longer withstand the enemy. If anyone boasted of his loyalty to his country and people, he merely said that he had '*kamped*' along with the *burghers* wherever they had '*kamped*.' We used in our conversation many military terms; for instance, 'to change one's position' was 'to go and lie with your saddle on another place.' 'I shall mauser you' meant 'I shall strike you.'

At Grootpan General Beyers again joined us, after having done the enemy some harm at Boksburg. He addressed us and explained his reason for countermanding the attack on Krugersdorp. He had told the secret to a few of his officers, who made it public property, so that the enemy had heard of it and were prepared for the attack.

Moreover, a great fault of the *burghers* had come to light at Nooitgedacht—namely, that they shirked their duty in their eagerness for plunder. He was afraid that if they took the town their plundering spirit would get the better of them and so give the enemy a chance of catching them or putting them to flight. Lastly he said that he was going to act in opposition to the orders received from the commandant-general, and would send the Zoutpansbergers and Waterbergers home that evening, as it was impossible for them in their condition to undertake any military operations. He himself also was going home, but would return after a few weeks, as a large commando, led if possible by himself, was to invade Cape Colony.

Kemp was made fighting general; the Rev. Mr. Kriel left with General Beyers; Klaassen took the place of Kemp, and Liebenberg was appointed Field Cornet of our commando.

The return to their homes of the Waterbergers and Zoutpansbergers roused a feeling of dissatisfaction in us. Owing to the horse-sickness in those regions, and the home-sickness of the men themselves, we concluded that we were not likely to see them again. We also thought it would have been better to have invaded the Colony long ago, instead of aimlessly wandering about the Hoogeveld as we had been doing. In all probability our generals put off the invasion as long as possible because many of the men—nearly all the Waterbergers and Zoutpansbergers—were against it. Such were the difficulties against which our generals had to fight.

In private, both Kemp and Beyers acknowledged to me that a march into the Colony was strictly necessary. I do not mean to criticise, but only to give an idea of the spirit reigning among the *burghers* at that time.

CHAPTER 16

Camped Near Tafelkop

General Beyers' force was again split into small commandos, which it was the intention of our officers to join into one large force, and so make their way through the ranks of the enemy. But this plan was not a success, for the enemy were too strong for us.

The Krugersdorp and Pretoriadorp commandos one night crossed the railway within sight of the khaki camp-lights at Irene Station —quite close to our capital, in full view of khaki's warning, 'No admittance!' We passed Zwartkop, crossed Dwarsvlei, and had to turn back to the right through Hartleyskloof, as we came across a camp of the enemy. We then entered the Moot district, dreaded for its terrible horse-sickness, and in the beginning of March we arrived at Tafelkop, to the northeast of Lichtenburg, near Mabaalstad.

Once, as I lay resting against my saddle, I heard an old Boer telling of the courage and hopefulness among the *burghers* from whom he came. They talked of nothing but peace. It was their belief that a European sovereign on marriage may make a request which must be granted. He may even ask a million pounds or somebody's head, and cannot be refused. So, they said, Queen Wilhelmina had risen to make her speech at her wedding, and had requested absolute independence for the Republics. The kings and princes were against it, but could not break the old custom, and therefore peace would soon reign over our country. But such talk of 'peace' was an exception, not the rule.

After the terrible experience of the last months, we had become resigned to our fate, and did not try to anticipate the future. We knew that we must fight with courage and energy, and the rest we left in God's hands. We had ceased to be curious about the plans of our generals, which were never made known to us. Exhausted in body and spirit, we took no account of time. It was all one to us whether it were morning, noon or night; whether we had to march one, two, or three hours longer; whether we had to march at all, or to remain where we were. But we were not demoralised, not unnerved. An overworked horse allows himself to be caught and ill-treated afresh. The enemy had only to fire at us to rouse our slumbering energy, for we suffered voluntarily, and were a support to each other, because of our firm conviction that we were giving our lives for the sake of our independence.

It rained when we arrived at Tafelkop, and when we had been there a week it still rained. The only clothes we possessed were beginning to rot on our bodies. Some of the *burghers* had a change of clothes on the trolleys; others made themselves trousers of their many-coloured blankets, in which they cut a remarkable figure. Others, again, were in tatters, and had to disappear on the few occasions that any lady visited us. Most of the men had no mackintoshes, but always looked forward to the sunshine that was sure to follow a heavy shower. But if the rain continued, we made huts of grass, or clubbed together in the few remaining tents, or if there happened to be an unburned farmhouse, we made for that.

When the rain continued at Tafelkop, and our limbs became stiffened with the cold, some of us went to an outhouse belonging to a neighbouring farm to seek shelter. During the day we sat there in our wet clothes staring dismally out into the rain. At night we tried to warm our naked bodies by covering ourselves with the dirty wool that happened to be lying there. All the outhouses in the neighbourhood were crowded with armed *burghers* in tatters. On the eighth day, when the welcome sun made its appearance once more, our clothes were still dripping.

Lately we had had fruit as a substitute for sugar; but the fruit season was over now, and we had to go back to meat and mealie-porridge, or mealie-porridge and meat.

In the Moot our horses died in such numbers—particularly the 'unsalted' mares—that many of our men had to walk. On March 10 my faithful brown pony Steenbok died of hors-sickness. For over a year he had carried me through thick and thin, and I could not bear to see his suffering. A few weeks later we got another lot of horses; I will not mention how, as the information might fall into the hands of the enemy. The people who still lived on their farms often told us that the few remaining fowls instinctively recognised khaki as an enemy, and made for the hedges and shrubs whenever they caught sight of him. So here, also, Nature looked after the survival of the species. The cows taken by the enemy also made their way back to their calves that khaki stupidly left behind, and so the little children could again have milk. Even the bees were not left undisturbed; but the bee is an enemy of any nasty-smelling thing, and therefore the dirty, perspiring khakis got many a sting, and the honey usually remained in the hives.

The enemy probably thought that we were helpless in our poverty. But a Boer is not easily made helpless. We patched our own shoes and carried the lasts about with us. Horseshoes and nails we made from the tires of wheels and telegraph-wires. Instead of matches we used two stones. When the enemy have burned and destroyed all our corn-mills, we will still have coffee-mills, and when those are gone we will do as the *kaffirs* do, and grind our corn between two stones—and crushed and roasted maize is very good to eat.

The old *voortrekkers* wore trousers made of untanned hide. We can do the same if khaki does not supply us with sufficient clothes. Our wives and children and our exiled men we cannot get out of khaki's hands, and that is the greatest difficulty in our way.

One of the greatest advantages we have over the enemy is that we are among friends, and can move about in small troops without having to depend on a base of operations, whereas they do well not to divide themselves in too small groups, or to venture too far from their base—even in large numbers.

The services in our camp were held by the Rev. Mr. Maudé—a man who kept the courage and the moral sense of the *burghers* up to the mark with his meek Christian spirit. He also formed the debating club that was such a welcome recreation to us. We often thought that the enemy would be surprised if they could know of the debates we had—for instance, 'Must the "hands-uppers" be allowed to vote after the war is over?' 'Must the *kaffirs* or natives have more rights?' 'Is intervention advisable under the circumstances?' etc. The men in the neighbourhood of Tafelkop were mostly 'hands-uppers,' so we confiscated their property, and their grain and cattle we took for the use of the laager, but we always left sufficient for the use of the women and children.

The future of a farm on which a *laager* had camped for some time was dark indeed, for even the grain in the fields was destroyed by the demon of war. If the owner of the farm were not a 'hands-upper,' our officers usually succeeded in preventing the destruction. Sometimes the pulling up of the fencing was inevitable, as we were so short of fuel. The Boer women were sometimes forced to accept the protection of the enemy, after their farms and property had been destroyed by friend and enemy alike.

The negotiation of February 7, between Kitchener and Louis Botha, was read out to us at Tafelkop. The *burghers* were unanimous in condemnation of Kitchener's conditions, and were fully satisfied with Botha's short, vigorous answer. Had we indeed fought so long and so fiercely only to become an English colony, and not to be allowed to carry arms unless we had a license? And for the *kaffirs* to be eventually allowed to vote? The men who were attached to their families and farms, but preferred losing all to becoming 'hands-uppers,' were unanimous in declaring Kitchener's conditions unacceptable, and all were ready to fight to the bitter end. We often spoke of the terrible suffering of our women and children in the refugee camps, and sometimes doubted whether it were not better for their sakes to give in. We did not know whether patriotism were worth the shedding of so much innocent blood. It cost us more than we can tell to remain firm and brave in our undertaking.

At that time we also heard of De Wet's retreat from Cape Colony, but not officially. It was broken to us gently, and at first as if he had been successful, so that we all thought peace was to follow soon.

How we rejoiced!

But a few days later De Wet's official report was read out to us, and then our courage sank indeed. What was the good of our fighting if the Colony would not help us?

The disappointment was not great enough to make us lay down our arms, but we knew it would be many a long day before peace was in the land. How long should we still be chased from place to place? When would there be rest for our exhausted bodies? And how we longed for our dear ones, if only we should find them alive!

Conclusion

In the Hands of the Enemy

We stayed fully three weeks at Tafelkop. I was appointed commissary of the Krugersdorp commando, and rode round to all the farms to procure the needful for our commando. As General De la Rey had been camping close by at Rietfontein for some time, there was not much left to commandeer, unless we deprived the women whose husbands were in the *veld* of the necessaries of life.

Our laager was moved from Tafelkop to Rietpan, from whence a few hundred of our horsemen started with some guns and a few trolleys for Groot Kafferkraal, in Hartbeestfontein district. General De la Rey had come over to organise the expedition in person, and accompanied General Kemp. I went with a man called Jooste to the neighbourhood of Lichtenberg and Klein Kafferkraal to commandeer cattle. There I heard many tales of the enemy's behaviour as they passed through a week before.

For some reason or other the houses there had not been burnt, perhaps owing to the verbal negotiation between Botha and Kitchener. I know of only one house that was burned down there. That was the finest house in the neighbourhood and belonged to Willem Basson. Mrs. Basson herself told me how it happened. Her husband had fled with the cattle when the enemy came along. The soldiers asked her for money. They said such a fine house must contain a great deal of money, and when she refused they became most impertinent. The finding of a packet of dynamite in the coach-house afforded a fine excuse. The dynamite was used by Basson for the making of wells. On finding the packet they shouted 'Hurrah!' and rushed off with it to the camp close to the house. They came back after a while and stormed the house, smashing the windows with stones. Truly a heroic storming of a fortress held by women! They destroyed everything in the house, and the women and children were obliged to flee to Mrs. Scheffers at Klein Kafferkraal, where I met them.

We know of many cases of cruelty and violence, cases that have roused us to a passion of hatred.

I do not believe that the cases of violence, which are not spoken of because of the horror, are tolerated by the military authorities, who are probably ignorant of them. One can understand that the worst were committed by isolated patrols who could give free vent to their evil passions. We cannot always hold the chief officers responsible for acts committed by individual soldiers, neither are our officers responsible for the unlawful acts of individuals on our side. But if the English, with their national pride and obstinacy, deny these acts of violence, we can give them sufficient proof of more cases than one.

I was not present when the Krugersdorpers attacked Babingtons force near Lensdenplaats, in the neighbourhood of Groot Kafferkraal. But the following morning, when they were retreating, I joined them with some cattle, and was present at the Battle of Stompies. The night before the battle I heard De la Rey's order given to Kemp to march his men at four o'clock the following morning in the direction of the enemy. He was told to retreat fighting, in case the enemy attacked, so as to give our reinforcements an opportunity of attacking in the rear. Kemp ordered the *laager*, or, rather, the few waggons, to retire to Bodenstein's farm the following morning.

While we were busy inspanning we heard the enemy's bomb Maxim, and before the waggons had forded the dangerous *drift* of the *donga* near Bodenstein's farm the bullets flew over our heads from the *bult* behind us. The women fled into the house and the *burghers* retreated as fast as they could. The enemy had surrounded us in the night, and each *burgher* had to do his utmost to escape from out of the half-circle. The few who stayed behind to defend the guns were soon obliged to fly after the rest, and to abandon one gun still on the other side of the drift. The others might have been saved if the women's *laager* had not impeded their flight by obstructing the way.

We retreated to Vetpan. Those of the *burghers* who retreated more to the right in the direction of Stompies were the best off, as the right wing of the enemy had to be on its guard not to enter the wood there. The enemy fired at us from horseback to enhance our panic, which was clever of them, as it was impossible for us to turn in any direction. My horse was overworked, and had changed its pace into a heavy gallop, a sure sign that it would not last much longer. When I looked round, I saw a few khakis riding on ahead, making our *burghers* 'hands-up.' Fortunately, someone released a spare horse; I mounted it without a saddle and made good my escape, but was incapable of riding for several days after.

Our men made no attempt to check the enemy's progress. They all fled, each one bent on saving himself. A Boer, if once he flies, is not easily turned aside. But it must be remembered that our horses were terribly overworked. They had to live on nothing but grass, and very little of that. We all also recognised the impossibility of checking the enemy, as we ran the risk of shooting our own men and women; so our only chance lay in flight.

The horses of the enemy were soon 'done up,' and they had to satisfy themselves with our guns—two large ones that we had taken from them at Colenso, a damaged bomb-Maxim and several smaller ones. They took 136 prisoners, among whom were Lieutenant Odendaal, 32 artillerists, 13 *burghers*, and for the rest women and children and some big, full-grown cowardly men who were in the habit of fleeing with the women and children. The greater part of the women's *laager* fell into their hands. The few waggons of Generals Smuts and Kemp that they captured were of no importance. Jooste and Malherbe were also taken prisoners.

I rode with General De la Rey to Tafelkop, where our laager was stationed. In a week's time I was back again at Stompies. I had been there scarcely an hour, when the tidings came that the enemy were camped on Willem Basson's farm. The following morning before daybreak I was on my way to Rietfontein. There, too, I had been only about an hour, when another column came down upon me from the direction of Ventersdorp, I fled to Tivee Buffelgeschiet with two boiled mealies and a piece of meat in my hands. Before I reached that farm, half an hour's ride, my horse was done up. I crept behind an anthill and prepared to defend myself against four scouts who seemed to be coming straight towards me. Suddenly, however, they turned off in the direction of their main-guard, because, as I afterwards heard, they were threatened by eight of our scouts.

But the khakis were nearing me, and I was obliged to lead my horse into a mealie-*veld* and to lie down full length in the rain. They did not appear, however, and I concluded that they had camped at Rietfontein, so I walked my horse to the farm of Mrs. Jansen, one of the few hospitable women in that sparsely inhabited country. She hastily informed me that the khakis had been there.

The eight *burghers* soon returned, among them a young man who was nursing a wounded man on the farm. In the night we went into the *veld* with a small brother of his, who rode a mule, and returned in the morning to watch the enemy's movements from the roof of the house. My horse was so ill with horse-sickness that it shook under me. The enemy suddenly appeared on the long *bult* (hill) along which I had come the day before. I carried my saddle into the house and fled into the *veld*. From behind an ant-hill I watched the enemy shooting my poor sick horse. They passed by me several times, but at last I was discovered, and had to give up my beloved Mauser without a chance of defending myself. My two companions escaped. This happened on April 3, 1901.

Fortunately, I fell into the hands of decent khakis who did not insist on examining my old *veld*-shoes that I was using as a money-box, so I was able to keep my precious four pounds. They took from me only a few trifles by way of curiosities, and said I was sure to be robbed of them sooner or later by the soldiers in the camp. I was told that I could congratulate myself that I was made prisoner, as many columns were coming down upon us from all directions, so that we would be obliged to surrender that very day. I answered that the war had given sufficient proof that their expectations were not always realised.

When the officers of the guard were told that I was taken under arms, a curt order was given to 'Let him walk.' When I protested, and pointed out that I was a prisoner of war and not a criminal, I was treated with consideration as an ordinary soldier. I was taken by Babington's force.

The following day the waggon *laager* arrived at Tafelkop, and the cavalry that had been sent on to capture our *laager* joined the camp minus any prisoners. When the enemy's *laager* arrived at Potchefstroom a week later, it brought along seventeen or eighteen 'hands-uppers,' one ambulance doctor, several families, and one prisoner of war. Six of the 'hands-uppers' told me that the whole month we were camped at Tafelkop they had hidden from us in their bedrooms so as not to be obliged to break their oath of neutrality.

I came across an old acquaintance of mine in the *laager*—Phister, who had served under Commandant Boshoff. I knew that he had been wounded in the leg at the Battle of Stompies and taken by our men to Rietpan. On the trek from Ventersdorp to Potchefstroom I discovered him lying on his back in the blazing sun on an open trolley, near to Potchefstroom; he shouted to me that he had had nothing to eat during the whole of the eighteen hours' trek.

In Potchefstroom our trolley, with the twelve 'hands-uppers,' the ambulance doctor, and myself, was sent in the direction of the prison. People came towards us from all directions. Some women called out to us: 'Why were you so stupid as to let yourselves be caught?' Others inquired, weeping, after husbands and sons.

When we got to the prison I alone was detained, and had the disagreeable experience of being locked up. The ambulance doctor was dismissed, as he was 'Not guilty'; and the 'hands-uppers' were taken to the refugee camp.

The treatment that the prisoners of war receive varies, and depends very much on the prisoners themselves and on the men into whose hands they fall. I was allowed to see my mother and sister, who obtained a pass to come from Pretoria to see me. But I have seen the guards roughly send away weeping women who were begging to be allowed a few words only with their dear ones.

At Elandsfontein Station the Transvaal colours worn by some of the prisoners of war were taken away by force. On the long journey to Ladysmith we were packed like herrings in open trucks, with insufficient covering for the cold nights.

The Ladysmith camp contained chiefly *burghers* who had been 'tamed' by the enemy, and were ready to take the oath of allegiance. They were well treated.

On April 3 I was taken prisoner, and on May 6 I was on board the *Manila,* together with 490 other prisoners of war, on our way to India.

The *burghers*, accustomed to a free, independent life, suffered horribly from want of space and insufficient and bad food. They could not get over the idea of having to appear twice daily for the roll-call, although there was no escape possible. But their sense of humour did not suffer.

Our *burghers* acknowledge that travelling is an education in itself, but they one and all prefer travelling as free men—first or second class—and they even prefer the high walls and limited space of the fortress to being a prisoner-of-war passenger on board the steamer.

The long, galvanized iron bungalows in which we live here have zinc roofs to guard against the heat of the tropical sun, but at any rate the wind can blow through the openings on either side. The *burghers* are kept alive and in pretty good health by an extremely temperate manner of life. Once a week they are taken by a strong guard for a walk an hour beyond the fort. They never get out on parole. As far as we are concerned, they might even take cannon along with them to guard us, if only they would take us out oftener.

Here, too, the moral tone of the *burghers* is kept up by religious services, and by the great devotion of the Rev. Mr. Viljoen, clergyman of Reitz, in the Orange Free State, who is a fellow-prisoner of ours. The gaiety is kept up by sports and by the companionship of many children. The sorrow is enhanced by the presence of many gray-headed old men and by sad and heart breaking tidings. 'Guard, is there any news this morning?'

We are grieving with the grief of the exile, but we are waiting patiently, and hoping still that a dove will bring us a branch with our colours—Orange, green, red, white and blue: peace and independence.

www.ingramcontent.com/pod-product-compliance
Lightning Source LLC
Chambersburg PA
CBHW021959160426
43197CB00007B/186